Marketing Automation with Mailchimp

Expert tips, techniques, and best practices for scaling marketing strategies and ROI for your business

Margarita J. Caraballo

BIRMINGHAM—MUMBAI

Marketing Automation with Mailchimp

Copyright © 2023 Packt Publishing

All rights reserved. No part of this book may be reproduced, stored in a retrieval system, or transmitted in any form or by any means, without the prior written permission of the publisher, except in the case of brief quotations embedded in critical articles or reviews.

Every effort has been made in the preparation of this book to ensure the accuracy of the information presented. However, the information contained in this book is sold without warranty, either express or implied. Neither the author, nor Packt Publishing or its dealers and distributors, will be held liable for any damages caused or alleged to have been caused directly or indirectly by this book.

Packt Publishing has endeavored to provide trademark information about all of the companies and products mentioned in this book by the appropriate use of capitals. However, Packt Publishing cannot guarantee the accuracy of this information.

Group Product Manager: Alok Dhuri

Publishing Product Manager: Akshay Dhani

Senior Editor: Nithya Sadanandan

Technical Editor: Maran Fernandes

Copy Editor: Safis Editing

Project Coordinator: Deeksha Thakkar

Proofreader: Safis Editing

Indexer: Tejal Daruwale Soni

Production Designer: Shyam Sundar Korumilli

Marketing Coordinators: Deepak Kumar and Mayank Singh

Business Development Executive: Puneet Kaur

First published: June 2023

Production reference: 1180523

Published by Packt Publishing Ltd.
Livery Place
35 Livery Street
Birmingham
B3 2PB, UK.

ISBN 978-1-80056-173-1

www.packtpub.com

To my loving partner, Ryan, for being such a calm, loving constant in my life. Your steady belief that I can do and accomplish anything inspires me to actually pursue those accomplishments. To my mother, Mimi, your sacrifices and perseverance are a constant reminder that I am loved. And to my beautiful baby boy, Leonardo. Pregnancy, birth, and writing all in the same year has been a truly unique challenge, but I have cherished every moment of my time with you and look forward to many more.

– Margarita J. Caraballo

Contributors

About the author

Margarita J. Caraballo is a senior technical product manager at Mailchimp, a marketing automation platform that has joined the Intuit suite of products as of late 2021. She lives in Atlanta and has been with Mailchimp for close to a decade and has seen its growth from a bulk email web app to a multi-channel marketing automation platform. Throughout that time, she has worked in every major customer-focused pillar of the company: product, engineering, and support. Throughout her career in tech, she has worked directly with users, as well as embedded with engineering teams. She is often described as equal parts data-driven and practical, helping others learn how to connect the pieces of their data together to tell a compelling story.

About the reviewer

Teddy Herbert helps medium and large businesses get the most out of their Mailchimp experiences. As an early Mailchimp employee with vast experience in the Mailchimp ecosystem at all stages of its growth from a bulk email marketing web app to a marketing automation platform, Teddy is one of the most knowledgeable and technically savvy customer success managers in the business. Teddy's 9 years of experience working with and consulting customers on how to use the Mailchimp platform gives him credibility in content creation and configuration within the platform.

Table of Contents

Preface — xiii

Part 1: Introduction to Mailchimp

1

Welcome to Marketing with Mailchimp — 3

A glance at Mailchimp's journey — 4	Digital content creators — 8
Understanding and using online marketing with Mailchimp — 4	Brick and mortar — 8
	Service providers — 8
Mailchimp-specific terms — 5	Mensa marketers — 8
Channels — 6	E-commerce marketers — 9
Campaigns — 6	Creating an account — 9
Classic Automations — 7	Summary — 12
Customer Journey Builder — 7	Further reading — 12
Common utilizations — 7	

Part 2: Getting Set Up

2

Basics of Account Management and Audiences — 17

Account management and setting an industry — 18	Help us improve your stats — 21
	Default Email Builder — 23
Details — 20	Email from Mailchimp — 23

Manage automatic replies	24	The purpose behind using a central versus various list	31
Setting up an audience	25	Summary	31
Why is it important to know about different contact statuses?	26	Further reading	32
Information you need to make your first list	26		

3

Importing and Combining Audiences 33

Merge Tags	34	The Combine Audiences tool	44
Put this tag in your content	35	Exporting and importing	44
Default merge tag value	36	Summary	45
How to import a list	37	Further reading	45
Combining audiences	41		
How to combine audiences	42		

4

Understanding the Difference between Groups, Tags, and Segments 47

How targeting can lead to higher engagement	48	Segmenting tools	56
What are groups and tags?	49	Basics of segmenting logic	56
Groups	50	Summary	59
Tags	53	Further reading	59
Importing to groups or tags	55		

5

Strategies and Tools for Managing Inactive Contacts 61

What are inactive contacts?	61	Summary	66
How to develop our own definition	62	Further reading	66
To unsubscribe or archive? That is the question	64		
When do I delete?	65		

Part 3: Basic Channels

6

Setting Up and Customizing Various Form Types — 69

Why are forms necessary?	69	Embedded and pop-up forms	83
Hosted forms	71	Embedded forms	83
Navigating to the hosted form builder	71	Pop-up forms	85
Categories of hosted forms you can edit	74	Summary	87
Creating a form on a landing page	78	Further reading	87

7

Establishing Your Brand with the Content Studio — 89

What is the Content Studio?	89	Giphy	95
Individual features and channels nested under Content Studio	91	Instagram	95
		My Logo	96
Creative Assistant	91	Summary	96
My Files	94	Further reading	97
Products	95		

8

Outreach Marketing with Templates and Campaigns — 99

Templates and how to start them	99	Campaign scheduling	118
What is a Template?	100	Types of emails to pair with targeted segments	120
Template Editor	100	Summary	123
Choosing a template	103	Further reading	124
Using the Campaign Editor	111		

9

Setting Up Your Marketing Presence with Websites — 125

What is a domain?	125	Where do I get one and what if I have one?	127
An additional entry point and sign-up portal	126	Making a website	133
Personalizing your domain settings	126	Editing settings	139
Improving deliverability	127	Summary	140
Having an authentic appearance	127	Further reading	140

Part 4: Refine and Automate

10

Understanding Reports and Analytics — 143

Technical requirements	143	How you can use and interpret these reports	153
The types of information that are accessible in Mailchimp's reporting	144	Expanded/advanced reporting features	156
Why opens and clicks?	148	Comparative Reports	159
General stats overview	148	Summary	163
Click performance interface	151	Further reading	163
Predicted Demographics interface	151		

11

Implementing A/B and Multivariate Testing — 165

Why experiment with engagement?	165	How do you take information from the results to better understand your audience?	171
Multivariate options and what elements you can experiment with	166	Summary	174
		Further reading	175

12

Strategies for Automating Using the Customer Journey Builder — 177

Technical requirements	177	Date-based events and data	183
The basics of automation and events	178	Marketing channel activity	184
Types of automation, journeys, and their logic	179	Integration and API events	184
Common use cases and recipes	180	Setting up a Classic Automation or Customer Journey Builder	185
Audience/contact activity	181	Summary	195
E-commerce activity	182	Further reading	195

13

Setting Up a Mailchimp E-Commerce Store — 197

Technical requirements	197	Setting up automations specific to e-commerce	213
What is a commerce feature?	198		
Setting up a Mailchimp store	199	Summary	216
The expansion of a contact dataset to include commerce/purchasing data	209	Further reading	216

Part 5: Get Smarter and Connect

14

E-Commerce Integrations — 219

Technical requirements	219	How to expand your marketing efforts with your commerce data	229
Featured commerce integrations	220		
Movement of information between these platforms	227	Summary	230
		Further reading	231

15

Form and Survey Integrations — 233

Technical requirements	233	How to find the right integration and connect it	238
Using form and survey integrations to build your audience	234	Summary	243
		Further reading	243

16

CRM and Connectivity Integrations — 245

Technical requirements	245	Zapier integration	252
Popular CRM and connectivity integrations and why to connect them	246	Understanding where data is present when syncing is initiated and associated advanced features	256
What the various integration paths are and how to find and use them	247	Summary	261
Browsing for integrations	247	Further reading	262
Sample integration walk-throughs	249		

17

Use Cases and Real-World Examples — 263

Starting a business or online presence	264	Next goals and vision for growth	267
Type of business	264	Ideal Mailchimp usage for this business	268
Background of the business	265	Service-based business model	269
Next goals and vision for growth	265	Type of business	270
Ideal Mailchimp usage for this business	265	Background of the business	270
From bricks and mortar to a digital presence	267	Next goals and vision for growth	270
		Ideal Mailchimp usage for this business	270
Type of business	267	Summary	273
Background of the business	267		

Index — 275

Other Books You May Enjoy — 282

Preface

I've always quite enjoyed writing, and writing a book synthesizing years of my experience with the Mailchimp platform felt like such an interesting opportunity to try and put together something that told a cohesive story about developing your marketing strategy. After over a decade in the technology space, and a huge chunk of that with Mailchimp, writing this has felt like such a fascinating and new challenge. I've moved from customer-facing roles to infrastructure roles throughout my career, but what has always kept me grounded and coming back to thinking about the strategic use of technology is the people and organizations I've encountered along the way.

I am a first-generation, American-born child of Cuban immigrants. Growing up, we didn't have very much, but I watched my family hustle to support each other, and I saw first-hand the value of a community that supports one another. In a way, I think that an immigrant story, or any story of struggle, really creates this clear-sighted belief in the power of investing in your community at every opportunity, big or small. My Tia Maggie was so good at community building, raising money, and really engaging with people. While she ran a non-profit, at the center of her role was telling a story, marketing the benefits of public radio dedicated to jazz music, and compelling people to invest in the public good for the community. Growing up, our family watched and supported her as she grew that radio station from a trailer in a rural area outside of Miami to a multimillion-dollar, multi-use arts and music facility in the heart of the city of Miami.

Sometimes, in the early days of Maggie's marketing, my cousins and I spent days leading up to fundraising drives stuffing flyers in envelopes (these were the days before affordable internet) to help her market her station. This was in the 1990s, before she had many other volunteers or employees. Even much later on, into my 20s and 30s, when the station was more successful and well known, a marketer's job was never done. She would sometimes call me to ask about the latest in marketing technology and talk through how technology might benefit the marketing she was trying out. It's a perfect illustration of how the means of marketing might change over time, but at the end of the day, it's always about developing a plan to keep in touch with your audience and get them engaged with you and your business or organization. If I could tell a story a fraction as well as she did, I would count myself lucky to be that skilled.

My mother's family really instilled in me this belief that being involved in your community, supporting people in your family, and really going out on a limb to build something new was the way to build a community. For my part, that included volunteering, but it also meant that, when I had the chance, I preferred to think of my own personal buying power as a small way to vote with my money and invest in my community. So, buying from small, local businesses is just one small way you can turn a day-to-day action, such as making a purchase, into one that also invests in your local community.

Working at Mailchimp for so long, I've had the pleasure of interacting with so many of our customers. Sometimes, this meant interacting with them directly at their most tired, when they're just trying to piece together their business needs with the best action to take in the app, or chatting directly with entrepreneurs and business owners who shared their precious time with our company to help provide us with context for their daily needs. I've heard first-hand from entrepreneurs how excited they were by their first-ever purchases, how pleased they are with the first person who buys a new product from them, and how flattered they are when people share some kind feedback to their newsletters. How could I not become fond of such earnest moments and want to invest in those small businesses, both professionally and personally, when I buy from them?

So, this guide is written with some hope that I can help make the road to successfully marketing and expanding small and mid-size businesses and organizations a little smoother. Whether you're new to the Mailchimp platform or you've been leveraging it for a while, and you're not quite sure how to leverage as much of it as possible to actually serve your business, this book has something for you. Mailchimp is a marketing automation platform that specializes in email and automations. The content of this book is based on years of watching businesses grow, seeing how businesses operate, and seeing how their audiences respond to their efforts. It's a strategy that's based on years of feedback and the development of new needs in the market, as the demand for more digital channels expanded for businesses. The book starts from the most common channels progresses to more advanced channels as you go along, ensuring that if you need to hit the ground running, you can focus on the most valuable channels for you and get back to building your brand and community.

Who this book is for

This book is ideal for a small-to-mid-size organization, business, or entrepreneur who is just starting their marketing journey, enjoys researching engagement strategies, and wants to take initial hands-on ownership of designing their marketing voice and channels.

What this book covers

Chapter 1, *Welcome to Marketing with Mailchimp*, introduces some of the terminology and language conventions used throughout the Mailchimp platform and some common user types.

Chapter 2, *Basics of Account Management and Audiences*, explores some valuable account settings you should consider updating early in your marketing journey, as well as how the audience feature plays a central role within your Mailchimp account.

Chapter 3, *Importing and Combining Audiences*, establishes a foundational understanding of audiences and how to structure your data for an import, and then execute on that import.

Chapter 4, *Understanding the Difference Between Groups, Tags, and Segments*, discusses the nuanced differences between groups, tags, and segments and how they can be used throughout the platform.

Chapter 5, *Strategies and Tools for Managing Inactive Contacts*, examines the different strategies to define what "inactive" means in the context of a business, and how those models relate to maintaining a strategy for targeted marketing.

Chapter 6, Setting Up and Customizing Various Form Types, demonstrates how to actively interact with your first channel and your contacts for the first time, as well as how to aggregate new ones.

Chapter 7, Establishing Your Brand with Content Studio, delves into how to establish your brand and its assets within your Mailchimp account, and how to bring images and other assets into an app and utilize them.

Chapter 8, Outreach Marketing with Templates and Campaigns, covers the two basic channels and how to set the tone for your marketing and outreach to your contacts.

Chapter 9, Setting Up Your Marketing Presence with Websites, explores how to set up a consistent marketing presence in the form of websites and the benefits of determining a brand identity.

Chapter 10, Understanding Reports and Analytics, expands on the analytic options and even offers some pro features to leverage comparative reports.

Chapter 11, Implementing A/B Testing and Multivariate Testing, delves specifically into the advanced marketing features available to gather additional data about your contacts/subscribers, helping you to determine what best engages them.

Chapter 12, Strategies for Automating Using the Customer Journey Builder, examines the marketing and product strategies to automate more outreach to your audience. This chapter covers the types of workflows and scenarios that can be automated within the Mailchimp platform and how to set up an ecosystem.

Chapter 13, Setting Up a Mailchimp E-Commerce Store, reviews how the platform can support the marketing needs of brick-and-mortar businesses or businesses with a physical inventory. This includes businesses with no online store and those who have an e-commerce platform but are looking to expand the reach of an existing solution.

Chapter 14, E-Commerce Integrations, explores the benefits of integrating your external commerce platforms, assuming that you leverage an existing platform to sell products, and the benefits to marketing initiatives if you do.

Chapter 15, Form and Survey Integrations, examines some of the more popular integrations for forms and surveys that can be connected to your Mailchimp account to elevate your forms.

Chapter 16, CRM and Connectivity Integrations, looks at some of the common/popular integrations to connect Mailchimp with another CRM or leverage a connectivity application. This chapter is of particular benefit for service-based businesses and agencies.

Chapter 17, Use Cases and Real-World Examples, delves into some of the real-life applications and common uses for a marketing platform. Each section focuses on some top scenarios where an application is used and then how to leverage a marketing strategy to build on your existing work.

To get the most out of this book

The best way to go about using this book is to ensure that you have opened a Mailchimp account. The book does go through the use of both free and paid features, so when you start each chapter, keep in mind to check for notes about whether the channel addressed in that chapter requires a specific account type. To see more information about current Mailchimp plans, feel free to check out their website here: `https://mailchimp.com/pricing/marketing/compare-plans/`

Software covered in the book	Compatible web browsers
Mailchimp	Google Chrome, Mozilla Firefox, and Safari (11 and above)

Download the color images

We also provide a PDF file that has color images of the screenshots and diagrams used in this book. You can download it here: `https://packt.link/RUXp2`.

Conventions used

There are a number of text conventions used throughout this book.

`Code in text`: Indicates code words in text, database table names, folder names, filenames, file extensions, pathnames, dummy URLs, user input, and Twitter handles. Here is an example: "The reason *|FNAME|* and *|LNAME|* are distinct is not just to indicate that they're first and last names, but also because the app will not allow them to both be *|NAME|*."

Bold: Indicates a new term, an important word, or words that you see on screen. For instance, words in menus or dialog boxes appear in **bold**. Here is an example: "Clicking that option will take you to the **Account Overview** page."

> **Tips or important notes**
> Appear like this.

Get in touch

Feedback from our readers is always welcome.

General feedback: If you have questions about any aspect of this book, email us at `customercare@packtpub.com` and mention the book title in the subject of your message.

Errata: Although we have taken every care to ensure the accuracy of our content, mistakes do happen. If you have found a mistake in this book, we would be grateful if you would report this to us. Please visit `www.packtpub.com/support/errata` and fill in the form.

Piracy: If you come across any illegal copies of our works in any form on the internet, we would be grateful if you would provide us with the location address or website name. Please contact us at copyright@packt.com with a link to the material.

If you are interested in becoming an author: If there is a topic that you have expertise in and you are interested in either writing or contributing to a book, please visit authors.packtpub.com.

Share Your Thoughts

Once you've read *Marketing Automation with Mailchimp*, we'd love to hear your thoughts! Scan the QR code below to go straight to the Amazon review page for this book and share your feedback.

https://packt.link/r/1-800-56173-3

Your review is important to us and the tech community and will help us make sure we're delivering excellent quality content.

Download a free PDF copy of this book

Thanks for purchasing this book!

Do you like to read on the go but are unable to carry your print books everywhere? Is your eBook purchase not compatible with the device of your choice?

Don't worry, now with every Packt book you get a DRM-free PDF version of that book at no cost.

Read anywhere, any place, on any device. Search, copy, and paste code from your favorite technical books directly into your application.

The perks don't stop there, you can get exclusive access to discounts, newsletters, and great free content in your inbox daily

Follow these simple steps to get the benefits:

1. Scan the QR code or visit the link below

```
https://packt.link/free-ebook/9781800561731
```

2. Submit your proof of purchase
3. That's it! We'll send your free PDF and other benefits to your email directly

Part 1: Introduction to Mailchimp

This initial section will lay the groundwork to understand the common terminology this book will use for user types and features and Mailchimp-specific terms, ensuring we're proceeding with a shared context.

This section has the following chapter:

- *Chapter 1, Welcome to Marketing with Mailchimp*

1
Welcome to Marketing with Mailchimp

Marketing and commerce – it's ultimately the crux of why you're here. Presumably, you're interested in growing your current efforts or verifying that you're making the best use of the Mailchimp platform if you're a current user. Platforms such as Mailchimp can be absolutely huge, and deciding what would serve you now versus what would work later in terms of your marketing efforts can be very overwhelming.

I don't want to discount the value of the robust knowledge base that Mailchimp's own technical content team maintains. It's been written by some of the smartest and kindest technical writers in the business, but what we can build together here in this book is a holistic vision for how the pieces that you're already using fit together and can be boosted by leveraging more of the platform.

Let's get right into a little background on Mailchimp and then define how we will be using both some general marketing terms in the broader context and terms you will see in the Mailchimp platform itself that deviate slightly from their typical utilization in the marketing industry at large. The goal here is just to set a solid foundation and understanding of words we'll be using throughout the book, but also in the event that you don't have an existing Mailchimp account to work with, we'll also be walking through creating an account quickly toward the end of the chapter.

In this first chapter, we will cover the following main topics:

- A glance at Mailchimp's journey
- Understanding and using online marketing with Mailchimp
- Mailchimp-specific terms
- Common utilizations
- Creating an account

A glance at Mailchimp's journey

Mailchimp, like many startups, started its life as a side hustle for its founders Ben Chestnut and Dan Kurzius. Ben and Dan operated a web design agency called *Rocket Science Group* and repeatedly noted that their smaller and mid-sized clients in particular mentioned their need for email marketing services. So, over time, on the side, they built the first Mailchimp email marketing service for small businesses.

Both Ben and Dan had parents who ran and operated their own small businesses throughout their childhoods and so they saw first-hand how difficult it could be for entrepreneurs to compete with better-equipped or larger competitors. This drove them to what ultimately became the mission of Mailchimp – to *empower the underdog*. In 2007, Rocket Science Group ultimately ended its agency work and turned all its efforts to developing Mailchimp into something specifically designed to provide small and medium-sized businesses with an email marketing tool as their initial entry point into marketing and staying in touch with their audiences.

Over the next decade, the needs of marketers steadily increased and became more complex. As the market pivoted more heavily toward diverse types of digital marketing, this drove Mailchimp to add more channels to be able to continue to equip the businesses that grew with them with what they needed to stay competitive. Of course, not only was this a benefit to long-time Mailchimp customers but it also ensured over time that Mailchimp stayed an ideal platform for new folks to *start and grow* with.

Over 20 years, this specific focus on small and medium-sized businesses and the commitment to the success of its users really propelled Mailchimp from being a bootstrapped, quirky, obscure, small email marketing platform into being a globally recognizable brand that does so much more. It kept much of what made it quirky and scrappy but certainly made its way to the front of the pack. This brings us to the current-day Mailchimp marketing platform.

Now that we have had a look at Mailchimp's journey, let's walk through a quick overview of the online marketing universe and then define some general terms and specific terms used in Mailchimp.

Understanding and using online marketing with Mailchimp

Online marketing specifically refers to platforms that empower you as the end user to use multiple, digital channels to reach an audience. Most commonly, since the 21st century, the drivers that foster the prevalence of online marketing instead of other traditional marketing channels are the internet, big data, and smartphones. Additionally, if we consider that market trends overwhelmingly point to each new generation leveraging more digital screens than the one before it, we can see that creating a holistic, data-informed marketing strategy becomes more and more critical.

Trend predictions from industry leaders such as Forbes, for example, point specifically to the need to think about your marketing strategy as *omnichannel* or *multi-channel* instead of as completely distinct efforts from one another. Businesses should consider all-in-one platforms as the predicted trend in terms of leveraging data about their contacts to build an overall journey. This empowers them to guide their audiences through all of their marketing content instead of maintaining them nested to specific channels.

As you begin your journey into considering different platforms, the key pieces of information to think about as you assess various marketing platforms is to think about categorizing their available channels into one of three buckets for you and your needs:

- **Non-negotiable**: These are the channels that are either already critical to your marketing or are biggies, such as emails
- **Known growth**: These are the channels that you know would be helpful but that you haven't attempted to work into your marketing efforts
- **Curious**: These are the channels you're either unfamiliar with, or you haven't previously considered how they would fit into a marketing effort for your needs

In *Figure 1.1*, we can see these hierarchies illustrated as a hierarchy from bottom to top; highest priority to lowest:

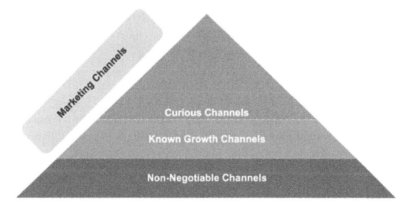

Figure 1.1 – Hierarchy of marketing channel needs

The reason I think of these needs as a hierarchy or categorization when considering platforms is that if you are starting with growth in mind, thinking of at least the two first categories when choosing a platform means that you have a longer runway for the growth of your marketing efforts. This is, of course, where multi-channel marketing platforms such as Mailchimp, instead of single-channel marketing applications, come to the forefront of your mind.

In the context of what we'll be discussing, we'll be thinking very specifically about Mailchimp-specific terms and then the most common digital marketing channels, which we'll define a bit more in the following section.

Mailchimp-specific terms

Mailchimp is most popular for (and built its business on the basis of) its email marketing features. However, the reality in the platform today is that you can manage more of your business and content creation within various channels all from one place, instead of needing different applications for each channel beyond the email channel. Today, it would be most accurate to refer to Mailchimp as a marketing and commerce platform.

Digging in, let's get specific with how we will be using some general marketing terms to refer to something more targeted within the platform itself before we get into the features themselves.

Channels

Speaking more generically, a **channel** is defined as *the people, organizations, and activities that make goods and services available for use by consumers*. When using it, people may be referring to a myriad of formats, such as direct sales, outbound calling, conference and industry events, and, of course, bulk or targeted emails.

Within Mailchimp's platform and knowledge base, a **channel** has a narrower definition – here, we're specifically referring to the mechanisms available to you within the application using which you plan to connect your business or content to your contacts. This is a narrowed definition to largely digital means of design and communication with your target audience.

Campaigns

When we say **campaigns** in a marketing context, we are usually referring to a set of strategic efforts and outreach to promote something or put certain content in front of your audience by leveraging various means. These are typically coordinated but different types of media, such as print, radio, and online platforms.

Within the context of Mailchimp, we are specifically referring to email marketing campaigns when we use the word *campaigns*. Even if we talk about classic automation and customer journey builders later on in the book, when we begin to turn our eyes to automating contact with our subscribers, these are collections of *campaigns* that rely on events occurring between them. More on this later though in *Chapter 12*.

Additional terms will be defined within the relevant chapters, but *channels* and *campaigns* are persistent terms that we will use throughout the book using their narrower scopes defined here.

So, keeping those key terms in mind and the relative hierarchy for how we should be considering these various channels inside the Mailchimp platform, next, let's take a look at some of the common reasons people come to Mailchimp. This will include a very high-level definition of some of the most popular *channels* such as *Classic Automations*, in addition to common reasons people generally use Mailchimp. So, let's take a quick, high-level view of these automated channels.

Classic Automations

Throughout the application, there are several features that, at least conceptually, seem to be a product that will automate something for you. You'll see as we go from feature to feature within the product that some of these things really will automate more for you than others. In the context of the platform itself though, you will see references to **Classic Automations**. These are sequences of emails that the Mailchimp application will generate for you with event-related logic in between. The terminology here refers to linear, prebuilt automation. What I mean by *linear* specifically is that these automation styles rely on single emails with single events between them. They will not fork or diverge to alternating emails. For example, the automation sequence might look something like this:

- **Event 1**: New subscriber joins **Audience A**
- **Email 1**: 1 hour after subscription, the application sends **Email 1**
- **Event 2**: Subscriber opens **Email 1**
- **Email 2**: 1 day after **Email 1** is opened, the application sends **Email 2**

As we can see here, there are no forks or deviations from a single thread of logic.

Customer Journey Builder

This is also an automation-based feature. The main difference between **Classic Automations** and **Customer Journey Builder** is that **Customer Journey Builder** does enable you to apply forks to events. You may have heard the term *customer journey* elsewhere specifically in the context of product management and development. You can think of it as a feature within Mailchimp that empowers you to create more advanced marketing pathways for your audience to move through. When we refer to a **customer journey map** specifically in *Chapter 12*, we will talk about the visual that the application makes for you as you develop your event and email maps that relate to how your audience members move through the content that you've pre-made.

Common utilizations

Let's get into some common utilizations in which multiple channels might be helpful. At the very end of the book in *Chapter 16*, we'll dig deep into these use cases and talk more about the business models and how they connect and ladder into the Mailchimp platform. Here, we'll take a look at *who* you might be as a marketer or commerce customer.

Let's check out some quick profiles for the following:

- Digital content creators
- Brick and mortar
- Service providers

- Mensa marketers
- E-commerce marketers

Digital content creators

This is a huge umbrella – it includes traditional internet denizens such as bloggers, but is now synonymous with anyone on the internet who creates content for education, entertainment, or both. Most commonly, it's associated with digital content creation and platforms such as Mailchimp that offer a home from which these creators can drive a lot of their content channels.

Brick and mortar

There's little I love quite like a small, independently owned, local business. Maybe that's a side-effect of working on products to support them for so long or growing up in a Latin community with bodegas on every corner and entrepreneurs hustling to build a new life. Mailchimp makes a great platform for businesses with physical locations or popups looking to expand brand awareness in their city or even outside of their immediate area.

Early industry estimates project that global events such as the COVID-19 pandemic may have sped up the rate at which Mom-and-Pop shops and other small stores will pivot to a digital presence. Pre-pandemic estimates predicted that the pivot would likely be within the next 5-10 years, but that gap has been narrowed to 1-5! With platforms such as Mailchimp, brick-and-mortar businesses selling goods can marry their email marketing efforts with basic e-commerce store features that empower that pivot to a digital presence.

Service providers

The service industry has been a steadily increasing portion of the commerce space for years and with that in mind, there are specific channels designed to empower this use case specifically. With appointment features, you can add to your omnichannel strategy, which likely includes things such as emails and automation as its foundation. Mailchimp can help you even if the items you're selling or promoting are more intangible than your brick-and-mortar counterparts with physical goods.

Mensa marketers

I think of this utilization as graduating to letting the platform do as much for you as possible. This is probably the ideal state, in which you have a handle on your fundamental marketing needs and core brand identity. We can even think of this as being your own agency. In the event that you are an agency that manages client accounts, the goal is likely to make as many of your channels as accessible and on-brand as possible. In this category, you'd be leaning more into **Customer Journey Builder** and **Classic Automations** to automate outreach to your users and leveraging social ads to make sure that engagement continues outside of their inboxes wherever possible.

E-commerce marketers

This utilization is almost the opposite of brick-and-mortar utilization. These are direct-to-consumer businesses that started their company on the internet to begin with. Instead of looking to make a digital pivot, they're likely to be thinking about how to expand their digital footprint or consolidate their marketing efforts into one platform. Mailchimp can help with integrating their e-commerce platform data with the campaign tools inside the Mailchimp platform itself to help automate outreach and better target their marketing to the purchase behavior they may see in their e-commerce business.

So, now that we know a bit more about the terms we'll be using and the background of why we even want to consider a marketing platform such as Mailchimp, we've set the groundwork for jumping into the product itself.

Creating an account

We'll work quickly through this section, since presumably if you're interested in optimizing or making ideal use of Mailchimp for your marketing, you likely already have an account.

> **Important note**
>
> A couple of things to note: by default, when you create a Mailchimp account, the default pricing plan selected is the free account. That being said, because the book will cover features from the basic email campaign features all the way through to reviewing integrations, commerce, and automation, the feature sets we'll be covering span various plans. However, even starting with a free account, we'll be able to cover quite a bit of ground.

To start with, you won't necessarily need a wealth of information just to create the account, as it can be edited in the account settings later. Indeed, if your Mailchimp account is going to be the centralized home for multiple businesses or audiences, you might not need or want to name your account after a single business anyway.

The main piece of information you will need to establish an account will be a personal email address for the account to be associated with (this can be at a private domain or with a popular email service provider such as Gmail, for example).

From there, you would take the following steps to create an account:

1. Choose a username and password for your account (your username can match your email address if you would prefer not to make the username distinct).
2. Choose your starting plan (this is where you can compare plans if you would like to start with something other than the free account).

3. Finally, input your first name, last name, business name, and, optionally, your website URL for your business if you already have one. *Figure 1.2* shows the **Account Set Up** page with the details filled in:

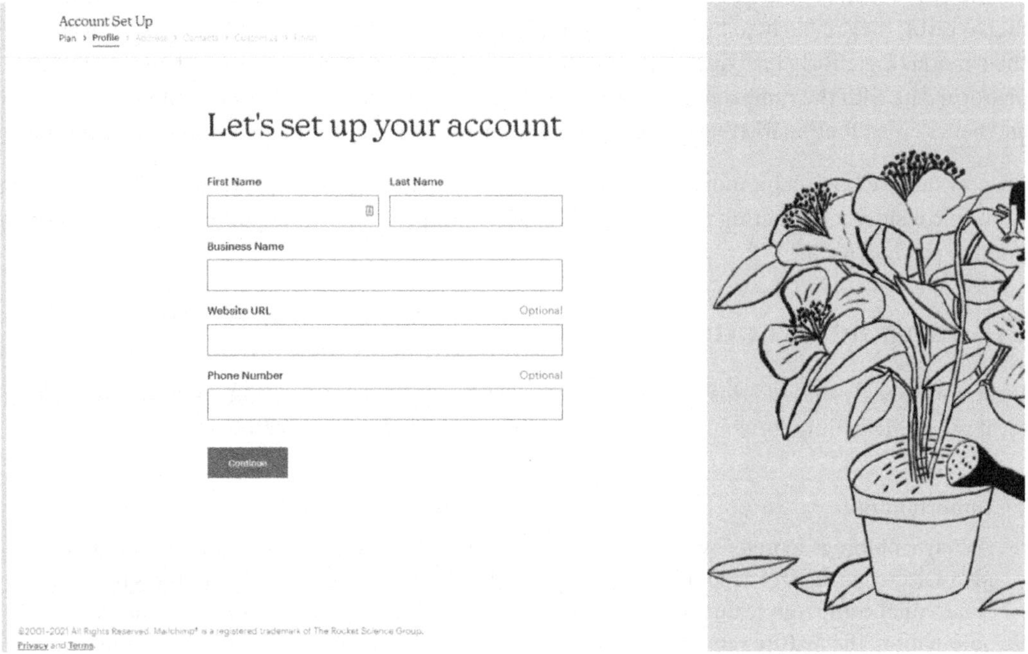

Figure 1.2 – Account Set Up page

As you move through the account creation pages, you will eventually arrive at your new account dashboard. Here, we conceptually see the three primary tasks that any new marketer should be thinking about as their starting point. In *Figure 1.3*, we can see the new account dashboard for a sample account, and the three sections identified there:

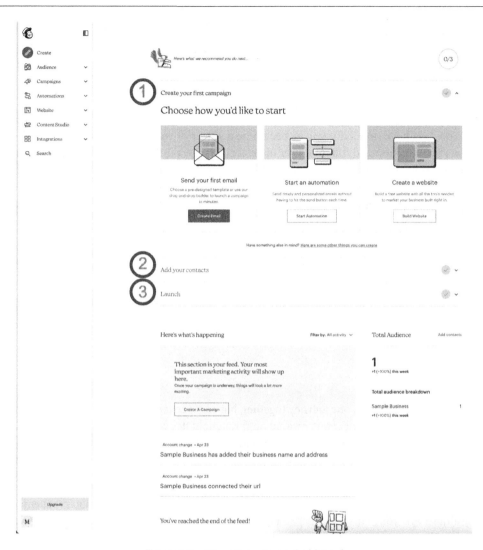

Figure 1.3 – New account app dashboard

The Mailchimp platform points out these three main calls to action to consider as you begin because you can think of them as the foundation of how you will start building your marketing effort. These three sections are as follows:

1. **Create your first campaign**: In this section, you will have the option to choose the type of campaign or channel you would like to start with. For example, as we can see in *Figure 1.3*, you were prompted to begin thinking about whether you would like to start with an email campaign, automation, or a website as the starting point for how you are going to interact with the audience. We will talk more at length on each topic in *Chapter 10* and *Chapter 11* respectively later on.

2. **Add your contacts**: Here, you will be focusing on importing your subscribers, cleaning up your existing list, or if you're early in your marketing journey, how to set yourself up to capture an audience.

3. **Launch**: Then, of course, the final initiating step is launching your new channel or campaign, whichever you choose as the right one to start your journey with!

Now, as you may have noticed if you've been a heavy user of web-based applications in the last decade, account creation and different user interfaces change a little bit over time. This is generally rooted in experimenting with small ways to help you get more use out of an application. These types of experiments are to help you understand what you're most interested in over time and how the application can help you find a feature most relevant to you.

While I've highlighted the most critical pieces of information to provide if you're in a hurry and trying to speed through the rest of the account creation process, depending on when you're reading this, it might be advisable to check out the additional, optional questions posed by the Mailchimp application as you create your account.

As Mailchimp adds more features in the future, signing up will change incrementally with more prompts being created in the app or even sometimes adjustments to what you see in the main calls to action I have referenced here.

Summary

So, we only just kicked off on our journey together, but we've covered a lot of ground already. Much like the journey Mailchimp as a company went on throughout its evolution, we'll be following in those same footsteps. If we keep in mind the hierarchy of needs outlined in *Figure 1.1*, we'll be starting with an exploration of audiences and the email campaigns that cater to them – every marketer's bread and butter.

Our modern lives revolve around our screens and particularly our inboxes so much that email has become almost everyone's first non-negotiable channel. Throughout the book, we'll spider out our strategy based on the use cases for additional channels.

So, in the next chapter, we'll start where everyone starts – audiences!

Further reading

Each chapter moving forward will have this section listed at the end to help provide you with some additional resources in case you're interested in further reading on the topics covered in the chapter. In this case, you'll find links to the definitions I referenced and articles discussing the broader digital marketing world:

- *The Evolution and History Of Digital Marketing:*

    `https://online.uwa.edu/news/history-of-digital-marketing/`

- Forbes overview of the future landscape of digital marketing:

  https://www.forbes.com/sites/forbesagencycouncil/2018/03/28/what-is-the-future-of-digital-marketing/

- Glossary definition of a *marketing channel:*

  https://www.gartner.com/en/marketing/glossary/marketing-channel

Part 2: Getting Set Up

Here, we will cover some of the highlights of setting up a Mailchimp account and ensuring that it is equipped with an audience to work with moving forward. Whether you're a new or an existing user of Mailchimp, this section features some helpful tidbits to adjust your settings, ensuring that your account is set up to serve you as you move into more complex feature utilization.

This section has the following chapters:

- Chapter 2, Basics of Account Management and Audiences
- Chapter 3, Importing and Combining Audiences
- Chapter 4, Understanding the Difference Between Groups, Tags, and Segments
- Chapter 5, Strategies and Tools for Managing Inactive Contacts

2
Basics of Account Management and Audiences

As you begin to use your Mailchimp account, you will discover that there are settings you can adjust. Changing these settings will make sure that you can more easily adopt analytic and benchmarking features further down the line. In general, taking these kinds of initial steps helps to ensure that you get the most pertinent results for your marketing efforts.

That being said, if you already have your account set up, you can go directly to *Chapter 3*, jump right into working with your audiences, and then can come back to this section later to check your settings. Some of the things we'll be setting here include indicating your industry so that Mailchimp's data-backed infrastructure can serve you benchmarks for your performance, and setting details about your business to streamline how data populates later. We'll take a look at some of these benchmarks in *Chapter 10* when we review some reporting features.

However, since you can come back to that later, if you'd like to jump straight into getting familiar with and importing your audience, you can skip to the *Setting up an audience* section of this chapter.

We will cover the following main topics in this chapter:

- Account management and setting an industry
- Setting up an audience
- The purpose behind using a central list versus various list

By the end of the chapter, you should understand some of the pros of managing your lists in different ways so that you can make the best decision for your efforts when you move on to importing in *Chapter 3*.

Account management and setting an industry

The essential goal here is just to cover and understand what information you can provide or set in your account to ensure that the data you see in the platform over time, in places such as reports, is as usable and relevant as possible as you scale your channel use. So, let's take a look at where we can either add or edit some settings in your account.

From the primary account dashboard, shown in *Figure 2.1*, you can access all of your account settings, and even all of your features as you move forward, in the left navigation menu. To specifically navigate to the settings for the overall account, follow these steps:

1. Click on the avatar/icon square in the lower left-hand corner, as shown in *Figure 2.1*.
2. A menu will appear; click on **Account & billing**.

Figure 2.1 – The account dashboard

Clicking that option will take you to the **Account Overview** page. Here, as you begin to actually import and send campaigns, you will be able to see account statuses and any notifications about compliance needs and tips for your audiences that the Mailchimp app needs to communicate with you. This is the page where you have menus available to you to make a plethora of changes. You'll have menus for billing changes and plan changes that will enable more features as you develop your marketing plans. Other menus will provide you with access to integrations to pipe in usable data from other platforms and apps that you might be using to run things, such as your commerce efforts, if they already exist outside of Mailchimp.

However, for what we're trying to accomplish in this section, the menu we're most interested in to set the industry details and other information about your business and organization is in the **Settings** drop-down menu. Here, select the **Details** option (as shown in *Figure 2.2*):

Figure 2.2 – The Account Overview page with the open Settings drop-down menu

This page contains five sections:

- **Details**
- **Help us improve your stats**
- **Default Email Builder**
- **Email from Mailchimp**
- **Manage automatic replies**

If nothing else, we should focus on these first two sections, **Details** and **Help us improve your stats**, as they'll be the two settings categories that, in the long-term, will impact some of the information you see about campaign details and benchmarking for reporting. We'll go over each setting within the sections specifically and highlight which settings influence data elsewhere.

Details

In the **Details** section, you can set information about your business and organization, the timezone you're working from, the date format you prefer, when your week starts, and the currency format you prefer your billing to be reflected in, as we can see in *Figure 2.3*:

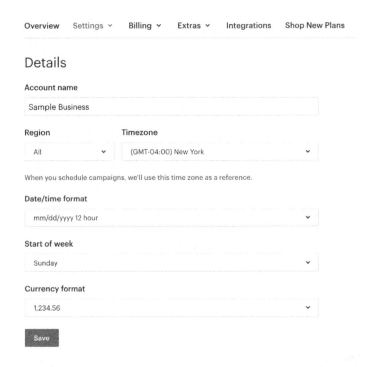

Figure 2.3 – Account Settings – the Details section

Let's take a look at what each setting here influences:

- **Account name**: This field is internal to you as a user specifically. This is the business or organization name you'll see associated with the account, but ultimately, unless you choose to later use the same name with an audience, this will only be visible to you and any other users you grant access to in the future. This allows for flexibility if you manage multiple businesses with distinct brands, if you're an agency or consultant and use various lists for your customers, and so on.

- **Region** and **Timezone**: This will be the referenced time used for your campaigns. It's the time zone you'll see reflected in the send date and time on the **Campaign Overview** page later on. Additionally, when Mailchimp gathers data about your subscribers as you grow your audience, it will be the default timezone used in the event that you leverage features such as **Scheduled send time** and **Timewarp** (there'll be more on these later in *Chapter 8* when we review campaigns).

- **Date/time format**: This, very simply put, is the format you would like dates and times to be displayed in. If you have an existing audience with associated date data, this is the format the information would appear in.
- **Start of week**: Again, this is largely about how you would like your data to appear. However, as charts begin to populate with information such as the weekly performance of campaigns, if you're a frequent sender, this information helps to indicate the starting point for your work week.
- **Currency format**: This is also an internal setting. Because audiences are designed to be flexible and accommodate different currencies, this setting is just specific to you and how you would like your personal billing information to be displayed and calculated for you. For example, if your organization is based in the United Kingdom but you have subscribers across Europe and the United States, your individual contact data can be modified to be region-specific, while this setting can be adjusted to **British Pounds** (**GBP**). This way, you can make sure that the billing information that displays elsewhere in **Account Settings** is displayed in GBP.

Help us improve your stats

This is where you can share a little bit of information about your organization that will help Mailchimp provide more specific feedback and stats, using different reporting features that can tell you more about how you're doing (see *Figure 2.4*).

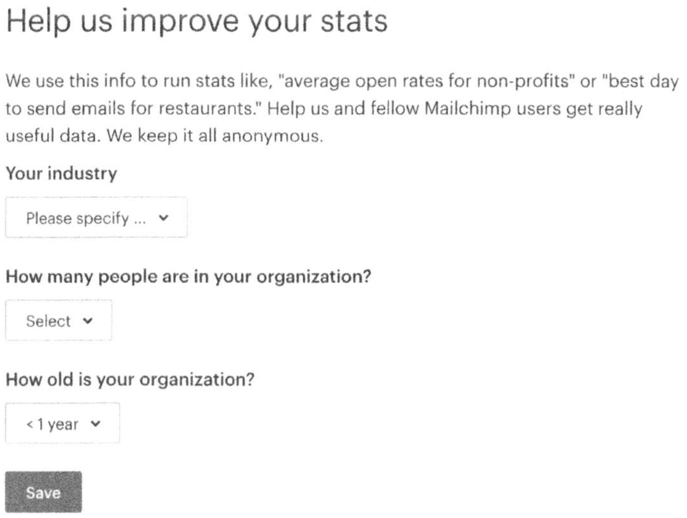

Figure 2.4 – The Help us improve your stats section

> **Tip**
> These settings, in my opinion, offer the best long-term return on the short time you spend making your selections.

Let's break this section down as we did for the previous section:

- **Your industry**: This section has a plethora of options. It features some broader choices if your business or organization offers a lot of different options, such as an **eCommerce** industry option, or more specific non-traditional commerce options, such as **Non-profit**. The benefit of selecting your industry is that it tells the Mailchimp app about a specific slice of business or organization that you would like to be benchmarked against. Throughout the reports, you will see benchmarks for performance against other users who are similar to you (which we will cover further later on in *Chapter 10*). Over time, this enables you to consider things such as **A/B testing**, where you can create two slightly different versions of the same campaign. This enables you to gauge the change in engagement with your marketing efforts, not just against your own past campaigns but also against other people in the same market space. You can also take comfort in knowing that Mailchimp anonymizes data before using it. So, while you can get an averaged insight into things such as click and open performance, Mailchimp doesn't share your granular performance information with another user, and vice versa.

- **How many people are in your organization?**: This is where you can choose to get a little more granular about the scale of your organization. Again, the goal here, if you wish, is to be more specific about the types of businesses you would like to be benchmarked against. For example, if you are a small beauty and personal care business, you may have less than 10 employees. In that case, you might be more interested in how your campaigns perform in comparison to businesses of a similar size, instead of a much larger business such as Sephora. In this example, based on the size of your operation, the Mailchimp app benchmarks you and compares you to other businesses in the **Beauty and Personal Care** category with fewer than 10 employees.

- **How old is your organization?**: Again, this is a way to slice your data and add more nuance to the types of stats and benchmarks that you would like to be compared to. Continuing the previous example, outside of size, you as a small beauty brand might not want to be benchmarked against a retailer such as Sephora, not just due to size but also the age of the business. It may make more sense for your business to be compared to other beauty companies of a similar age.

Next, let's quickly walk through the remaining three sections!

> **Important note**
> These next three sections are designed to influence the information you receive from Mailchimp. If you would like to receive tips and tricks from the platform, you can select your editing experience and indicate to Mailchimp's platform how you would like it to help you manage automatic replies from your audiences as you begin sending email campaigns in the future. If you want, you can just think about this later and keep the default settings for now, proceeding right to the audience setup section without worrying too much that you might be missing out on enabling a niche feature.

Default Email Builder

Default Email Builder allows you to toggle between Mailchimp's two campaign editors. Mailchimp has offered a drag and drop email building experience since late 2011, and in early 2018, it launched a new email builder to modernize the platform and experience. When you create a new account, the more recent editing experience is the default setting, and because it's the up-to-date builder, it's the one that future content in the book will largely focus on, specifically as we move into the sections about campaign building. However, even if you choose **Classic Builder**, there's a significant amount of overlap, and we will touch on some of the differences in template options in both. The flexibility here is that you can change your selection and test-drive both experiences if you wish.

Email from Mailchimp

In the **Email from Mailchimp** section, you can choose what kinds of newsletters you will find most helpful. Some of these are stats about your accounts, which you can have sent to your email if you're on the go and want a quick snapshot of your weekly account summary, for example (and this is one of the places where selecting when your week begins comes into play too). However, you can also choose to opt into great tips such as the weekly round-up from Mailchimp's partner magazine **Courier** (`https://www.couriermedia.com/`), a London-based company that specifically serves and talks to entrepreneurs and small businesses. You can see all the options available to you in *Figure 2.5*:

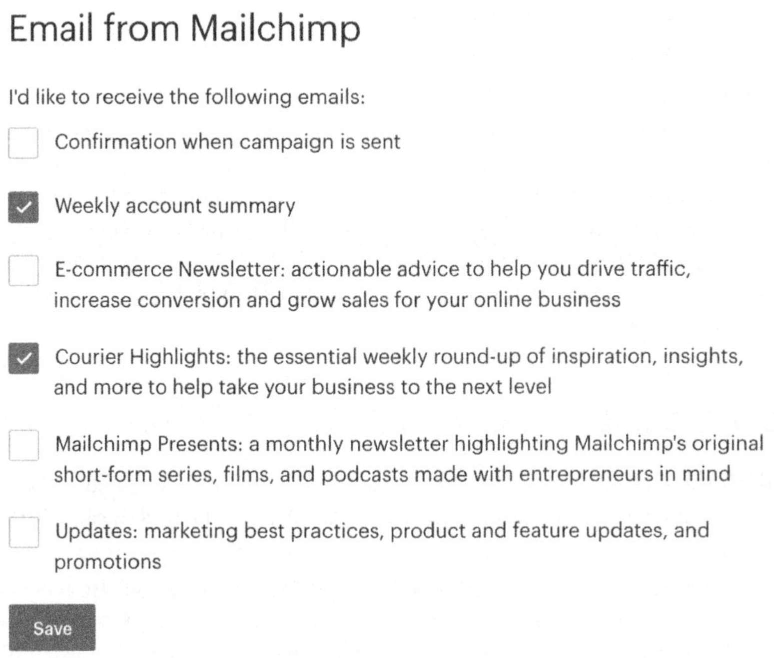

Email from Mailchimp

I'd like to receive the following emails:

- [ ] Confirmation when campaign is sent
- [x] Weekly account summary
- [ ] E-commerce Newsletter: actionable advice to help you drive traffic, increase conversion and grow sales for your online business
- [x] Courier Highlights: the essential weekly round-up of inspiration, insights, and more to help take your business to the next level
- [ ] Mailchimp Presents: a monthly newsletter highlighting Mailchimp's original short-form series, films, and podcasts made with entrepreneurs in mind
- [ ] Updates: marketing best practices, product and feature updates, and promotions

Save

Figure 2.5 – Options in the Email from Mailchimp section

Manage automatic replies

Finally, we have the **Manage automatic replies** section, which is quite straightforward. When you send a campaign, an email address you set will be used as the **From email address** setting. This means that when the email lands in a recipient's inbox, if they have an out-of-office reply set or any similar automatic email, the email address you set will typically be the one that the reply is sent to. However, if you have a huge audience that the campaign is being sent to, this might be undesirable. You could be in the position of accidentally swamping your own inbox with unhelpful emails. To mitigate that happening, you can enable the **Reject automatic replies to my campaigns** feature by checking the box to have those emails handled for you by Mailchimp, as shown in *Figure 2.6*.

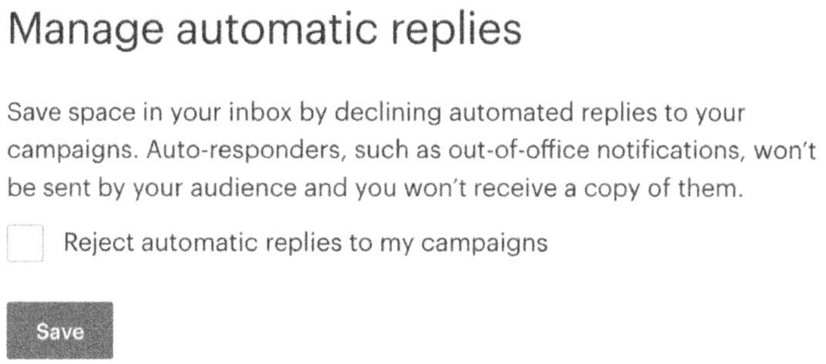

Manage automatic replies

Save space in your inbox by declining automated replies to your campaigns. Auto-responders, such as out-of-office notifications, won't be sent by your audience and you won't receive a copy of them.

☐ Reject automatic replies to my campaigns

[Save]

Figure 2.6 – Managing the automatic replies option

Once you've gone through the five sections on this page, you're ready to move on to creating your first audience. Similar to these previous account settings, audience settings help influence what information populates automatically for you in the future. So, let's take a look at these more granular, audience-specific settings.

Setting up an audience

Audiences are the *beating heart* of your marketing efforts, regardless of what platform you use. This is whether you're thinking about the traditional definition of an audience, meaning who you are writing or designing for or talking to, or the more tangible definition, namely a literal list of people you are intending to interact with to cultivate a relationship or connection.

The purpose behind having an audience is ultimately the same though. They're who you're trying to engage. They're the folks against which you're measuring the success or failure of your efforts. This is particularly true for small businesses and entrepreneurs. Successful engagement with the people your business or organization serves helps drive the peaks and troughs of your success.

Within Mailchimp, and indeed with most marketing platforms, there are various states and types of contacts. So, to set the initial groundwork, let's cover what those are:

- **Subscribed**: This is a contact that has at some point intentionally opted to receive your emails.
- **Unsubscribed**: This status is indicative that, at one point, this person was in your audience, but at some point chose to opt out.
- **Bounced**: This is a contact that has been sent emails various times, but the receiving email client indicated that the address was invalid or unable to be delivered.
- **Transactional**: This is usually a person who has interacted with your business – for example, with an e-commerce store – but would only like to receive critical communication such as receipts and shipping status. However, they have indicated that they would not like to receive marketing communications from you.

So, with that context as our foundational understanding of contact states, let's talk about why platforms such as Mailchimp even use this type of categorization.

Why is it important to know about different contact statuses?

Mailchimp is based in the United States, but it serves customers in over a hundred countries globally. This means that it operates and offers features in compliance with privacy and communication standards in those countries. For example, in the United States, there is a law called the **U.S. CAN-SPAM Act** (`https://www.ftc.gov/business-guidance/resources/can-spam-act-compliance-guide-business`). These are established rules around commercial email and messages, and most importantly, they *give recipients the right to have you stop emailing them*. As I'm not personally an attorney who can provide legal advice, you can read the full text of the regulation directly on the FTC's website.

However, this creates some ambiguity for people when they're first coming to Mailchimp or any platform, and they may wonder, *"I've already got a list of contacts I send emails to, who gave me their email addresses at my store, but can I use them in a marketing platform?"*

The answer is *yes*! As a rule of thumb, you don't want to include people who might have given you their email address over a year ago and haven't engaged with you or purchased anything in a long time, but an existing list of your clients, customers, and so on should be okay.

> **Important note**
> Keep in mind that if you purchased your list from a data broker, online, or some other means, I wouldn't recommend importing that list and marketing to them. It's always a much better and more sustainable idea to grow your own list.

Information you need to make your first list

First, let's just make the list you want these contacts to go into, whether you either import a list or create a form to start growing your own list!

When you first log in to Mailchimp, and throughout most of your experience with the application, there is a navigation menu on the left-hand side of the screen. There, you will see an **Audience** option, which will open a little menu in the left navigation column. This is the area where we'll predominantly be working to set up our lists and manage our contacts in the future:

1. Click **Audience** in the left navigation menu.
2. Click on **All contacts**.

When you select the **All contacts** option, you'll be taken to the audience table, as shown in *Figure 2.7*. Here, you will see an audience table with the email address you used when signing up, subscribed to the list to show you how information is organized in the audience.

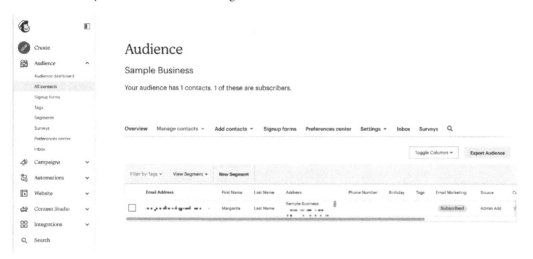

Figure 2.7 – The audience table

We can see a plethora of options here in the menu, but the ones I'm most interested in having us start with are the ones that will impact what your audience sees in forms in the future, and the information they will see in the footer of your email campaigns. So, we're heading into **Settings** and starting at the top, with **Audience name and campaign defaults**.

First things first, the audience name field is what will show up by default in forms; if you select double opt-in, it will show up in subscription emails and the interface that contacts might see if they go to update their profiles. We'll go into editing forms later, but in the meantime, if you want to skip the manual work of editing the name in the signup forms, you can edit it right here. Typically, the best recommendation would be to look at your list as a global or primary list and then use groups, tags, or segments to delineate and target different subsets of your subscribers.

So, name the audience as something that aligns with your business or organization but is not necessarily specific about who you're targeting. For example, you might just want to leave it as the name of your business if you're selling something, or you could name it after yourself if you're an artist or writer who is trying to build a following online.

There are three core sections that the audience settings page is broken down into:

- **Form settings**
- **Campaign defaults**
- **New subscriber notifications**

Basics of Account Management and Audiences

Each serves a distinct purpose and will cascade to impact your marketing efforts in different ways.

Form settings

In the first section, **Form settings**, as you can see in *Figure 2.8*, we see options related to the security and protection of your forms. Double opt-in and reCAPTCHA can seem like barriers to list growth, but in reality, they can be a good measure to ensure that the growth you're experiencing is steady, intentional, and healthy.

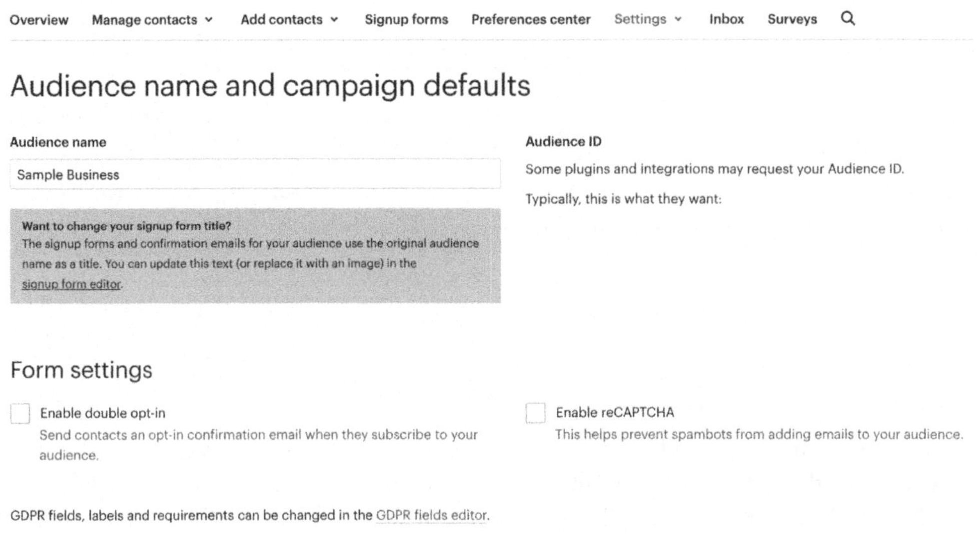

Figure 2.8 – Form settings in audience settings

If you are not familiar with **double opt-in**, it refers to a process where you are, in essence, confirming with the user that they would like to be added to your audience, and it empowers them by acknowledging that they know you'll be marketing to them.

The general pattern of a potential contact might go something like this:

1. They visit your website.
2. They sign up through an embedded form.
3. They receive an email thanking them and asking them to confirm whether they would like to be added to the marketing list.
4. Mailchimp adds them to your list as **Subscribed**.

reCAPTCHA is wonderful because it can help protect your audience from spambots. Spambots are programs that will frequently scrape through the internet, plugging garbage email addresses and other text lines into fields such as your signup forms. reCAPTCHA requires potential subscribers to check a box to complete the signup process to indicate they're not a robot (you've probably encountered plenty yourself!).

The reason I think this can be such a simple and powerful tool is twofold. One, most platforms such as Mailchimp charge based on contact volume in your account. Clogging up your list with lots of contacts that, in most cases, can't even receive email and who aren't genuinely engaged with you or your marketing can end up costing you *actual money*. The second reason is that if want to make use of performance stats and other indicators throughout the app, you'll want to make sure your list stays healthy. With lots of spambot email addresses on your list, you'll see those stats showing that you're receiving fewer successful sends, fewer opens, clicks, and so on – all because some percentage of your audience isn't even human.

Campaign defaults

In the next section, as shown in *Figure 2.9*, you can set some default information that's populated into campaign headers for you so that you don't have to fill it out every time.

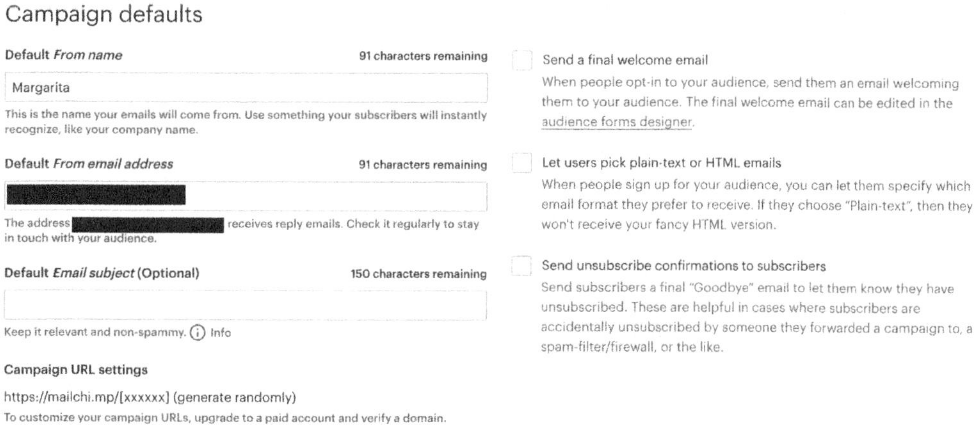

Figure 2.9 – Campaign default behaviors

You can set a name for your emails – for example, if you have a nickname or brand identity that you would like to use. You might use your brand's name, a pen name, the name of your mascot, and so on. Critically, if you want to keep the email address you initially signed up for with your Mailchimp account private, you can input a business-related email address here. To use an email address here, you have to actually be able to receive emails at that address, and if it's at a private domain, you will have to complete an email verification process similar to when you signed up for a Mailchimp account originally.

Optionally, you can also set a default campaign subject line. If you decide to use this, I would generally recommend choosing something that's not a hard sell on a specific behavior. For example, something more specific to a business or organization tends to perform better than something generic. Mailchimp has been in the email marketing space for over a decade, and in that time, research there and in the industry broadly indicates that subject lines with lots of unrelated emojis and that are excessively long tend to see lower engagement than those that are concise, specific, and descriptive.

> **Tip**
> You can check this URL to understand best practices for email subject lines: `https://eepurl.com/dyikT9`.

On the right-hand side in *Figure 2.9*, you can make some decisions about some very simple automatic emails that you can set up quickly to engage your new subscribers, or attempt to re-engage them should they choose to unsubscribe. These options in *Figure 2.9* can be something great to set up while you take the time to customize and design a full-fledged welcome automation.

New subscriber notifications

The final section on this page, **New subscriber notifications**, has more to do with how you would like information about a specific list to be sent to you if you wish. This is totally optional, and as you scale, you might grow less and less interested in having data this granular. But it really all depends on where you are on your journey! If you're new to marketing platforms, it can be really exciting to get the one-off notifications when people subscribe or unsubscribe. You'll have two one-by-one options here, where you can enable an email to be sent to the email address of your choice about each subscription and unsubscription, and then one report that's a weekly summary.

You can experiment and toggle these off or on as you figure out what works for you. Personally, my recommendation would be to use the mobile app if you have a smartphone because you can self-serve a dashboard at will if you're genuinely curious, avoiding filling your personal inbox with stats.

> **Tip**
> Before moving on, remember to save any changes you made on this page!

The last setting for each audience I want to focus on, particularly if this is your first list, is **Required email footer content** in the **Settings** menu. The reason I'm highlighting this is that information in this section must legally appear in marketing campaigns that your contacts receive. Mailchimp uses a placeholder in your campaigns to display this information for you, but you want to make sure that it's information you're comfortable with your subscribers seeing. Ideally, this should be a physical address associated with your business or organization, but it can be something such as a post office box but not an email address or website.

The key behind a great many of these settings, either for lists or for the account overall, is that taking a little extra time when setting up ensures that you don't accidentally present information to your contacts that you don't mean to be sharing; additionally, it helps to make sure that what you do show your contacts is consistent and clear from the outset of your marketing. Next, we'll talk a little about the benefit of using a central list versus several lists.

The purpose behind using a central versus various list

Should you already have multiple lists, that's okay. In *Chapter 3*, there will be an entire section dedicated to combining lists and the pros and cons of those actions. However, before we move on to that, I'd like to talk about the purpose of having a different strategy at the outset of your account. The ideal situation would be to combine them into one primary list and utilize features such as segments, tags, and groups to organize subscribers for specific sends.

One of the main reasons is that each list in the platform is viewed as completely distinct and is largely what billing is based on. For example, if you have the email address `example@example.com` listed as a subscriber in *audience A* and *audience B*, then that contact would count as two distinct contacts and be billed accordingly. But instead, if we have the address in a single, centralized list and use groups or tags to indicate they're in *Group A* and *Group B*, then that contact would count as a single contact but still enable you to identify that address for distinct marketing purposes.

The benefit here would be that your billing would be lower over time, but you'd still have the ability to better target your sends for different purposes.

We'll go further into these list management strategies in the next chapter!

Summary

By doing things such as editing our account and audience settings, we've set a solid foundation for actually building out our lists. It gives us some insight into the inherent benefits of choosing the number of lists we'd like to use and other neat fringe benefits that allow us to plan a little.

Specifically, in this chapter, we learned things such as what basic information we need to have set up in an account for compliance purposes, and how to ensure that data from the platform is as usable and relevant as possible as we scale. We also learned what an audience is and what purpose it serves in the entire Mailchimp ecosystem, as well as how to edit the settings of your first list to best serve you. Finally, we learned the impact of maintaining one list versus multiple lists, ensuring that you can make an informed decision about your billing and data utilization that makes the most sense for your business.

In the next chapter, let's dive deeper into our audience and importing so that we can get the core of our application running.

Further reading

- *Best Practices for Email Subject Lines*: `https://eepurl.com/dyikT9`
- *Anti-Spam Requirements for Email*: `https://eepurl.com/dygYDH`
- *View or Change Account Contact Information*: `https://eepurl.com/dyinqr`
- *Why We Require an Unsubscribe Link*: `https://eepurl.com/dyinv1`

3
Importing and Combining Audiences

It's not uncommon to start your business in-person, online, or locally in your community without using a marketing platform such as Mailchimp. This might mean that you've been sending emails one by one to your contacts or collecting interest for your content or products at events such as craft fairs, conferences, or expos. As long as you were clear with people that their information was being collected to contact them for the marketing of your products or services, you can import that list into Mailchimp. If you previously used another marketing platform, but maybe it didn't quite work for you, you don't have to leave your contacts behind when making the switch to Mailchimp.

Most platforms don't make the assumption that you have no audience and are looking to build one from scratch, but Mailchimp makes it possible for you to import contacts if you have them and collect new contacts using forms and landing pages (which you'll learn more about in later chapters).

You also might already be a Mailchimp user and looking for better ways to manage your lists. In that case, you might want to particularly think about checking out the *Merge Tags* section to make sure you're making the most out of the data you collect. Alternatively, you can jump to the *Combining audiences* section of this chapter if you have lots of lists and want to try not only to cut your billing, but also to make the most of all of your contacts.

In this chapter, we will go through the following main topics:

- Merge Tags
- How to import a list
- Combining audiences

By the end of the chapter, we should have a solid system for our audiences and how we organize that data. So, let's jump into it!

Merge Tags

Merge Tags is one of my favorite simple yet powerful functions built into the Mailchimp platform. It makes all of your data more useful. It's a text-based identifier for account information and audience field content such as **First name** or **Email address**.

It's powerful because you can use these placeholders to make your bulk marketing emails a little more personal and special for your contacts. You can also use them, and you'll see them appear by default, in the footers of campaign templates to pull in account information to keep all your emails and content compliant with laws such as **CAN-SPAM**, as we noted in an earlier chapter.

More recent trends identified by Mailchimp show that contacts are 29% more likely to open personalized emails and those emails drive six times more transactions than generic ones.

The more specific emails are, the more engagement they will drive over time.

Additionally, as you add merge tags, you can also choose to just toggle them on and off on your sign-up forms in the future – another bonus to thinking about fields and their merge tags a little in advance!

So, to add fields and edit the merge tags for each of those fields, when you're looking at the **All contacts** table, you would do the following:

1. Click on the **Settings** menu.
2. Select **Audience fields and *|MERGE|* tags**.

We can do so much from this interface to set ourselves up for an easier time in the future, which is so exciting. So let's take a look at our options in the **Audience fields and *|MERGE|* tags** section of the **Audience** settings.

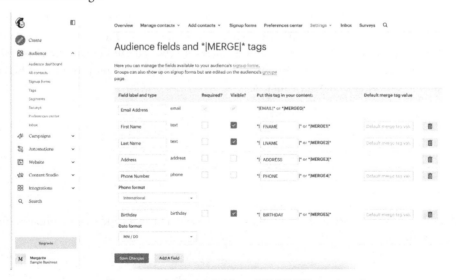

Figure 3.1 – Audience fields and *|MERGE|* tags interface

Let's look over each of the columns we can see in *Figure 3.1* and talk briefly about what it impacts:

- **Field label and type**: This is the name of the field and it should identify the type of format in which you would like the information to be saved in the Mailchimp database. There are over 12 field types. We'll look further into the options when setting up sign-up forms, but they are fairly straightforward. For subscriber data, we can see the most common use cases in the preceding screenshot and for the most part, beyond that, fields are most commonly **text** fields.
- **Required?**: This is how you enforce any of these fields being necessary in order for contacts to be added to your audience.
- **Visible?**: As the column title implies, this is the setting for whether you would like a field to be visible to contacts on default sign-up forms in the future.
- **Put this tag in your content**: When you import data into Mailchimp, by default, this field will generally be populated for you with some version of the column names you indicated during the import process.
- **Default merge tag value**: This is the value you would like to appear in a campaign or automation email in the event that the contact doesn't have information in the field.

Specifically, the two columns we'll be focusing on from the preceding settings are **Put this tag in your content** and **Default merge tag value** since these are the ones we'll get the most use out of when we actually begin sending out campaigns.

Put this tag in your content

This is the super-powerful part. These are text identifiers you can put into your campaign text in the future to have the Mailchimp platform replace the text with the contact's specific profile information. For example, you can use the * | FNAME | * merge tag in a campaign, like in the following text snippet, and two different contacts will see two different sentences:

*Hi *|FNAME|*! I'm so excited to tell you about my newest project. I think you'll really like it.*

A contact with the name *Freddie* in their contact profile would see the following:

Hi Freddie! I'm so excited to tell you about my newest project. I think you'll really like it.

Whereas a contact with the name *Jane* in their contact profile would see the following:

Hi Jane! I'm so excited to tell you about my newest project. I think you'll really like it.

Now, of course, personalization should and absolutely can go well beyond just your contacts' names, but it's a really wonderful starting point for getting comfortable with the purpose and function of merge tags in your content. You can use it to input interests your contacts might have logged in a field during signup or their birthday for an automation to wish them a happy birthday and provide them with a discount. It has so many applications.

During setup though, the most important thing to consider is how easy some of these merge tags are for you to remember. By default, for example, first name is given the *|FNAME|* merge tag. But if that's not super-memorable for you, you can change it to something such as *|FIRST|* – whatever works for you to minimize the frequency with which you might need to refer back to this page while you're working on your campaigns in the future.

> **Important note**
>
> Merge tags are not duplicative, meaning you can't have two merge tags that use *|NAME|*, for example. The reason *|FNAME|* and *|LNAME|* are distinct is not just for indicating that they're first and last names, but also because the app will not allow them to both be *|NAME|*. Every tag should be unique in order for the app to replace it during a campaign send.

Default merge tag value

Now, in the event that you're making some information optional, you'll want to set a default value for your merge tag. This is something that the platform will input for you in the event that when you use a merge tag in a campaign and the contact doesn't have information for that field, the app still has something to input into the blank space. Building on the last example, we might want the default value for **First Name** to be something generic but on-brand for your business or organization, such as **buddy**. So, using the same example, if we set the default field to **buddy**, we will see the following:

*Hi *|FNAME|*! I'm so excited to tell you about my newest project. I think you'll really like it.*

A contact with the name *Freddie* in their contact profile would see the following:

Hi Freddie! I'm so excited to tell you about my newest project. I think you'll really like it.

And a contact with *no information* in the *First Name* field in their contact profile would see the following:

Hi buddy! I'm so excited to tell you about my newest project. I think you'll really like it.

Another cool detail about merge tags is you can even get a little fancy. Sometimes you may want to format the information that people input themselves into fields of your sign-up forms. Some contacts type super-fast or use things such as autofill on their browsers and might end up inputting their first name like this: *freddie*.

Obviously, this isn't necessarily ideal when using a merge tag in a campaign because it would be very clear that we didn't personalize these campaigns for each contact, and we're looking for something polished. So, we can ensure that the automatically input content meets our stylistic preferences. We can use the following to change the format for us so we don't have to worry about the formatting choices contacts might have made when working quickly:

- **Title case**: This formatting option will capitalize the first letter of each word
  - `*|TITLE:FNAME|*`
  - **Example**: `Hi *|TITLE:FNAME|*! I'm so excited to tell you about my newest project. I think you'll really like it.`
    - **Result**: *Hi Freddie! I'm so excited to tell you about my newest project. I think you'll really like it.*
- **Uppercase**: This formatting option will capitalize all the letters
  - `*|UPPER:FNAME|*`
  - **Example**: `Hi *|UPPER:FNAME|*! I'm so excited to tell you about my newest project. I think you'll really like it.`
    - **Result**: *Hi FREDDIE! I'm so excited to tell you about my newest project. I think you'll really like it.*
- **Lower-case**: This formatting will change the value to be all lowercase
  - `*|LOWER:FNAME|*`
  - **Example**: `Hi *|LOWER:FNAME|*! I'm so excited to tell you about my newest project. I think you'll really like it.`
    - **Result**: *Hi freddie! I'm so excited to tell you about my newest project. I think you'll really like it.*

So, get adding! Edit the merge tags so you're comfortable with the code! And don't forget to save at the end. Next, we'll get into how to add contacts to an audience we can actually leverage these merge tags with.

How to import a list

As is true with a couple of other basic features of your Mailchimp account that are central to the whole platform being able to function, there are a couple of ways of navigating to **Audience** and starting a new import. As we saw in *Chapter 1*, in *Figure 1.3*, with a brand-new account you'll see a prompt on the home page of the app called **Add Your Contacts**. This is probably the quickest initial path to the import wizard, but of course, even if that prompt isn't there because you've done at least one small import, you can reach it by selecting **Audience** from the left-hand navigation panel, which will take you to the **Audience Dashboard** screen, as seen in *Figure 3.2*:

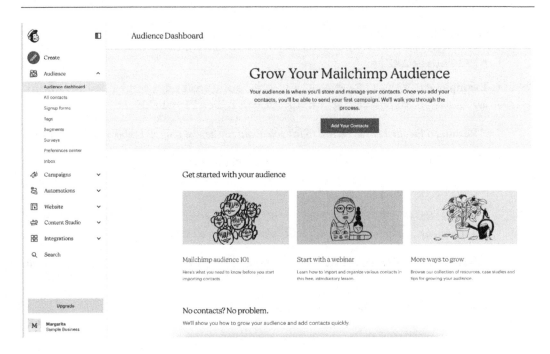

Figure 3.2 – Audience Dashboard

When you click on the **Add Your Contacts** button at the top, you'll be given three options for importing your existing contacts:

- **Import from another service**
- **Upload a file**
- **Copy and paste**

The two most common options are **Upload a file** and **Copy and paste**. In *Part 5, Get Smart and Connect*, we'll look a little more into integrations. In order to use the **Integration** options, you would have to connect through the **Integrations** menu option first. In the **Integration** options, you'll have commerce platforms such as Shopify, **customer relationship managers** (**CRMs**) such as Salesforce, and workflow automation software such as Zapier that you can connect to. But as a starting point, I would recommend starting with a standard import option.

With the **Upload a File** option and the **Copy and Paste** option, you're still ultimately looking to use information from a spreadsheet. You'll want to make sure that the file you're importing or copying from is a **comma-separated values** (**CSV**) or a **TXT** (**plain-text**) file. These are the formats that allow the application to automatically understand where the columns of data exist. For example, if you are copying and pasting, ultimately, what you paste into the block might look something like the following:

```
First name, Last name, Email address
Freddie, Von Chimpenheimer, sample@sample.com
Margarita, Caraballo, sample+margarita@sample.com
John, Doe, sample+john@sample.com
```

The pattern we see emerge here is that if we look at the first value of each line, it's the column name at the top and then the first name of each entry. So, this would be the equivalent of telling Mailchimp what kind of data is in each column.

Once you've selected your import file or copied and pasted from a CSV or TXT file, you will be asked to confirm the status the contacts should be imported with. Reminder: as we began to cover in *Chapter 2*, your options are the following:

- **Subscribed**: This is a contact that has at some point intentionally opted to receive your emails.
- **Unsubscribed**: This status is indicative that at one point this person opted to receive your emails, but at some point indicated that they wanted to opt out.
- **Cleaned**: This status allows you to indicate email addresses you might have but you know are invalid. You can identify addresses that would *bounce* if you attempt to send an email to them. The goal with importing these addresses would be to make sure that you don't spend time sending emails to email addresses that were ultimately invalid when you sent to them in the past.
- **Non-subscribed**: During the import, this is your chance to bring in information for people who in the past might not have opted in on your other platforms for marketing, but who perhaps might have purchased from a store and requested transactional emails such as invoices, receipts, order notifications, and so on. This is the desired status for *transactional* contacts, as we noted in *Chapter 2*.

A key thing to keep in mind about how you organize your data or choose what order to import your data in is you will want to group your contacts by the preceding categories if you plan to import to more than just the **Subscribed** status.

So, for example, if I wanted to import people into the first two contact types, I'd divide my **Subscribed** contacts into one import and **Unsubscribed** into a second.

After you choose the contact status type, if you have an existing list, you can also check the box next to the option to update any contacts that might already be in your audience.

> Important note
> If you choose this option, note that the subscriber profile information already in the Mailchimp account for each email address will be overridden with the data in the imported file.

In the next section of the import wizard, you can create a tag to identify this particular import if they have something in common. So, leveraging one of the earlier examples, if you collected these email addresses at a conference, you might want to tag all of these contacts with a tag to indicate the name of the conference where you met the contact. We'll go further into the use and purpose of tags, groups, and segments in the next chapter, but they're essentially mechanisms for organizing the data in your list to empower you to use one main list as opposed to several separate lists, while still allowing you to connect to niche sub-sets of contacts for different purposes or for different brands.

The final step is to match the columns of data in your file to the merge tags or categories your list is set up for. In *Figure 3.3*, we see the results of the copy-and-paste information from the earlier example:

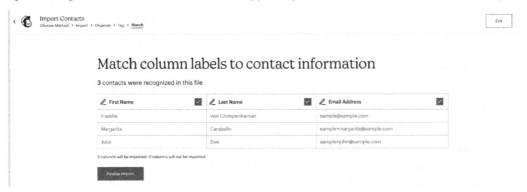

Figure 3.3 – Match step of the import wizard

At this point, we see the app attempt to match the file information it sees in what you attempted to import with known data points. Mailchimp, at its most basic, is a marketing email and automation platform. In order to move forward, at the very least, it will identify email address information. However, you can choose to edit any of the column names if you feel there's a better or more descriptive name to give the content of a column.

Once you click on **Finalize Import**, you will get a confirmation screen informing you of how many contacts will be imported and what kind of impact it might have on your billing. This, of course, will vary slightly depending on the plan you have and then you can confirm that you would like to start the import. You'll see a page indicating whether your import went through, which will tell you a little more about the number of contacts that have been updated and then how many were added as net-new to your audience, as in *Figure 3.4*:

Figure 3.4 – Import success page

Again, the nice thing about audiences being core to using Mailchimp is that there are a couple of different places you can start an import from. The same wizard experience we just talked through on the last several pages can be initiated from the following places:

- **Primary Account Dashboard**: As long as you haven't attempted an import before, you will have the option to start an import to your first list from the home page as soon as you log in to the Mailchimp app.
- **Audience Dashboard**: This is the experience we went through in more detail in the last several pages, but it's the default option as soon as you click on **Audience** in the left navigation panel, again if you have not completed an import yet.
- **All contacts**: If you have completed at least one import, this will be the path you use to import every subsequent time. From this interface, you can select the option to **Add contacts** and then **Import contacts** and it will take you to the same import wizard.

> **Important note**
> If you don't yet have a file of audience members and you would like to try out this import function first, you can download a sample file directly from Mailchimp that will allow you to run through an import as described and check out the formatting of a file prior to import. You can find it in the *Further reading* section at the end of this chapter; it's called *Format Guidelines for Your Import File*.

Combining audiences

Finally, let's talk about why using a primary audience is generally a better experience over time.

The first short-term benefit is the obvious monetary angle. Marketing platforms and CRMs tend to charge based on utilization and they tend to define that utilization by contact number and feature access. Within Mailchimp specifically, there are different packages depending on the features you're interested in, but within those tiers, the price goes up depending on the number of contacts you have in your audiences.

As noted before, each audience within Mailchimp is viewed as being completely separate from one another. This means if you have `Audience A` and `Audience B` and the `example@example.com` email address is a contact subscribed to both lists, then that email address would count as two contacts for your billing.

Now, arguably, the monetary benefits would be applicable in the short term and long term, since those cost savings would carry over the life of your use of a marketing automation platform such as Mailchimp, but the additional benefits are slightly more conceptual at first.

As you scale your use of Mailchimp, the application will log information about your subscribers' behaviors, such as the frequency with which they engage with your content, to their subscriber profile. The longer your audience is active, the more behavioral data you'll have access to in order to segment, group, and tag your audience members. As we noted earlier in this chapter, more targeted and personalized campaigns perform better over time and drive more engagement with your products and brand. Since audiences are distinct from one another, this means that you'll have the most complete data about your contacts by keeping them on the same list.

Now, before we walk through the two options for how to actually combine your audiences inside Mailchimp in the event that you're already a user, let's cover some of the reasons and use cases for keeping separate lists:

- You're an agency managing the marketing efforts for several different companies or brands within a single Mailchimp account.
- If you are in need of GDPR features for one set of contacts but not another.

    GDPR features, when they are enabled for the audience, would apply to all contacts and forms when they have opted in.
- You are a long-time user of Mailchimp and have lots of engagement data on both lists.

When you combine existing lists, the list being combined into another will not combine or transfer engagement metrics such as opens and clicks, but it will transfer the contents of the subscriber fields such as **First Name**, **Last Name**, **Email Address**, and so on.

In the next couple of sections, we'll run through a couple of the different ways you can combine your audiences.

How to combine audiences

To actually combine audiences, you have two options:

- Use the **Combine Audiences** tool
- Export and then import the audiences you want to combine

Generally, though, I would recommend exporting your lists to keep a backup either way; it's always better to be safe!

To export any audience in Mailchimp, you would navigate to the specific audience, then take the following steps:

1. Select **All contacts** from the left-navigation menu.
2. In the upper right of each contact table, click the **Export Audience** button, as seen in *Figure 3.5*:

Figure 3.5 – Export Audience button on the audience contact table

Once you have the exported files as a backup, you can head into whichever option you prefer. I've put together a quick workflow in *Figure 3.6* to help you determine whether combining audiences is right for you:

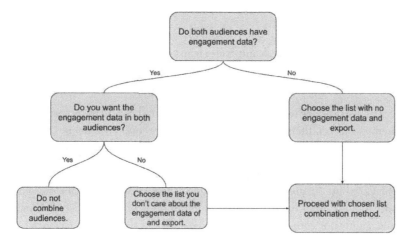

Figure 3.6 – Should you combine your audiences?

The preceding workflow should help you come down on a decision related to your existing audiences if you are already using multiple lists either inside Mailchimp or in another platform that you plan to import into Mailchimp. Largely, what you should be thinking about is what data is most important to you. Ultimately, you should strongly consider streamlining your audiences as much as possible at an earlier stage in your marketing journey. This will help to manage your costs, but also provide you with a more centralized home for your audience data.

Finally, let's take a look at a tool exclusively designed to achieve this type of combination.

The Combine Audiences tool

This option is probably the simplest, assuming the audience you are combining into another is relatively unused or lacks much engagement data. When you're ready, you would navigate to the list of all of your audiences at once, which you can find by heading to **Audience Dashboard**:

1. Select **Manage Audience**.
2. Select **View audiences**.
3. Once there, you will identify the name of the audience with the engagement data you either don't care about or that doesn't have engagement data.
4. Next to the **Stats** button, there's a drop-down arrow menu.
5. Click on **Combine audiences**.

A pop-up modal will appear, and there, you can indicate the primary audience you would like this list to be combined into. This will let the Mailchimp platform do it for you and then you can opt to delete the old list once you review it and make sure you feel comfortable. Next, let's take a look at another method of combining audiences.

Exporting and importing

This is a slightly more manual process and really leans on the audience import process from the beginning of this chapter. You'd essentially be putting together the audience export process noted at the beginning of the *How to combine audiences* section and then the import process in *How to import a list*.

This doesn't necessarily produce radically different results, but it can be more comfortable for people who want to manually match their data to the new or primary audience fields. One is not markedly better than the other, but depending on your comfort level, this process can feel more visual.

That being said, without using the **Combine Audiences** tool, you could risk temporarily inflating your billing. The **Combine Audiences** tool is designed to execute the transfer/merging of contacts for you all at once. On the other hand, the export and import process, because audiences are viewed as distinct, would count your audience members twice until you either unsubscribe the contacts from the old audience or delete the old audience.

> **Important suggestion**
> If you choose this option for combining your audiences, you should use the contact archiving tool. Archiving a contact will remove the audience member from being an active recipient to a separate designation that allows you to retain their data but does not allow you to send emails to them and does not impact your billing. We'll discuss inactive contacts and how to manage them further in *Chapter 5*.

Summary

This chapter was really all about marrying adjustments in your settings and audiences with practical steps and changes you can make to make your marketing automatic and a little more thoughtful as you build out your channels. Because we know that more personalized marketing tends to experience more engagement, how we responsibly use our contact data can really be the difference between a good campaign and a great one.

In this chapter, you learned how to leverage features such as merge tags to serve you just a little more in modifying your marketing efforts without having to make a single campaign for every single contact. We also learned what types of files are platform-compatible, what limits exist, and how to think about organizing your data before importing it. And finally, we learned how different list management strategies can help reduce duplications and billing, but also the pros and cons of each choice you might consider with respect to organizing your contacts.

In the next chapter, let's put some of this into practice. We'll be digging into how we actually leverage features such as groups, tags, and segments to identify and organize our contacts for targeted campaigns in the future.

Further reading

- *What is personalized marketing?*: https://mailchimp.com/marketing-glossary/personalized-marketing/
- *Format Guidelines for Your Import File*: https://eepurl.com/dyilKP
- *Compare Mailchimp pricing plans*: https://mailchimp.com/pricing/marketing/compare-plans/
- *Archive or Unarchive Your Contacts*: https://eepurl.com/gn3WJj

4
Understanding the Difference between Groups, Tags, and Segments

In a world that is more interconnected now than ever before, with more options for content and an increasing number of screens to pay attention to, it becomes really critical to think about how to stay relevant to your audience. In the context of marketing, we only have a short time to make an impact as people skim their inboxes or their social media feeds. The more generic or bland your content is, the less likely you are to get engagement. This, of course, means that the more you understand why people engage with you and what they like about you or your product, the more specific and on-brand you can make your campaigns.

To that end, while we should always be mindful and respectful stewards of the data that people entrust us with, we should always think a bit about how we can target what we send out to people. This chapter is going to focus on what we mean when we say *targeting*.

We will cover the following main topics in this chapter:

- How targeting can lead to higher engagement
- What are groups and tags?
- Importing directly into groups or tags
- Segmenting tools

So, let's take a look at the theory behind targeting and then get into these tools!

How targeting can lead to higher engagement

Targeting your marketing drives higher engagement, and if you're promoting products or services, it also drives higher revenue. But you don't have to take my word for it – in a report published by the *Harvard Business Review* in 2018, *The Age of Personalization*, they preface their findings by discussing how using and developing a strategy for personalization, including personalizing things such as the products and services you offer or your website, can have a positive impact on your revenue. This also demonstrates that your business or content is really focused on and understands its audience, which in turn makes for a more engaged and loyal customer base. You'll find a full link to the report in the *Further reading* section at the end of the chapter.

When you show your audience that you understand why they've subscribed to your content and what they come to you for, you tend to see higher rates of engagement.

So, what do we mean when we say targeting?

We can think of **targeting** as how we think about customizing our content to be a little more specific for a subset of our audience.

For example, let's say that I sell books online only. I want to get a sense of how the business works and what I like about selling books before committing to a brick-and-mortar location.

My audience is currently 2,000 contacts. I think a pretty easy first assumption we can make is that if I were to ask even 100 random people what their favorite kind of books are, there would be a pretty low likelihood that all 100 would like the same genre of books.

So this means that the most valuable initial piece of information I can gather about my contacts is what genres of books they are most interested in. That way, when I send campaigns, I can do things such as the following:

- Use dynamic content to customize my emails to be more specific to the genres people like, which is covered in detail in *Chapter 8*.
- Use tools such as segmenting to create a different campaign specific to different genres of books, which we will cover later in this chapter in the *Segmenting tools* section.

If we think about it from the perspective of the customers in that scenario, aren't they more likely to consider a book or even click on a link to read the summary of a book if they know that it's a genre they usually read? The closer we can get to making our audience open a campaign, read a campaign, or even click through to a store, the more revenue we can drive for our businesses.

The reality is that personalization is a slightly moving target. That means that as your business evolves and grows, your audience is changing and growing with you. Therefore, keeping up with industry trends and experimenting with your marketing and personalization is always important. We can even look to the tech industry itself for the personification of this behavior. It's an industry that is constantly changing because what we want from our tech is constantly growing. We want to be more connected, we want more information… we want more!

This desire for more tech and to get more *out of* that tech means that tech companies are moving quickly to keep up. What worked 5 years ago may not work now, and tech companies aren't usually precious about tossing aside a strategy that might have worked before in favor of a strategy built for now, and experimentation is at the very heart of that. This involves trial and error and then enough humility to balance changes with feedback from your users.

Now that we have a shared understanding of what we mean by targeting, let's actually start looking at some of the features that we can use inside platforms such as Mailchimp to actually empower you to employ that targeting yourself.

What are groups and tags?

We can think of both **groups** and **tags** as how we can take steps to organize our audience into more niche subsets during importing or when designing our forms. You may even remember that earlier in *Chapter 3*, when we covered **combining audiences**, we briefly discussed how you could use tools such as these to indicate sets of contacts that belonged to different parts of your business.

For example, let's say that I run a beauty company and it has two distinct brands. One brand is geared toward skincare and anti-aging products, and the second brand makes nail polishes. These two brands are marketed separately and have distinct domains and online presences. By using groups, I can set up checkboxes on a signup form and allow contacts to choose whether they'd like to hear from one brand or both. And in that way, when I inspect the audience, I can see which contacts are interested in one brand or another, and I can *target* my campaigns more accurately by using that group information. There will be more on that later in this chapter when we talk about **segmenting**.

Similarly, tags can be used to identify subsets of your audience, but they're largely more for internal use. Using the same business as an example, let's say the first brand goes to a beauty expo to demo some products. While there, we let people sign up to hear more about the brand and company. When I get home and I import those contacts, during the import process, I can add a custom tag such as **2022BEAUTYEXPO** to identify those contacts for future sends, as shown in *Figure 4.1*.

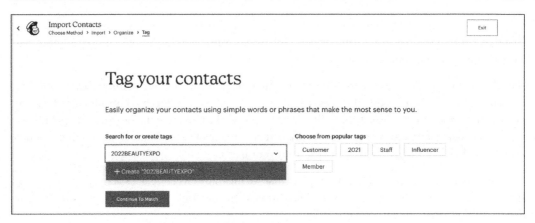

Figure 4.1 – The import step to tag contacts

And again, once we apply this tag, we can inspect the audience and easily identify contacts from the expo that we can specifically target and follow up.

So, now that we understand why we might want to use these tools, let's jump into how we can create them and what the differences between them might be.

Groups

By and large, groups are generally visible to your audience; they are something they can opt into to inform you about the kinds of things they're interested in. When you're creating a group within Mailchimp, you'll want to determine two things primarily:

- A group category
- Group names

The **group category** can be a question or a single phrase that conveys what you're trying to understand about your audience. The group names would then be the items or options under that category that the subscriber is, in theory, selecting from.

Continuing the example from earlier in this chapter, let's say I wanted to understand what kinds of products each subscriber was most interested in for my skincare line, or perhaps I wanted to know what kinds of products to recommend to different subscribers. I might make my group category and group names the following:

- Group category:
  - How would you classify your skin type?

- Group names:
  - Dry skin
  - Oily skin
  - Combination skin

In this way, as a skincare company, I can gather a bit of information from my subscribers as they sign up so that as I develop new product lines for different skin concerns, I have a built-in set of information about my audience to help me choose specific contacts to market to. Let's say, for next winter, I developed a family of super-hydrating products to combat dry skin. I know I can start the marketing for that line to audience members who indicated they're prone to dry skin.

So, let's get into how to set up your first group category:

1. When you log in to your Mailchimp account, you need to click on **Audience** in the left navigation panel and then select **All contacts** from the menu, as shown in *Figure 4.2*.

Figure 4.2 – The All contacts option in the left navigation panel

2. From the audience contact table, click on the **Manage contacts** menu and head into **Groups**.

3. Here, choose the **Create Group** option, and under that, you'll head into the editing interface to create a group category and group names. However, your primary concern is really going to center on whether you want the group to be visible to contacts on the form later and then how you want the groups to appear to them if they are visible.

   Generally, if you plan on having many group names under a category, it would be best to choose a drop-down option where contacts can only select one. The reason for this is that exceedingly long and visible group lists can be overwhelming when people go to use your sign-up forms. Therefore, be sure to balance your desire for information with making your forms appear accessible.

4. By default, the application will give you three blank fields for group names, but you can always add more if you need them.

> **Important note**
> The application will allow for a maximum of 60 group names per audience. However, the group category names will not count toward that maximum.

Your editing interface will look like *Figure 4.3*:

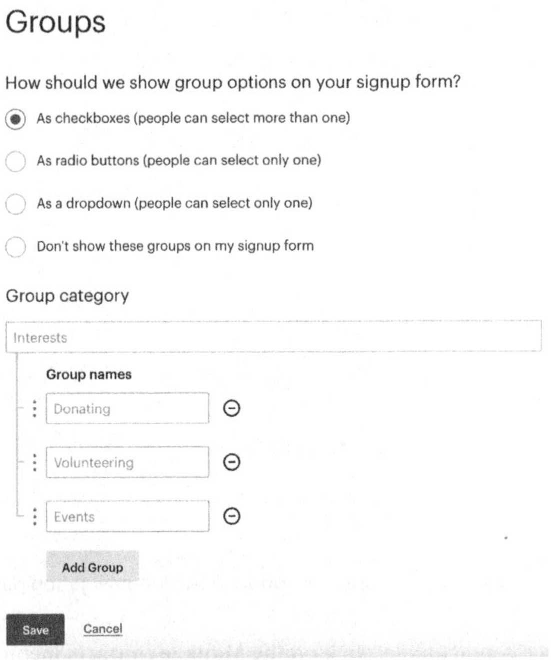

Figure 4.3 – The Group category and Group names editing interface

> **Important note**
> Be mindful when creating groups that you carefully consider the group options, as these cannot be edited later on.

There are a couple of things to keep in mind when creating these groups. There are some parts that you can edit in the future and some that you can't, which I've categorized for you here:

- These can be edited:
  - Group category
  - Group names
  - Group names can be added later
- These can't be edited:
  - Group options

We'll get further into sign-up forms later on in *Chapter 6*, when we start setting up and customizing our sign-up form. However, group fields generally will show up at the bottom of sign-up forms, due to their being a different type of group field from all the other ones you might have created during importing in *Chapter 3*.

So, now that we know how to create subsets of contacts that are predominantly visible to your audience, let's take a look at tags.

Tags

Similar to groups, the purpose of tags is to empower you to know more about and categorize your contacts. Then, you can later use that information to make sure that the marketing you send them is customized to them to ensure they're engaged. Tags, however, can be thought of as more of an organizational tool internal to you. They're a bit more flexible, in the sense that you can make them suit your needs at the time.

For example, you might want to choose tag names to identify where you encountered a person being added to your list if you met them at a particular event, or you might want to associate the contact with a particular role, such as an influencer or a member of staff.

> **Important limitation**
> Tags cannot exceed 100 total characters per tag.

We briefly saw how to add tags during the import process we walked through in the previous chapter, but generally, during these imports, the idea is to mark all the contacts in that import with one or a collection of tags. We'll go further into importing into groups and tags in the *Importing to groups or tags* section later on in this chapter.

However, the basics of creating these tags are very similar to creating groups.

When you're viewing the contacts table, you do the same thing you did when you created groups. You click on the **Manage contacts** menu and then select **Tags** this time. In the tag creation interface, click on the **Create Tag** button on the right-hand side, and a popover modal will appear for you to enter the new tag name, as shown in *Figure 4.4*.

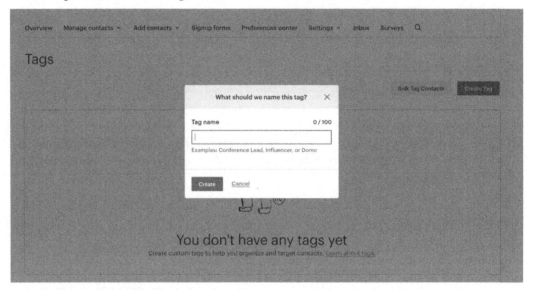

Figure 4.4 – The tag creation popover modal

This is also the interface where, in the future, you can take a look over a full list of all of the tags you're using and even delete them.

> **Important note about deleting**
> These deletion actions are permanent. If you delete something accidentally, you will likely need to repeat the same actions you took to categorize the contacts in the first place. So, please be mindful of what you intentionally delete.

Once you have your groups and tags in place, you can begin to import or add contacts directly to the subsets you've created.

Importing to groups or tags

As with many platforms, there are a variety of ways you can accomplish the same task. The general idea here is that different users might have different usage patterns, so tools should be accessible in multiple ways to empower you to find the mechanism that works best for your workflow. The method we're most familiar with at this point is the import process.

Let's go back to the example at the beginning of this chapter. In that example, all the contacts in the file that we imported in *Figure 4.1* were all people we had met at a conference. The implication here is that when we choose to use the tag function during the import process, we are indicating that this tag applies to 100% of the contacts in the import. Although that might work for some use cases, in others, we might want a tag or group to apply to some contacts but not others.

If you're trying to import a fairly large audience, you can also do a little leg work in advance to organize these contacts into their groups simultaneously as they are imported.

You can do this by creating another column in your CSV/TXT file, where the column title is an exact match for your group category and then the group names the contact belongs to is the contact data (again, these should be an exact match for the group names you created in the app).

Using the same skincare categories that we used earlier, our import document might look like *Figure 4.5*.

Email	First name	Last name	How would you classify your skin-type?
sample@sample.com	Sample	McSample	Combination skin
sample+1@sample.com	Sample	Sample	Dry skin

Figure 4.5 – A sample group import file

What's great is if you have groups in which your contacts might be members of more than one group at a time, you import them into multiple groups at a time using the same mechanism. The core difference would just be that you would separate the group names with a comma. For example, looking at the first row in *Figure 4.5*, if we wanted to let subscribers choose both combination skin and oily skin, that cell would read as follows: `Combination skin, Oily skin`.

Then, when the import is completed, they'll have been added to both groups.

You can also initiate the import process through the **Manage contacts** tools, where we created the groups and tags originally.

As we can see in *Figure 4.6*, when we look over our groups, we can see that each group name has an **Import** option listed. This will trigger the import option you're familiar with but also allows you to bring in contacts to one group or tag specifically.

Figure 4.6 – A group overview and import page

Now that we have a baseline for how to add groups and tags and how to import contacts into them, let's take a look at what we can do with them!

Segmenting tools

We'll be using the word **segment** in two different ways. The first is perhaps the most literal way, the action of breaking or identifying a subset of your contacts, and the second is to refer to the abstract object we create in your audience. When we save a segment we create, we'll still refer to that subset as a segment.

Segmenting is the application of all of this prep work and what makes this juice worth the squeeze. By setting specific logic within a segment, we can use both data the audience members provide you with and the actions those contacts take in response to your campaigns to better understand what engages them. This is the tool we will use to let the application do the heavy lifting of applying logic to your overall list and sending it to the right audience members each time.

Basics of segmenting logic

Segments are exclusively driven based on conditions and logic. We are essentially giving the platform a list of requirements to create subsets of our contacts, and then it will keep the segment updated as people join or leave your audience. This way, over time, less manual management is demanded of you.

When we refer to **conditions**, we mean the specific rules that you set to determine whether a contact will or will not be in the subset you're creating.

When we refer to **logic**, we are referring to variables that tell the app whether any or all of the conditions need to apply.

Each segment can consist of *five conditions* at a time, and then, between each condition, you can choose whether *any* or *all* are required for a contact to be included in the segment.

To create a segment, navigate to **All contacts** for the audience (the table of all of your audience members), and then, at the top of the table, you will see an option that says **New Segment**. This will open a menu over your table that looks like *Figure 4.7*, where you can start choosing your conditions.

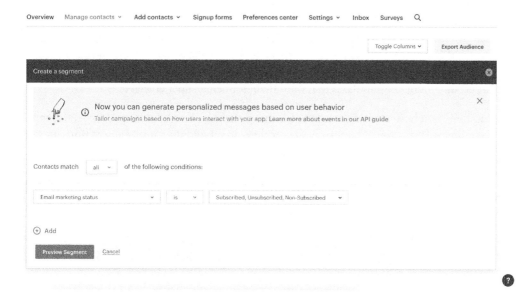

Figure 4.7 – Creating a segment interface

Now, it would be a thoroughly and absurdly long table to cover 100% of the segmenting options. Additionally, Mailchimp's wonderful technical content team has an excellent resource with this identical information (which I've linked at the end of this chapter as an additional resource). However, I do want to go over some of the categories that exist and how they can be enabled if you don't currently have them:

- **Subscriber data**: This is the most common category of data and it's predominantly what we've been talking about up to this point. This is the very basic data we have about each contact, such as their email address, first name, and last name. This data is limited to whatever your subscribers gave you at sign-up or additional information that you imported.

- **Activity data**: This is information collected by the platform about how each contact is or is not interacting with your campaigns, automation, or other channels. It lets us do things such as sending a campaign to everyone who has opened the last five emails so that we can target our most engaged subscribers. Alternatively, if they didn't open all of the last five emails, maybe we want to target people we think might be disengaging with our content.

- **Groups and tags**: This is, obviously, the application of using groups and tags. It's the category that allows us to identify one of the subsets that we've already created.
- **API/integrations**: If you end up using integrations, sometimes you can segment based on whether the contact migrated to your audience through a specific integration. This might be a little variable, as it depends on whether the third-party developer for the integration provides Mailchimp with enough information about itself, in order to allow the platform to tell you the specific name of the integration a contact came from.
- **Commerce**: If you're using either Mailchimp Stores or a third-party e-commerce integration such as Shopify, you will also see purchase activity and behaviors that contacts have undertaken with your store as options as well. For example, you could look for people who have made over a certain number of purchases to reward them for being super engaged.

The additional benefit to creating a segment is that once you've saved the conditions, the app will continue to update it for you. Therefore, you don't have to rebuild the same segment time after time.

For example, upon saving for the first time a segment created with the conditions in *Figure 4.8*, the app will inform me that five people make up the segment. However, as more people subscribe to my audience and engage with my content, the app will continue to update it, and after a month, the segment might show as having 15 subscribers.

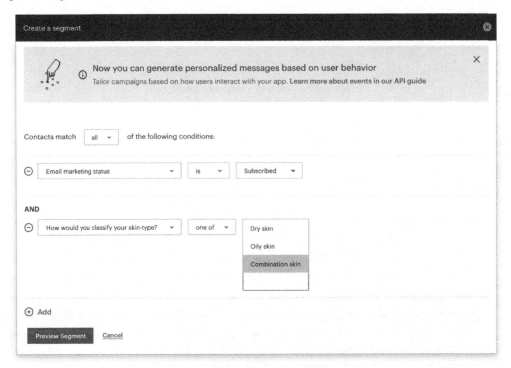

Figure 4.8 – Creating a new segment

You can also access the segmenting interface when building a campaign, which you'll see later on in *Chapter 8*. Segmenting is a continuous and practical way to use targeting practices to ensure that your content is specific to the people you're reaching out to.

Summary

This chapter discussed taking the next steps to ensure that your content is specific and relevant to the people in your audience and the tools available for identifying different subsets of people. This is because we know that a more engaged audience generally results in higher metrics and revenue.

In this chapter, we have gained a sense of why we want to be using groups, tags, and segments and how targeting more specific content can lead to more engagement. We also nailed down how to set up groups and determine the reasons we might want either a visible group option or hidden groups. There is some difference between groups and tags, and we learned how tags can be used to build up contact data and how that helps us to get the best initial use of segments. Finally, we learned how to use segments in the audience interface and enable the app to update and maintain these for us.

Now that we know the basics of segmenting, let's next take a look at how we can use it to manage inactive contacts and potentially remove them to ensure we're managing our spending.

Further reading

- *Harvard Business Review: The Age of Personalization*: `https://hbr.org/resources/pdfs/comm/mastercard/TheAgeOfPersonalization.pdf`
- *All the Segmenting Options*: `https://eepurl.com/dyikND`

5
Strategies and Tools for Managing Inactive Contacts

If you're using Mailchimp or a similar platform, chances are that you've come to it to help manage or drive tasks relevant to your business, organization, or content that you're trying to get off the ground. In any of these cases, managing your contact lists for engagement is important for decisions you make about your billing and business expenditures.

Before we delve into this chapter, it's important to highlight that when we say "inactive," we're talking about both contacts who are currently **subscribed** but maybe haven't engaged with your content at all as well as contacts in different statuses, such as **unsubscribed** or **cleaned**, as discussed in *Chapter 3*. When we talk about "billing" though, it only applies to subscribed contacts, so don't worry too much that keeping data relevant to unsubscribed and cleaned contacts is hurting you in the long term.

This chapter will go over some of the different strategies for maintaining a healthy and pruned list, why you might consider maintaining a strategy for defining what "inactive" means in the context of your business, and how those models relate to maintaining a strategy for targeted marketing.

We will cover the following main topics in this chapter:

- Understanding what inactive contacts are
- To unsubscribe or archive? That is the question
- When do I delete data?

So, let's go over some of these types of contacts and how we might want to manage them on the platform.

What are inactive contacts?

There are some intrinsic benefits to defining what an *inactive* contact is in the context of your business or organization. As we learned in the previous chapter, segmenting is a powerful tool and can be leveraged with inactive contacts. In some cases, you might choose to create a custom campaign specifically for people who are subscribed to your audience but maybe haven't opened or clicked on a campaign in a specific period of time. This can be over 3 months, over 6 months, and so on – you can experiment!

Alternatively, once you've attempted to re-engage this subset of your subscribers, you might determine that keeping them in your audience as subscribed just might not make sense for your business. Email, in particular, demands that we walk a fine line between reaching out to our audience and making sure that we're not perceived as "spammy." Mailchimp does quite a lot of work to make sure that it's compliant with laws such as CAN-SPAM, but as a user, you will have the best sense of what your contacts do and don't like over time.

So, much like with anything related to technology, experimentation is going to be the key to understanding what does and doesn't work for your audience.

How to develop our own definition

I think the key to developing and refining your definition of an inactive subscriber is to consider creating or thinking about different customer personas and what they come to your content looking for. You can think of this as being your own Product Manager. By better understanding and bucketing your audience, you make your segments more powerful. You can think of a *persona* as an avatar, representation, or archetype of the type of audience member you're trying to understand.

You'll be using segmentation here because, ideally, your personas should be developed using a mix of real data (which we can get from Mailchimp) and the instincts you have about your business. I'm a big believer in being data-informed in the decisions and designs you make. By finding the right balance of qualitative data and quantitative data, you allow yourself the freedom to make instinctual decisions for your business driven by qualitative data, and you can prioritize your decisions to tackle your problems by using quantitative data.

Creating *personas* is a mechanism by which you combine important information you've learned about your users or customers to categorize different types of people that engage with your product or content. This can be data you access through the Mailchimp app but also interviews with your users, or information you might glean through reviews of your products.

Personas are made up constructs of behaviors and characteristics of a hypothetical user and what their perspective on your business is.

To get to our starting point specific to your Mailchimp account and your usage of the platform, we'll start by asking ourselves:

> What does my ideal audience member look like? What are they doing and not doing?

By understanding what we want to see from our audience, even at a minimum, we can begin to understand what it might look like to define a contact that isn't doing any behaviors you're interested in such as opening campaigns. For example, if you want your ideal contact to *at least* open one of every five campaigns, then you can set a segment to constantly comb through your audience for contacts that meet the following conditions:

- **Contacts match all of the following conditions:**
- **Email marketing status | is | Subscribed**
- **AND | Campaign activity | opened | Any of the Last 5 Campaigns**

We can see what this looks like in the segment builder in *Figure 5.1*:

Figure 5.1 – The segment builder for inactive subscribers

Critically, we start our segment with the indication that the contact should be **Subscribed**, because the goal is to understand how many people in our audience aren't as engaged as we would like. Don't be discouraged if this figure seems high compared to your overall number of contacts; the goal isn't to eliminate all of these people but rather to learn enough about our audience to engage with more and more of them over time.

Additionally, depending on what you're trying to do with your business or organization, you might have other or secondary definitions for what someone **inactive** might look like. For example, if I have an e-commerce business selling books, I might also use a definition based on whether they have ever purchased something from my store.

I would recommend having a couple of different definitions and then, before making any choices about whether to mark people on your list as subscribed or not, try a re-engagement strategy. The platform provides a couple of different options for what that re-engagement looks like, and the ideal one depends on how much you know about your contacts. Different tools accomplish different tasks.

For example, if you're at an early stage in your marketing journey, **A/B testing** might be your best option. Generally, early in your efforts, you will know a little less about your contacts. The data you might have tends to skew more qualitative than quantitative, and using A/B testing lets you experiment with things such as your subject line, the content of your campaign, the from name, and the send time to see which version – A or B –receives better engagement. We'll go further into A/B testing campaigns in *Chapter 11*.

You can also automate the process of re-engaging your contacts! For example, let's say you really, really like your segmenting conditions because you feel like you know pretty definitively that if contacts haven't engaged in the last 10 campaigns, they're not going to engage at all. You can set an automation to trigger on conditions you're comfortable with and have it send a re-engagement email or two (whatever you feel is the right number of last chances customized with this user persona in mind), and then automations has a very neat feature called **post-sending actions** that you can enable to make the platform unsubscribe people for you. We'll cover all things **automations** and **customer journey builder** in *Chapter 12*.

And that brings us to the next decision in this process, which is whether to unsubscribe the contacts or not. So, let's look at reasons for which we might take one action or another.

To unsubscribe or archive? That is the question

Now, let's say you have tried some re-engagement campaigns or automations and you feel like you've tried your best to get some of these contacts to interact with your content, but, as you expected, some of them aren't engaging over time. Sometimes, this can happen, but you now have to make the decision as to whether you would like to keep them in your audience for a while, or whether you would like to move them from **subscribed** to another status so that they're not contributing to your billing. Doing the latter also reduces the risk that they might report your campaigns as abuse over time.

So, if you decide you're ready for the next step, you then have to decide how you want to handle the contacts going forward. Important questions to ask yourself include the following:

- *Do I want to keep the data?*
- *Are the stats for these contacts important to me?*
- *Do I want to keep a visible record of these contacts?*

These will really be the crux of how you make a decision, and it essentially boils down to whether you want to **archive** or **unsubscribe** a contact and whether you want to see them in the contact table when you load the audience. The platform does a tidy job of moving archived contacts to its own filtered table, which you can see by clicking on the **Manage contacts** menu and then selecting **View archived contacts**.

Personally, I think this is the ideal way to handle inactive contacts. It allows you to keep data in an individual contact profile, reduces the impact on your billing plan, and keeps these inactive contacts from clogging up the view of your overall subscribers.

However, if you prefer to be able to see them in your **All contacts** table, then you can choose to move their status to **Unsubscribed**. This will keep them in your visible table but still nets you the other two benefits.

The bonus to both of these methods is if you take these actions, these contacts can still resubscribe themselves to your audience later. So, this doesn't have to be a permanent action, since the contact themselves can choose to re-engage with your content down the line.

Once you've determined what actions or statuses are best for your business, you can then think about what data you actually need to keep and what you can remove.

When do I delete?

The direct answer to that question should be made carefully and with forethought. Deletion actions are permanent and cannot be reversed.

It's a feature that was added in response to users' need to stay compliant with the European Union's **General Data Protection Regulation (GDPR)**. GDPR was adopted in spring 2016 and became enforceable in spring 2018, which meant that businesses and organizations that collect or utilize personally identifiable information of people located in the EU needed tools to help them stay compliant. Mailchimp offers tools to add to your sign-up forms to gather GDPR-compliant consent in the event that you have EU contacts, but it also offers a GDPR-compliant deletion mechanism, which is more relevant to this chapter.

The way this deletion deviates from archiving and unsubscribing is that it will delete all information associated with the contact profile and anonymize their email address in your reports. Once a contact has been deleted, it cannot be added again to a list manually through imports or by manually adding them to the audience. In order to return to your audience, the contact would need to choose to resubscribe themselves through a form, essentially providing their consent all over again.

> **Important note about deletions**
>
> Archiving and unsubscribing are quite different from contact deletion. If you choose to do a permanent deletion, the data will truly be gone, as that deletion was designed to be GDPR-compliant. So, exercise caution when using a permanent deletion; the application will issue you a warning to indicate that *the action is permanent and cannot be reversed or recovered by Mailchimp*.

The GDPR-compliant deletion should really just be utilized for contacts you know you have absolutely no interest in, or to comply with a direct request from a contact who has asked to be permanently forgotten in compliance with GDPR, should they reach out to you directly.

However, the general takeaway here is that when we make decisions, we should try to make informed ones about how we would like data to be leveraged.

Summary

This chapter was really about how we can apply what we learned about segmenting tools in the previous chapter – not just to help us engage contacts but to also manage our business or organization internally to ensure we're making the best use of the platform and the tools it equips us with. All businesses require some amount of balance between external expenditure and revenue generation, and this is your first step toward automating that balance.

In this chapter, we learned more information about the nuances between different types of inactive contact statuses and what they could mean for your account. We also worked on how to develop an understanding to determine a definition of inactivity that best works for your marketing strategy, and how to leverage this definition as you gain more insights into your audiences. Having developed that, we learned about the nuances between archiving, unsubscribing, and deleting, and why in some cases one option might be more valuable to you than another.

Now that we know how to manage our billing and different inactive statuses, let's check out how to begin setting up different types of sign-up forms, in the event that we don't have a robust audience or we want to grow our existing audience of contacts.

Further reading

- *Silicon Valley Product Group: Personas*: `https://www.svpg.com/personas-for-product-management/`
- *GDPR-Compliant Delete Contacts*: `https://eepurl.com/dyilrv`
- *About the General Data Protection Regulation*: `https://eepurl.com/dyiknH`

Part 3: Basic Channels

This section begins by exploring some of the most basic, but also incredibly fundamental, channels in a Mailchimp account and some of the strategies you will use to set these up.

This section has the following chapters:

- *Chapter 6, Setting Up and Customizing Various Form Types*
- *Chapter 7, Establishing Your Brand with Content Studio*
- *Chapter 8, Outreach Marketing with Templates and Campaigns*
- *Chapter 9, Setting Up Your Marketing Presence with Websites*

6
Setting Up and Customizing Various Form Types

In this chapter, we will spend some time talking about the various types of forms you can create inside the Mailchimp application to drive engagement in your funnel. There is a good spread of different form types, so this means that even if you don't have a pre-existing website in which to use forms, Mailchimp has options for you that don't require one.

We will cover the following main topics in this chapter:

- Why are forms necessary?
- Hosted forms
- Landing Page Form
- Embedded and pop-up forms

We'll go from form types that require very little information or resources for you to establish or set up to more advanced form types that you will have to place on an existing website outside of Mailchimp. The sections on hosted forms and website forms will involve Mailchimp hosting the form for you so that you don't need your own website to start collecting audience members – then, embedded and pop-up forms are specifically for folks with an existing website that they'd like to collect audience members from. By the end, ideally, you'll have a notion of which form type is best for your current needs and be able to create a pipeline to help you grow your audience further.

Why are forms necessary?

If you're new to Mailchimp, or maybe you have only been using it to contact a pre-existing set of contacts, you might be asking yourself how you can start to grow your audience. For most businesses and content creators, larger audiences have a direct connection to either revenue for your business, or for content creators, the size of the partnerships and sponsors that they can attract. Even if you are thinking in the context of a non-profit organization's usage of a marketing platform, having a larger audience can mean more people you can connect with to either serve or even receive donations from.

To that end, if you don't have a funnel through which you can gain more audience members, this means that your business growth can be a little challenging. You might be facing a relative plateau in engagement or relying exclusively on word-of-mouth. Especially if you're a business trying to drive sales or a content creator trying to drive partnerships, brand awareness is critical.

When we think of a funnel conceptually, we can lean on a traditional **sales funnel** as seen in *Figure 6.1*:

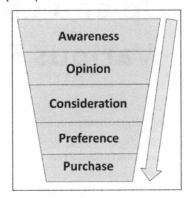

Figure 6.1 – Traditional conceptual sales funnel

With a conceptual sales funnel, we're meant to observe the steps a buyer goes through in the run up to making a purchase – not so much the physical actions, but the behaviors observed.

In order to purchase something from you, somebody must become *aware* of your company first. This can be achieved through some of the marketing efforts you've already tried before, marketing efforts that you might attempt to implement later in this book, or even through your own social media if you leverage something such as Facebook, Instagram, Twitter, or TikTok.

As noted in *Chapter 1* of this book, people develop their initial opinions pretty quickly. The nature of digital marketing is that the opportunity to make an impact is brief and that people become *aware* of something and form an *opinion* on it almost simultaneously. Next, somebody will then *consider* the fit of your product or service for their needs and this window of deliberation is an ideal point at which to engage with this person so you can continue to develop a relationship. Funnels are never 100% at capturing all of the people who enter them. You're never going to gain the attention of all of the people who develop an awareness of your product or service, but the more points of contact that you can develop from the people who become aware of you or your business, the higher engagement you will see overall. The end goal, of course, is to drive a *purchase* – or engagement for content creators or non-profits, for example.

So, with that baseline context for why we might want to grow our audience and leverage tools to do so, let's take a look at these forms!

Hosted forms

If you'd like to get something quick and simple out the door with minimal manipulation required on your side, the **hosted form** is the perfect option to start with. In this builder, you'll largely be manipulating the fields and colors and what the audience can see or not, depending on whether you configured any hidden fields in *Chapter 3*. Within Mailchimp, you have the option to create a hosted form per audience in an account. Again, because every audience within a single Mailchimp account is treated as completely separate from one another, this means that a single signup form will only connect to one single audience.

Navigating to the hosted form builder

When in your account, to get to your hosted form builder for a specific audience, from the main dashboard, do the following:

1. Select the **Audience** menu option in the left-hand navigation panel.
2. Click on **Signup Forms**.

This will then show you a menu of some of the form types that we'll be able to work with:

- **Form builder**
- **Embedded forms**
- **Popup form**
- **Contact form**
- **Form integrations** (We'll be going further into integrations in *Chapter 16*)

Here, we'll be starting with **Form Builder**. If you click on **Select** next to the form type, it will send you right into the builder for the hosted form connected to this audience, as seen in *Figure 6.2*:

Setting Up and Customizing Various Form Types

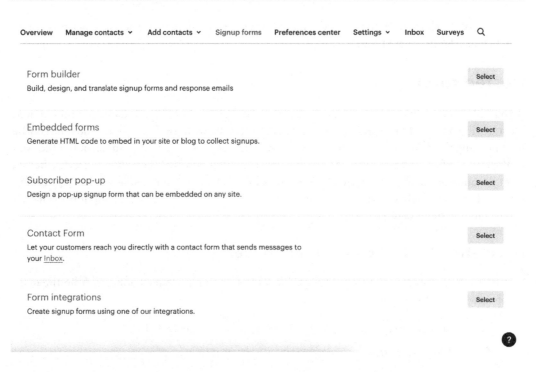

Figure 6.2 – The Signup forms menu for a specific audience

When the builder loads, you'll see that it's a fairly simple form, to begin with. What you'll see from top to bottom is the following:

- A drop-down menu for **Forms and response emails**
- The option to allow your audience to choose their email format
- The URL at which your form will be hosted by Mailchimp
- An editing menu with **Build it**, **Design it**, and **Translate it** tabs

Underneath, in the editor itself, you'll see the merge tag fields that you set up in *Chapter 3*, and this is where we can do some initial editing. See *Figure 6.3*, for example:

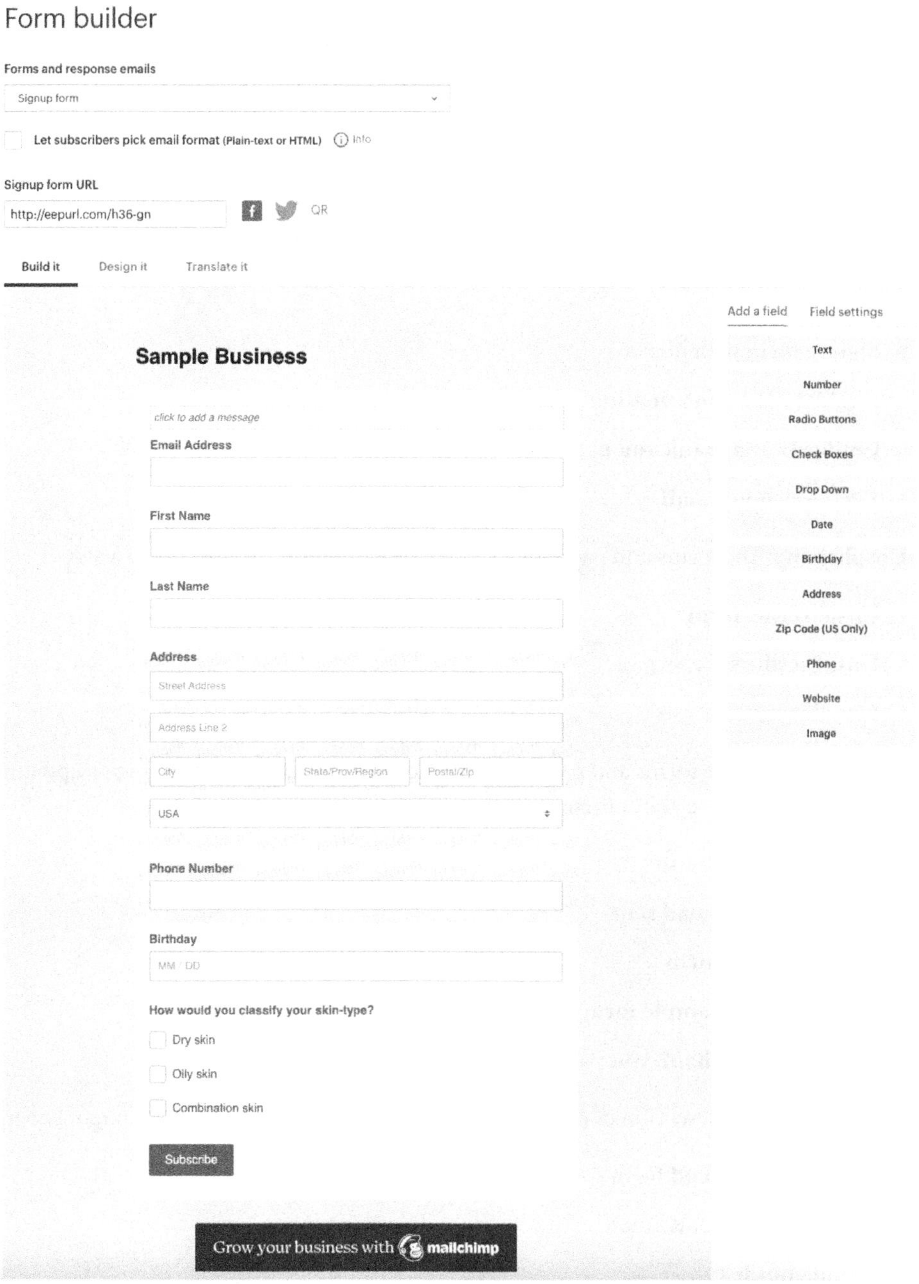

Figure 6.3 – Sample signup form editor

Categories of hosted forms you can edit

Before we get too far into editing together, I want to briefly mention the options available to you in the **Forms and response emails** drop-down menu. The really nice thing about this builder is that you can edit not just the initial form that your audience will see but you can also edit things such as a welcome email (if you'd like to set that up as a stop-gap before you get into more robust automation). You can also adjust things such as the form for updating personal preferences, or what audience members see if they unsubscribe if you'd like to make that a little more personal. A full list of what you can edit is as follows:

- **Subscribe**: The forms and pages contacts encounter when they first sign up:
  - **Signup form**
  - **Signup form with alerts**
  - **reCAPTCHA confirmation**
  - **Confirmation thank you page**
  - **Final welcome email**

- **Unsubscribe**: The forms and pages that contacts encounter if they decide to leave:
  - **Unsubscribe form**
  - **Unsubscribe success page**
  - **Goodbye email**

- **Update Profile**: The forms and pages that contacts encounter when changing or updating the information you have about them:
  - **Profile update email**
  - **Profile update email sent**
  - **Update profile form**
  - **Update profile sample form**
  - **Update profile thank you page**

- **Other Bits**: This is a section of miscellaneous forms and pages your contact might encounter:
  - **Forward to a friend form**
  - **Forward to a friend email**
  - **About your list**
  - **Campaign archive page**

- **Survey landing page**
- **Automation Landing Page**

It's not necessary to engage with each and every single option in this menu unless you absolutely want to change the text in every single one. The super nice thing about just editing the first option, **Signup form**, is that aesthetic choices you make in **Design it** for just this form will automatically be applied to the rest of the forms and response emails to make sure that your brand stays consistent. Such a nice timesaver!

So, to move on to actually editing the **Signup form**, let's start with **Build it**. In this interface, you can drag the blocks for your form around. That way, you can adjust the order in which potential contacts fill their information out.

> **Tip about fields**
>
> The longer your form, the more of the fields you should consider leaving as optional. People can develop survey fatigue and you don't want to create too much friction in becoming a member of your audience if you're trying to drive numbers. This means if you have various fields, make sure your most critical fields are right at the top.

Additionally, you might notice that at the top of the builder, you will see a space highlighted for you by a dotted line (the **click to add a message** label in *Figure 6.3*). This isn't a block that is visible in the actual signup form, but it's where the builder allows you to enter some text if you'd like to write a little something about your business or organization. Clicking on this space will open a small pop-up window in which you can edit the content that goes into that block, as seen in *Figure 6.4*:

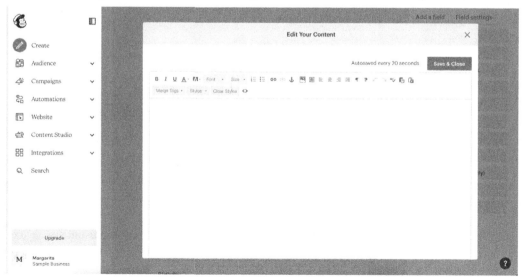

Figure 6.4 – Signup form at the top of the content editor interface

Now, there is the option in this editor to add images to the block if you would like. I recommend using them sparingly here, as the options for editing the alignment of the images are a little more limited within this interface. That's likely better to handle in one of the other more robust form options such as **Websites** in the next section of this chapter.

In this interface, I recommend focusing on one to three tight sentences – something such as what people might expect you to be communicating to them about, or even details about your business. Once you've landed on something short and snappy, you can click **Save & Close** and it will immediately be published to the builder.

Additional options in the **Build it** section include the **Add a field** option or the ability to select a specific field already in the form and edit **Field settings**. By default, the menu that appears on the right is the **Add a field** list of options, as you can see in *Figure 6.3*. However, when you select a field in the builder – for example, the **First Name** field – you will see the **Field Settings** menu for that specific field open on the right, as seen in *Figure 6.5*:

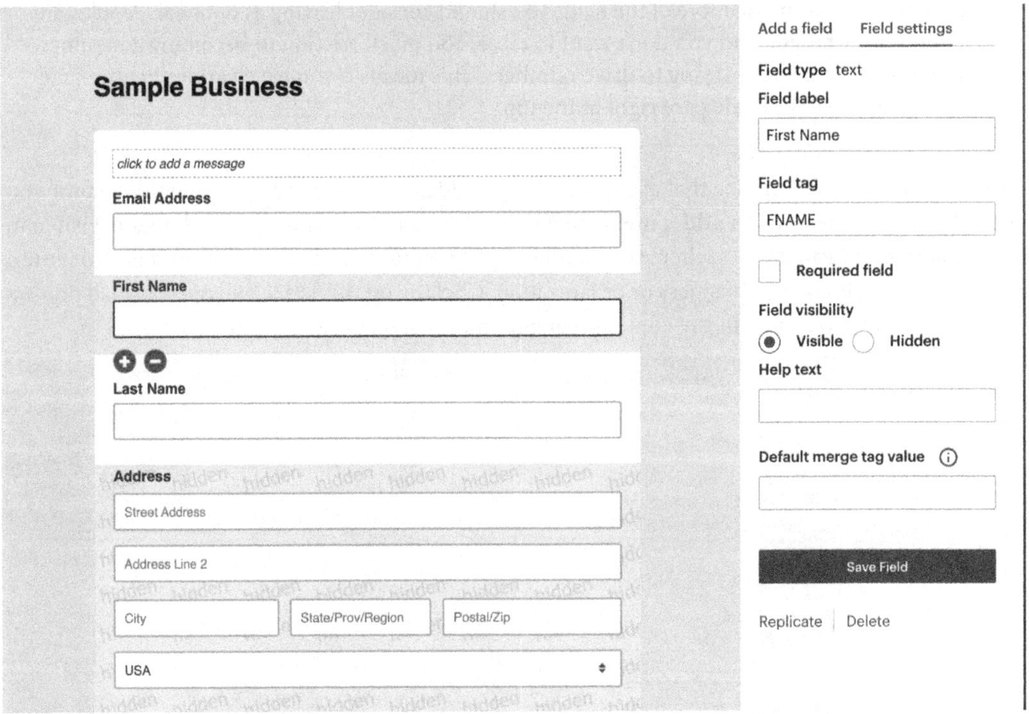

Figure 6.5 – Field settings menu for the First Name field

Here, you can make specific fields required, adjust the name of a field, and even adjust the merge tag you set in *Chapter 3*. Once you've made the edits you want, you then click on the **Save Field** button.

> **Important note about field edits**
>
> Changes made in the field settings here will be applied to the **Merge Tags** section that we covered in *Chapter 3*. This means you'll want to be sure that any changes you make to the **Field Tag** field here are ones that you intend to use throughout your marketing later.

The next section we want to look to in order to make the form a little more aesthetically appealing is the **Design it** section. By default, the form and background are fairly monochromatic, which is a fairly inoffensive default, but might not be the first impression you want to make. Alternatively, if you have a rough brand identity and designated color palette, you might want to adjust this form to fit with this identity better.

This part has four main areas that you can adjust:

- **Page**: This is the overall hosted page. It's broken down into a **Background** section, where we can adjust the color of the page, a **Header** section, where we can see the editable text, and then an **Outer Wrapper** section, to apply a custom color behind the title of a form.

- **Body**: This is the part of the form from the text you entered at the top to introduce your form or brand down to the **Subscribe** button. You have the option to edit the **Foreground** color, which is the color you will see behind the fields. You can also adjust the **Default text** settings if you'd like a different font, size, color, or even spacing of the text and its padding. Finally, you can adjust whether you would like the **Link style** option on the form to appear in a contrasting color. By default, most applications will differentiate normal text from hyperlinks by using a blue color, which is true here as well.

- **Forms**: In this section, you'll be able to manipulate the color of **Buttons**, fonts, and text, and the intensity of the color of errors should contacts encounter any. You'll be able to adjust these for **Buttons**, **Buttons hovered** (when a contact hovers over a button), **Field labels**, **Field text**, **Required**, **Required legend**, **Help text**, and **Errors**.

- **Referral Badge**: Here, you can choose the alignment of the Mailchimp referral badge at the bottom, as well as choose between different referral badge options.

> **Note about referral badges**
>
> If you are utilizing a free account type, it will not be possible to remove or hide referral badges. That being said, if you do have a paid account, you can adjust the visibility of the referral badges in **Account & billing** under the **Extras** menu.

In the final section, you can choose to translate the form if you would like to. If you have audience members from multiple places or who speak various languages, a really neat feature you can use here is **Auto-translate**. By enabling this feature, if the browser the contact is using is in another language and the app can detect that, the form will automatically translate the text for you. The option is seen in *Figure 6.6*:

Figure 6.6 – The Auto-translate feature for hosted forms

Once you've made all the adjustments you'd like to make to the form, you're ready to go. All you have to do is grab the URL found in the **Signup form URL** field, copy it, and then paste it wherever you would like to promote this new hosted form. For example, you can choose to promote it on your social media to drive engagement with folks who might follow you there but might not be formally subscribed to your marketing content. Additionally, this also allows people who follow you to retweet or generally repost the form for you. This allows you to leverage the people already engaged with your brand as a mechanism for not just spreading word-of-mouth but also equipping people within their reach to actively locate your business if they're curious about you.

Once you have this initial funnel open, it's a good opportunity to think about whether you might want something more robust or something compatible with adding more images if you think that would be more engaging for your brand. Next, we'll jump into some of the options for building a more customizable landing page.

Creating a form on a landing page

If matching your brand is a big priority and you don't have an existing website or much of an online presence outside of maybe a few social media accounts, you might want to use a builder in which you can more easily add images and maybe even hero images to land on a more robust look.

In *Chapter 9*, we'll dive deeper into setting up a domain and establishing a website with multiple pages if you would like, but in this section, we will specifically focus on creating a single page you can promote at which people can sign up to be part of your audience. Landing pages are really ideal for things such as hosting a signup form – or let's say your business is partnering up for a giveaway with another company and you'd like to create a joint landing page where people can join to take part. Landing pages are ideal because they're quick to set up and can be published and taken down fairly easily, so using them to achieve a specific goal is ideal.

When logged into your Mailchimp account, you can navigate to landing pages by doing the following:

1. Click on **Create** at the top of the left-hand navigation panel.
2. Clicking on **Landing Pages** from the menu that appears on the left.
3. Name your landing page and select your desired audience, as seen in *Figure 6.7*:

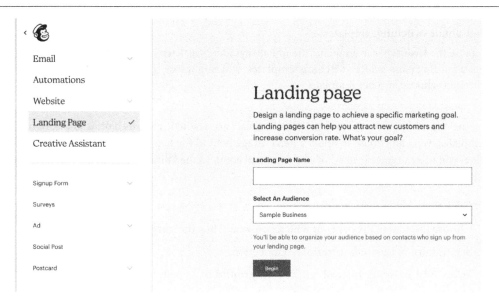

Figure 6.7 – Landing Page creation page

Once you've named the landing page and selected the audience that the people who use the page will end up in, you can click on **Begin** and select a template. Now, this really comes down to personal preference, but what you'll see on the **Templates** page will list some categories of landing pages:

- **Lead Generation**
  - This form type is ideal for adding new contacts to your audience, specifically for generating contacts who have shown some interest in your product or services but might be unverified

- **Promote Your Products**
  - This template is ideal for displaying a specific product or family of products

- **Grow Your List**
  - This template is very specific to increasing the size and the reach of your audience

For creating a landing page that allows people to sign up to be part of our audience, we're currently only interested in the **Lead Generation** and **Grow Your List** options. Some of the options are pre-designed and use placeholders to provide examples of what kinds of content you might want to put in – others are a bit more simplified for folks who maybe don't need or want as much guidance. This is the part that's really up to you. You're also totally welcome to choose one and then if it's not really your cup of tea, click on **Back** in the lower-left corner of the build and pick a new template to check out.

> **Note about switching templates**
>
> Because the layouts of the templates are not always identical, keep in mind that if you input text into a landing page before switching templates, you might lose some of the text and settings when you choose another template.

Lots of the choices once you've selected your template are aesthetic choices. For example, in many of the templates, you can choose to apply a **hero image** behind the text in a specific area. Hero images are when you use an image instead of a background color. In the builder, you can set this up by doing the following:

1. Click **Style** in the right-hand menu.
2. Choose the area of the page for which you would like the image to be the background.
3. Scroll down to the **Body Interior Style** section.
4. Select **Add an image instead** for the **Background** color item (*Figure 6.8*):

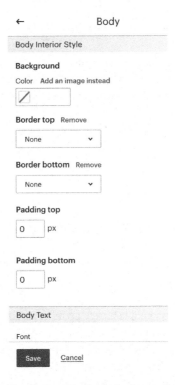

Figure 6.8 – The Body Style panel

The **Style** section is where you can adjust things such as colors, section paddings, and fonts for an entire section instead of doing it for every content block that you edit. Beyond these stylistic choices, you can and should edit all the content blocks with text. You can choose to delete them by hovering over the block and clicking on the trashcan icon if you don't feel they're necessary. Alternatively, just clicking on them will open the text editor in the right-hand panel to allow you to change the text to something that matches you and your brand (*Figure 6.9*).

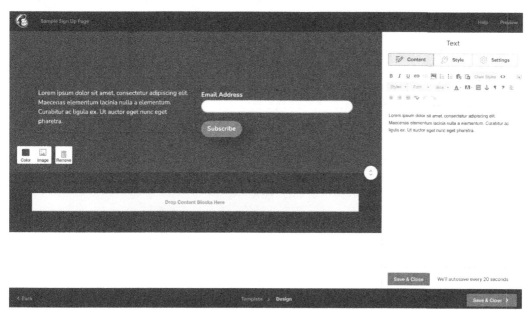

Figure 6.9 – Editing a Text block

Additionally, if you want to add content blocks and not remove them, you can do that too by clicking on the **Blocks** option on the left-hand side of the **Style** menu we used earlier, and you'll see a bunch of options for blocks that you can click on and then drag into whatever position you like.

Finally, regardless of the other content blocks you add, I would recommend clicking on the **Signup Form** content block, which in *Figure 6.9*, would be the block containing the **Email Address** field and the **Subscribe** button. The reason is that here, you can edit the fields that you would like folks to fill out when they subscribe, and you can even edit a custom success message. By default, the application will ask for an **Email Address** at a minimum because in order to create a contact, that is the minimum piece of information that the platform requires. Similarly, it will also pre-populate a success message for you, so you don't have to worry that if you publish it without editing the message that the contact wouldn't see any confirmation that they were successfully signed up.

Once you've made all the adjustments that you'd like, you're ready to publish the landing page! To do so, you need to click on **Save & Close**, and you'll be directed to a final checklist to edit some details about the page before publishing it if you would like. For example, you can edit the **Page Title** and **URL** settings if you would like to. **Page Title** is what the contact will see in the tab of their browser when the page is opened. A given **URL** is randomly generated by Mailchimp by default, but you can tweak it if you would like it to be a little more memorable (*Figure 6.10*).

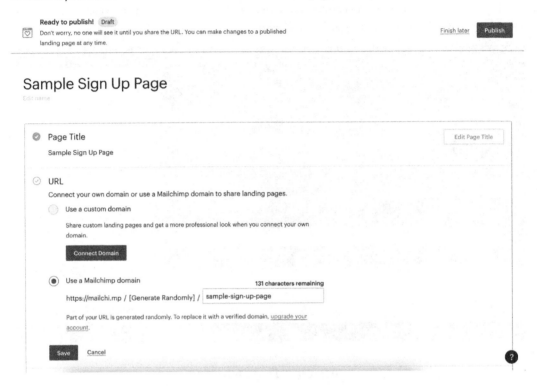

Figure 6.10 – Editing the page URL

You'll see the option to leverage a custom URL if you already have one or if you would like one. This allows you an even greater level of control over the URL people see when they head either to your landing page or a website in the future. If you're curious about that we'll be digging into that in *Chapter 9*, but again, the goal of this section is to focus on what the fastest ways to get a landing page out are to ensure that if you have no signup forms out in the world, you can get one out there while you focus on developing more robust channels.

Once you've made all the changes you want, you can click **Publish** in the upper-right corner and your landing page will now be out there in the world! You can always **Unpublish** it in the future, so you don't have to view this as a permanent option if a more robust digital footprint is something you're working toward building in the future. However, it's a great option for promoting through your existing channels, and as mentioned before, for setting up a quick page for partnered events.

Next, let's take a look at some options for folks who already have an existing website on which they'd like to embed a Mailchimp form.

Embedded and pop-up forms

Embedded and pop-up forms are pretty unambiguous terms, thankfully. They both go on an existing website and they do what they sound like they do. Embedded forms appear and are integrated more seamlessly into the makeup or scrolling mechanism of a specific page on your website. They appear as just another asset on a page overall. A pop-up form also does just about what it sounds like it does. When you arrive at a particular page or attempt to leave a page, the form will pop up over the main content of the site and appear almost out of nowhere.

You don't necessarily have to pick one or the other. Popups can be quite useful for grabbing someone's attention quickly and really drawing their attention to get them to become part of your audience. Embedded forms are also quite nice because they're relatively unobtrusive and can just be integrated into the flow of a website. They're also quite handy to use together.

If we think through a behavior many of us have probably engaged in, it makes sense to use both if you aren't sure which would be the best fit for you and your brand. As an example of pretty normal behavior, sometimes you might encounter a brand either through a friend telling you about it or scrolling through your preferred social media feed and deciding it caught your attention enough to check it out directly. You go to its site just to get a feel for whether what it sells or talks about is something you're more than fleetingly interested in and then a popup appears that offers you 10% off or just asks you to sign up. You think, "*I don't know enough to decide whether I want them to email me,*" so you dismiss the popup. However, then after some scrolling and reading, you decide you are probably open to subscribing for a discount to see whether you can get a deal later – but you've already dismissed the popup, so you either need to clear your cache and cookies or give up. Wouldn't it be better if somewhere on the page you're investigating there was also an embedded form to remove any obstacles to subscribing?

That's the advantage of ensuring your funnel has multiple entry points. By removing friction to engage with you and your brand and making sure people have multiple opportunities to sign up, you'll see more consistent traffic and growth. So, let's walk through the options for creating embedded and popup forms that you can place on your website.

Embedded forms

To get to the builders, we need to do the same things we did when setting up or checking out the hosted form at the beginning of this chapter:

1. Select the **Audience** menu option in the left-hand navigation panel.
2. Click on **Signup Forms**.

To start with, let's check out the **Embedded forms** option. When we click on the **Select** button, we'll be directed to the builder, where we can customize the text and other content of the form we hope to put on our website. In the builder, we'll have the option of editing the following fields:

- **Form Fields**
- **Settings**
- **Tags**
- **Referral Badge**

See *Figure 6.11*, for example:

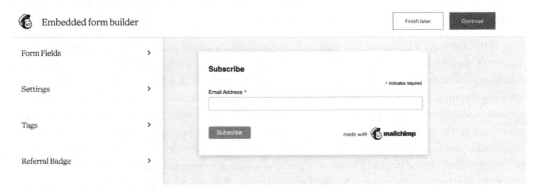

Figure 6.11 – Embedded form builder

Now, as noted earlier, referral badges, as you can see in the lower-right corner of the form, cannot be removed for free accounts. That being said, if you have a paid account, you can disable them in the account settings. For the embedded form builder, you have the option to toggle it off in the menu. Otherwise, you just have the option to choose the style of the badge that is visible.

Beyond that, as with the other forms, you can choose in **Form Fields** what information contacts will have to provide to sign up. Keep in mind that the more fields you have, especially required fields, the more space the form will take up on your site and the more friction contacts may experience when filling it out. You don't want to cause form/survey fatigue, so make sure that you're requesting the information you need without going overboard.

If you would like to change the heading that people see or the width of the form, you can adjust those settings in the **Settings** menu.

> **Special note for those more inclined to development**
>
> For those of you who might be a little more inclined to customize styles in the CSS sheets for your site, you can choose to disable CSS in this builder under **Settings**. This should allow your embedded form from Mailchimp to inherit styles that you set in your existing CSS sheet. Keep in mind that this is just for those who are inclined toward development, as Mailchimp does not currently offer custom development support.

Additionally, as a cool callback to *Chapter 4*, in which we talked about **Tags**, this builder also allows you to create a custom tag for any contacts that come through this embedded form once you place it on your site. For example, if the particular page of your site on which you're placing the embedded form promotes something specific – an event, a product, or a think piece, whatever it is – you can create a custom tag that is applied internally only (meaning it's not visible to the subscriber when they sign up) so that you can differentiate them from other contacts and segment them in the future.

Once you've made all your edits, you can click on **Done** in the upper right-hand corner, and it will take you to a final page where you can click on a **Copy Code** button to copy the embedded code to paste into the builder/interface of your personal website, wherever it is you would like it to appear. Because there are a myriad of different website providers, the steps here might vary, but generally, you're looking for the area of your website's builder in which you can edit the HTML for the page on which you'd like your form to appear.

Pop-up forms

Similar to the hosted and embedded forms, to navigate to the builder, we would do the following:

1. Select the **Audience** menu option in the left-hand navigation panel.
2. Click on **Signup Forms**.

Then, we'd click on the **Select** button next to the **Subscriber pop-up** option. This will direct us to the builder, where we will see a mocked-up website with a popup appearing over it, which is what we're here to edit. In the builder, we have the option of editing the following on the left:

- **Style**: This will allow you to edit the font, color, and size of the text in the popup.
- **Layout**: This will allow you to choose the orientation of the text and the signup fields relative to an image. For example, if you would like an image to appear on the left-hand side of the popup as opposed to the top, you can make that adjustment here.
- **Settings**: This will allow you to choose how opaque the overlay is, its position on the page, and when you would like it to appear, as follows:
  - **Immediately**
  - **After 5 seconds**

- **After 20 seconds**
- **Scroll to middle of page**
- **Scroll to end of page**
- **On exit**

In the central builder itself, you can edit the text, set an image, and add other fields to the popup, as seen in *Figure 6.12*:

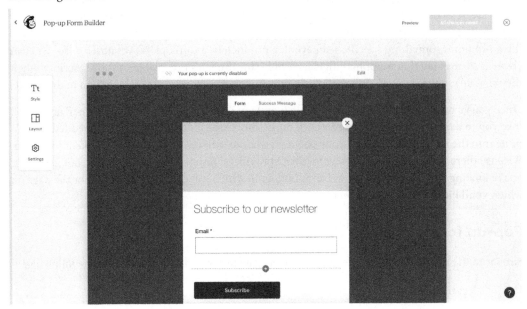

Figure 6.12 – Pop-up form builder

Once you've made the design decisions that are the best for you from the left-hand menu, you can then move on to the central builder, where the mockup of the popup appears. To edit text there, you can just click on the text you would like to change and type directly into the block that appears. If you click on the plus sign (+) under the **Email Address** field on the pop-up form (*Figure 6.12*), you'll be given the option to add additional fields, as with other builders. Finally, if you chose one of the layouts in which you have an image adjacent to the text and subscription fields, you can hover over the blank and click on the **Set Image** button to upload an image to the builder.

You can also adjust the **Success Message** option that your contacts will see when they submit the form so that they know that the form went through. By default, it'll be a simple **Thanks for subscribing!** message, but you can adjust it if there's something that's a little more on-brand for you.

If you've created a site with Mailchimp in the past, you will have the option of enabling this popup for that website – if not, you can input the URL for your site and then generate a JavaScript snippet to pop into the code of the page on which you would like it to appear. Even if in the future, you choose to make design changes to your pop-up form, the nice thing about this script is that you can edit it in Mailchimp, and when you click on **Save & Publish**, it should then push that change to your site as well.

With all these form options available to you, you can pick and choose the combination of them that makes the most sense for you.

Summary

In this chapter, we dug into the myriad of options built into the Mailchimp application. By considering all of them, you can think about what your strategy for growing your contact pool is. For example, you might decide you're early on in your marketing journey and want to opt for a simple hosted form until you make further decisions about your logo, language, and maybe even content. This will let you get a form out there while you're still developing your brand identity. Alternatively, you might know exactly what your brand looks like and what it's about, so maybe you already have a website and don't have an immediate need for a landing page or hosted form. However, leveraging embedded and pop-up forms allows you to open up your marketing funnel directly into your Mailchimp account so that you don't have to constantly import audience members or manage them manually – you can just let the application do that heavy lifting for you.

Fundamentally, we nailed down that understanding how to leverage one or multiple forms is possible whether you have a website or not. Additionally, we learned how to customize these forms so that they were more in line with your brand. Best of all, this leaves even more advanced form options available to folks even in a low-code format.

Up to this point, you may have noticed that the further we proceed, the more we talk about branding and establishing a general aesthetic. In the next chapter, we'll talk specifically about the **Content Studio** a bit more, and how the Mailchimp application can help you collect all the assets you import into one place, but still make them available to you across various channels. As we move forward, it will become more and more important for your images and assets to be cohesive.

Further reading

Here are some additional resources to dig further into some of the topics we covered in this chapter:

- *About Landing Pages*: https://eepurl.com/dyij9L
- *Add a Pop-Up Signup Form to Your Website*: https://eepurl.com/dyikvH

7
Establishing Your Brand with the Content Studio

We've talked about your brand a bit in the last several chapters. If anything, this becomes an increasingly important thing to consider the more channels you add to your marketing efforts. If you think about how tracking and content have worked for you in the last few years, you may have noticed that the ads you see across the internet have been familiar and consistent. The more you browse content and even products, over time, the more the ads you see, and the recommended content on your social media feeds are skewed toward showing you familiar content or previously viewed products.

The brands and their content also become pretty easy to spot because lots of these people and companies spend time thinking about their brand identity. As I noted in *Chapter 1*, generationally, people are using more and more digital screens, but the amount of time we have to make an impact per screen is compressed. This means that the more cohesive we make the content and marketing we send out across different channels, the easier it is for our audience to connect the dots between our channels. This also drives the perception that our content or products are potentially a good fit for them.

In this chapter, we will cover the following topics to help us with developing your brand:

- What is the content studio?
- How to establish your brand
- Individual features and channels nested in the Content Studio

We'll work through the features inside the Content Studio to make sure that by the end, you can create or import assets into the platform that can be used to ensure that your brand is consistent from channel to channel later on.

What is the Content Studio?

At a very basic level, the content studio is like a folder inside Mailchimp where you can save images, documents, and other assets you intend to use in campaigns, ads, and forms of automation throughout the app. The neat thing about the content studio is that if you connect an Instagram business account or you choose to create a store, you will also have those images available to you in the content studio.

By default, the **Content** studio is broken down into subsections inside the feature:

- **Creative Assistant**
- **My Files**
- **Products**
- **Giphy**
- **Instagram**
- **My Logo**

The great thing about having all of these assets and files in one centralized place within the Mailchimp platform is that you can begin to play around with and tangibly see how your visual and aesthetic choices play together. This is a very concrete way to visualize your brand and how others in your audience will experience your aesthetic choices.

We'll touch on these sections and features of the content studio individually as we go through the features and how they can serve you in building your brand. You can access this menu/section list by clicking on the **Content** studio menu option in the left-hand navigation panel.

The preceding bullet-point list is the order in which the sections are listed in the menu that opens when you click on **Content** studio in the Mailchimp app, and we'll walk through each. First, though, I think it might be helpful to understand how these pieces within the content studio contribute to establishing your brand identity.

So, how do you establish a brand?

Your brand, in the context of digital marketing, will be composed of various pieces:

- **Colorways** – This will be a family of about three colors that your content will be centered around. This generally consists of your brand's primary color and some complementary colors to go with it.
- **Logos/hero campaign images** – Whether it's a logo for absolutely all of your content or a set of two to three images meant to promote a specific campaign for a predetermined window of time, this will be the primary image associated with your content.
- **Font family** – As people engage with your content, some degree of consistency makes the brand feel comfortable to them to a certain extent. As you land on things such as a font, it's important to consider its readability and accessibility. Try to limit intense fonts to the logo or highly targeted assets within your brand.

- **Specific language** – When we think of large brands, there's usually a tagline or specific voice that the brand writes in. For example, Mailchimp's own brand is quirky and conversational, whereas you might think about the brand voice of a security software company as looking to sound trustworthy and honest.

Mailchimp can help you collect some of these pieces in one place and then make them accessible inside all of the channels throughout the app. This is where the content studio can help support you in making sure your assets are consistent, which is the feature family we'll focus on in this chapter. With that in mind, let's go through the subsections within the feature itself and talk a bit about what we can get out of each feature.

Individual features and channels nested under Content Studio

Creative Assistant

We'll likely spend the bulk of our time in this section. The nice part of this tool is that, although it's currently in beta, it will provide you with the opportunity to pre-identify things such as your logo, which will be shared with the **My logo** section for you. **Creative Assistant** is a tool within the application that will pull things such as fonts, colors, images, and logos from a website and puts them together into a neat, consolidated collection for you.

To hop into **Creative Assistant**, you would do the following:

1. Select the **Content** studio menu option in the left-hand navigation panel.
2. Click on **Creative Assistant** from the menu that opens in the left-hand navigation panel.

Creative Assistant can pull information for you from a pre-existing website if you have one. Alternatively, it can be a Mailchimp landing page if you set one up by following the previous chapter and that's the closest thing you have to a website thus far. But it's good to note that if Mailchimp is not your first attempt at marketing and you already have a website elsewhere, you can use that website, even if it's not a Mailchimp product.

Whether you're at the beginning of your branding journey or you have bits and pieces of a brand in various different places, the **Creative Assistant** tool gives you a solid starting point. In the main builder, we're given the option to input a URL and a logo if we have one or browse through some sample brands Mailchimp has pre-built for you to consider (*Figure 7.1*).

Figure 7.1 – Creative Assistant builder

If you have a website and you choose to import a brand using a URL, this can take several minutes as the application checks out the site and collects information about whether it can identify a specific logo, colors, fonts, and other images on the page you provided. Once it collects some data, it'll begin generating pieces of branding content for you to review and check out. And with every option it provides you with, you can opt to edit the design if you would like by hovering over it and then clicking on the **Edit Design** button, as seen in *Figure 7.2*:

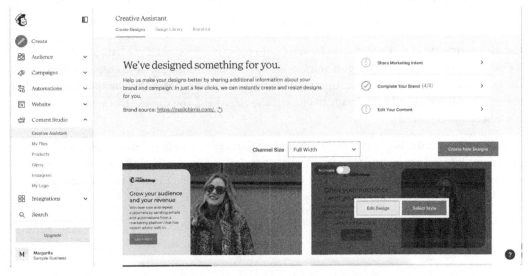

Figure 7.2 – Sample Creative Assistant design

Additionally, if you click on **Select Style**, you'll be shown additional designs that you can download if you would like to have options for channels both inside and outside of Mailchimp. **Creative Assistant** will generate designs for channels including the following:

- Email
- Landing pages
- Facebook
- Instagram
- Twitter
- LinkedIn
- YouTube
- Social ads
- Google Ads
- Postcards
- Presentation slides (16:9)
- Presentation slides (4:3)
- Zoom backgrounds
- Eventbrite backgrounds
- Pinterest

With every section, you can choose to either download these designs or edit the designs to tweak them a bit before using them.

> **Note about channel-specific designs**
> Not all of these designs are available with a free account. While you can preview them for ideas if you would like to, you will not be able to download them to use them without upgrading your account to a **Standard** account type.

Once you complete the steps marked by an exclamation point icon, as seen in *Figure 7.2*, you will have some designs to start working with, and if you click on the **Brand Kit** menu option at the top, you will see the following:

- Logos
- Fonts
- Colors

- Your brand personality
- Button styles

The app was able to collect these from your site.

At any point in the future, though, as your brand evolves, you can always edit this brand kit. Or if you would like, you can start over with a new site that you might have redesigned or that you'll maybe build with me later in *Chapter 9*. If that's the case, you would do the following:

1. Select the **Content** studio menu option in the left-hand navigation panel.
2. Click on **Creative Assistant** from the menu that opens in the left-hand navigation panel.
3. Click on **Brand Kit**.
4. Click on the **Reset Brand Data** button.

This will remove the old brand data, so you'll be asked to confirm that you want to start over.

When you've landed on a base brand that you're into, we can begin to check out some of the other features nested within the content studio.

My Files

This section should be pretty short and sweet. If you've used any product that lets you upload/import files, this interface will be super familiar to you. This is a straightforward interface that lets you add files to your Mailchimp account to use in a channel, or alternatively, where you can see all of the files you have uploaded in the past.

This is a very basic file hosting functionality so that you can choose to add images to your campaigns, or you can upload a document or something that you'd like to send to your contacts. The latter is conceptually similar to an attachment in a basic email; the only caveat is that bulk marketing emails with attachments will be filtered as spam for sure, so the Mailchimp application essentially allows you to link the file in your campaigns instead.

It's important to note that like with any form of file hosting, there are size and file type limitations to what you can upload, but most of the most common file types are compatible. Here's a list of file types, but if you'd like a full list of compatible extensions, I'll link the full list in the *Further reading* section at the end of this chapter:

- Images
- Documents
- Text

- Spreadsheets
- Audio
- Video
- Presentations
- Archives

Products

Once you set up your e-commerce store (which we'll cover in *Chapter 13*, if you don't have an existing store, and *Chapter 14*, if you do), you'll be able to review the products in your store all in one place. You can even edit the images associated with the product within this interface instead of bouncing between applications to make sure the right product image comes up in your campaigns or on your websites. This will enable you to make adjustments to the items your audience will see in places such as a landing page, website, or commerce store from one centralized place.

Giphy

If you're looking for a quick and fun way to spice up your content, who doesn't love a GIF? This is the internet classic of curating the perfect meme or visually representing your current mood. This tool is free and it's essentially an integration with `Giphy.com` that lets you use a search term in the search bar and choose a specific GIF to suit your message and content.

Instagram

If you have an Instagram Business account, you can connect your associated Facebook account through the **Integrations** interface. As long as it's the Facebook account associated with the Instagram Business account, images from your Instagram will appear on this interface. As with all the other **Content** studio sections, you'll be able to leverage those images in campaigns and other channels.

To connect your Facebook account, you would do the following:

1. Click on **Integrations** in the left-hand navigation panel.
2. Click on the **Facebook** icon.
3. Click on **Connect** to initiate authentication and log in to your Facebook account, as seen in *Figure 7.3*:

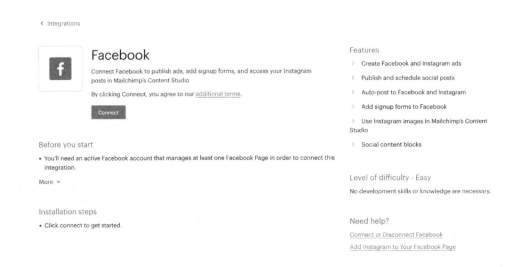

Figure 7.3 – Facebook integration connection page

You'll get to see more integrations in *Chapters 14* to *17*, but consider this an early taste of connecting your platforms!

My Logo

This is a pretty straightforward section, but the reason it deserves its own section is that very often, people have different versions of their logo on different channels. For example, your logo will likely have more text connected to it for a banner on a website versus a smaller logo for an ad that will appear on a social media feed. Similarly, people might have a simplified black-and-white version or outlined version of their logo with less color to ensure that, if it's paired with a very bright and vibrant campaign, the colors don't clash.

In this way, creating a section just for your logos leaves you room to grow your brand as you diversify your marketing channels and your audience broadens.

As you can see, the content studio is more than just the home of any content you upload into Mailchimp over time. It's a tool itself that you can leverage to refine your brand as you grow your audience and the variety of channels you use to engage with them.

Summary

In this chapter, we reviewed a really neat tool and family of features that helps us get a single look at our current brand and also equips us to think about evolving that brand into something more mature than it may currently be. The Content Studio, as it's the home of our images and styles, is really quite powerful because it provides us with the ability to edit our brand in one place and make it consistent across all of our channels. Additionally, we took a look at how information and assets come to be in the content studio and how we can personally edit or adjust them to best suit us. And ideally, we now have a notion of how to upload our logo and build a brand around it.

Next, we'll take a look at leveraging some of these content pieces to design a template and a campaign. We'll dig into all of the tools available to us in **Campaign Builders** and how we can customize the templates provided by Mailchimp to best suit our business.

Further reading

Here are some additional resources to dig further into some of the topics we covered in this chapter:

- *Use the Content Studio*: `https://eepurl.com/dyinjb`
- *Use Creative Assistant*: `https://eepurl.com/hg_5Dj`
- *Share Files Types with Contacts*: `https://eepurl.com/dyimK9`
- *Upload, Add, and Edit Images in Emails and Landing Pages*: `https://eepurl.com/dyim5D`

8
Outreach Marketing with Templates and Campaigns

This topic is very likely the reason why you picked up this book. In the 90s and 2000s, it very much seemed like email might be a technological trend that would eventually give way to a different form of digital communication. While these other forms of digital communication have absolutely come about, email has only gotten more robust and become more integrated into our everyday lives. As a direct result of that, marketing automation platforms, such as Mailchimp, have become central to how we approach bulk email marketing in particular.

In this chapter, we'll be looking specifically at two basic channels, very likely the exact ones that you initially came to Mailchimp for: **Templates** and **Campaigns**. These help to set the tone for your marketing. We'll be looking at the relationship between these two channels. So, overall, we'll be covering the following topics:

- Templates and how to start them
- Designing a Campaign
- Sending and scheduling strategies
- Types of emails to pair with targeted segments

So, let's start by looking at Templates.

Templates and how to start them

This might surprise you, but I think if used right, templates are a big deal and could be as useful as campaigns, if you're the type of person who prefers to put in some extra work upfront to reduce effort later. So, in this section, we'll cover a couple of things, such as what specifically a template in the Mailchimp platform is, the editor itself, how to choose a template base, and what to do with the template once you've made your choice.

What is a Template?

I really love templates: both the ones that you can select in the application that are sort of predesigned, but also just conceptually. I think templates can be really powerful. If you're looking at marketing with a longer lens, you should be looking at what steps you can take now that might make things easier in the long term. Ideally, you'd be thinking about the future of your business where you're sharing marketing responsibilities with another person, or even not doing it yourself at all; you might rely on others in your business to do it for you. In that scenario, you'd still want to maintain your brand identity. So, fundamentally, what we mean is that we should be asking, *how can I, as a nascent business owner, invest a little more time now to make things more efficient and consistent in the long term?*

And that's really at the heart of why I love templates. You can spend a little more time now, playing with and maybe even indulging in the aesthetics of an email without worrying too much about the content just yet. It's a neat way of focusing on the design and look of your future emails now so that you can just plug in images and text later on.

With that said, let's take a look at where we can find the Template Editor in the application.

Template Editor

Like we've done pretty consistently when navigating the application, we'll be looking to the left-hand navigation menu to find **Templates**. The editor is accessed by clicking on the **Campaigns** menu option and then selecting **Email Templates** from the list, as seen in *Figure 8.1*:

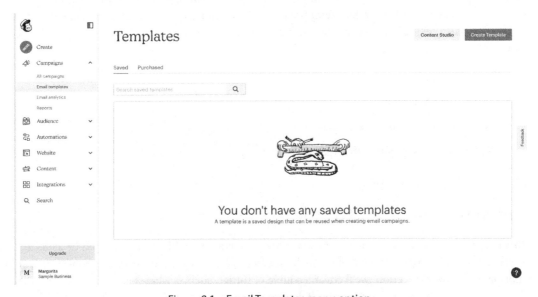

Figure 8.1 – Email Templates menu option

Click on **Create Template** to enter the editor. Here, you can begin to review and choose the layout type you like. Personally, I wouldn't worry too much about the color choices made for you in any of the predesigned templates if none of the color schemes are your cup of tea. It's all adjustable in the editor itself. The key in this part is really to focus on the layout. Here are a couple of things I recommend considering as you review your options:

- Do I want content to appear in a consistent order from one email to the next?
- Does my audience seem to have a preference for simple emails that favor just text or is an image-rich campaign necessary?
- Do I know whether my audience overwhelmingly uses one email service provider or application?

> Note about email inboxes and service providers
>
> Not all email inboxes receive and process information in the same way. For example, if you are sending emails to a large company that uses Microsoft Office, you'll want to experiment with templates. Outlook is so customizable that different types of elements might be blocked by your IT department, so experimenting with templates and content blocks is key.

It's absolutely fine to not know the answers to these questions or even to let the answers come to you over time as you begin to feel out what the aesthetic or design is that is right for your business or organization. But this is data that you can begin to collect over time if you're new to the marketing journey. We'll go over, in *Chapter 10*, where you can find information about email services your recipients are predominantly using when reading the reports of your emails.

But the essential goal in asking yourself these questions is to figure out what kind of layout and designs are best suited to your audience. Let's go over some of the reasons why I think these questions are ideal starting places and some examples before diving into where to engage with the Template feature itself.

Do I want content to appear in a consistent order from one email to the next?

This is an important question because some brands are built upon the idea that they are more spontaneous compared to other brands in their market. This means that on the opposite end, predictable brands likely lean on their audience knowing where they can refer to quick information in the email campaigns they send. When you have a notion of what your identity should be, you won't want to deviate radically from it. You can certainly reinvent your brand or your company, but when you get to a place where you're happy with your engagement, you will want to experiment with pieces of your design and content, but you won't want to change too much at one time.

For example, if you host pop-up dining experiences in your city, you may rely on allowing your audience to consistently know where, when, and what the new menu will be. Because what you're primarily marketing is the experience itself, you may not want your campaigns to be overly busy and cluttered, blocking easy understanding of what you'll be offering at the pop-up.

However, your business might be one where a surprise or some sort of unpredictability is what your audience wants from you. Or maybe you've seen that your audience really ebbs and flows with the seasons. Maybe you hold seasonal offers around the holidays, and during those times of the year, you may want to put more content into your campaigns than you might around other seasons. This means your audience might not have quite the same interest and bandwidth for cumbersome content in the off-season as they do when they're engaged with holiday shopping.

For example, say I own a bookstore. During the holiday season, when sales increase for my business, my content might include more detailed recommendations for buying different books for a young adult versus a 30-year-old science fiction fan.

Does my audience seem to have a preference for simple emails that favor just text or is an image-rich campaign necessary?

This is really for the purpose of consistent template design. The answer will inform the types of content blocks you might want to place in your template. You will have the option of a handful of content block types, and some will be geared toward text, some toward images, and some toward a combination of both, as well as buttons, dividers, and some blocks designed to help you link out to other sites.

If you were, for example, a writer who sends out a monthly newsletter, text-oriented would likely be ideal for you. Teasing new chapters to your audience or even novellas and short stories would help to keep your readers engaged.

However, you may be a photographer who provides their audience with sneak peeks of working behind the scenes, putting together a gallery show, or even demonstrating some of your work. In cases such as this, it's very likely that an image-driven campaign will be the most engaging to the folks subscribed to your campaigns.

Do I know whether my audience overwhelmingly uses one email service provider or application?

This one seems perhaps unnecessary, and to a certain extent, it definitely deserves to be toward the end of this list of questions to consider. But the format in which your content is viewed can be relevant to the images you select or even the order in which you want to present text-driven information to your audiences. Most marketing platforms, such as Mailchimp, predominantly design their base templates in a responsive fashion. This means that if you know most of your audience exclusively reads your emails from their phone, then you may want to ensure that your most important information is available right at the top since your audience may just be scanning the email.

On the other hand, if you know your recipients all use Gmail or another provider from their laptop or desktop, then you have a bit more flexibility to be creative and distribute the key information throughout the email's body.

> **Definition of "responsive" email design**
>
> Responsive email refers to emails that have additional coding applied to ensure that they are compatible with different device types. This means that depending on the size of the screen your contact is viewing the email on, blocks of text or images that sit next to each other can stack vertically to help make sure your contact only needs to scroll up and down and not left to right as well.

Let's take a look at some of the templates and begin to get a feel for what you should look for and where you can find more options.

Choosing a template

After you click on **Create Template** as you did earlier, you'll be taken to a page where you can see the default base template options, as seen in *Figure 8.2*:

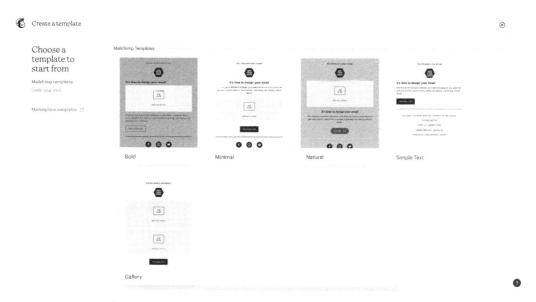

Figure 8.2 – Default template options

Here, we see a pretty decent and simple representation of what I was referring to when talking about templates and emails containing a spectrum of content, from text-heavy to image-heavy. For example, when we look at the previews of **Simple Text** versus **Gallery**, we see that they are almost the opposite of one another.

For **Gallery**, we can see that we have empty image blocks and just a simple opener where you can input a logo or a simple opening line. This would obviously be ideal if you're an artist or photographer, for example, looking to promote or tease your next pieces.

On the other hand, with the **Simple Text** template, we see a lot of placeholder text. While there's a simple opener and somewhere where you can input your logo again, the remainder of the content for you to replace with your own is text-specific. This would be geared more toward authors, bloggers, and so on who are looking to provide text-based content.

The other three exist somewhere in between these two. The other templates inject a bit of color as well (which you can absolutely change later in the editor), but as you can see, they contain the same logo and simple opener and then content blocks that are a mix of text and images.

These five templates don't have to be your only options though. Mailchimp has other predesigned templates that you can add to your account for free or at various price points, depending on how fancy you want to get without designing it yourself. Alternatively, if you're comfortable with HTML, you could also code your own template.

To review other predesigned templates, you would need to click on **Marketplace Templates**, as seen on the left in *Figure 8.2*. This will take you to the marketplace, where you can review some of the fancier predesigned template options if instead of customizing your layout more manually you would like to just edit the content and not the layout. As we can see in *Figure 8.3*, there are some paid options, and by selecting the **Price** dropdown on the left, you can also choose to view templates specifically based on a price range.

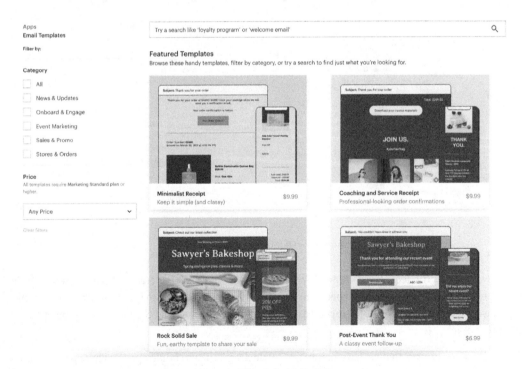

Figure 8.3 – Template Marketplace

They currently range from free to about $14.99, so feel free to browse. If you filter on **Free**, you'll see an additional five email templates, as seen in *Figure 8.4*, that you can then import into your account to work with.

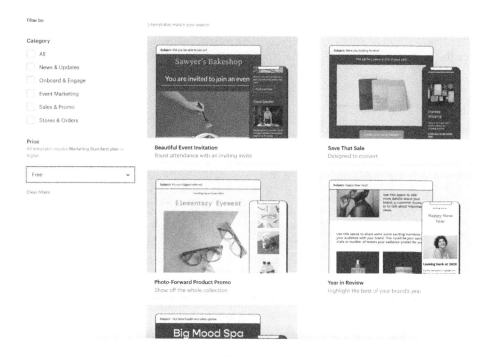

Figure 8.4 – Free-filtered Template Marketplace

If, for example, I were very fond of the colors and layout I see in the template named **Beautiful Event Invitation**, I would click on it, and the next page would tell me a bit more about the template and provide some examples of how it would look by default on a desktop. It'll also show me previews of what it looks like on mobile. There is also a button toward the top that says **Add for Free** to import it into your account.

> **Important note about Template Marketplace**
>
> As we move forward, some of these extras will require an upgraded account type. In the case of extra templates, we see in the Template Marketplace that these will generally require a Marketing Standard plan or higher. Generally, if you are still working with a Free account, you will want to utilize the templates already available in the account itself.

But whether you're using a template from the defaults available in the account or you choose a template from the Template Marketplace, once you make your selection, you will be taken into the editing interface itself. This is where you can begin to change the layout or add text/images to the content blocks themselves, whatever you're feeling.

If you followed along in *Chapter 7*, when you go into the editor, you will see whatever you set as your logo is input for you by default. But most importantly, to the left, you will see a toolbar where you can choose to add different content block types. These are consistent between the Template Editor and the Campaign Editor, which we'll dig further into later in this chapter. Now, let's take a look at these options and what they are.

We can see the menu itself here in *Figure 8.5*. Then, we'll list the options and what they mean:

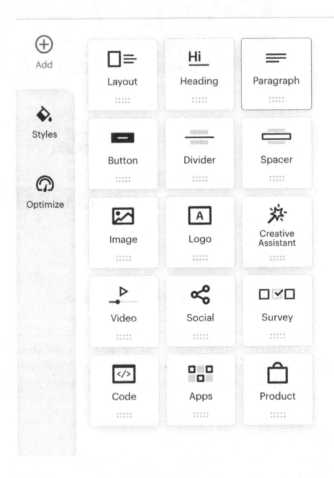

Figure 8.5 – Content block menu

As we review these options, it's important to note that many of them are menus themselves, meaning that when you select them, you will be given a couple of options for each. To select a content type, click on the block and then drag it over to the location in the template on the right you would like that content to be inserted.

So, now that we know a little more about how to activate the menu, let's review what is meant by each category:

- **Layout**: This opens a secondary menu on the left where you can choose to add a new layout/content to the area you dragged the *layout* box to. This sub-menu consists of the following:

  - **Text**: Provides you with three layout options for how you would like two areas of text to appear on the template, stacked on top of each other or two text bodies next to one another

  - **Text & Image**: Provides you with six options for text oriented next to or stacked above or below image spaces

  - **Image Gallery**: Provides you with four gallery options with your choice of two images, three images, four images, or five images grouped together

- **Heading**: A simple text block for the top region of your template where you can set text color, padding, and background color for the block and then input text for the opener of your template/campaign. This is best used near the top logo or in place of it.

- **Paragraph**: This is a simple text block that enables you to add text wherever you dragged the option to in the body of the template, where you can edit parts of the style, such as the color and size.

- **Button**: This option allows you to drag a button into your design that you can then link to a website or a file you've added to the content studio.

- **Divider**: Wherever you drag this content block, you will be adding a horizontal line between different content blocks/areas of your template or campaign.

- **Spacer**: This is similar to **Divider**, with the exception that it does not add a visible horizontal line but enables you to create a more natural space between different content blocks in your template. You can even choose the pixel height of the space if you would like to make the space greater or smaller.

- **Image**: This allows you to add space for a new image.

- **Logo**: This is a placeholder where you can select your logo or upload another to the body of your template or campaign.

- **Creative Assistant**: This option enables you to replace campaign images with images you may have worked on in *Chapter 7*. You can also edit images here and select **Generate Designs** to go into the **Creative Assistant** interface we used earlier in the book.

- **Video**: This allows you to add a video to a template or campaign.

- **Social**: This option adds social icons that you can then link to your company or organization's Facebook, Instagram, and Twitter. This is similar to the **Button** option, where the purpose is to link out elsewhere and help you promote your other channels outside of the platform.

- **Survey**: This option adds a button that will eventually lead to a survey you create inside the Mailchimp application. For context, the **Template Builder** is not specific to or connected to a specific audience. This will just help you with the design of the button itself. Once you utilize the template in an audience-specific campaign later, you can choose a survey associated with that audience.
- **Code**: This allows you to add a custom HTML block wherever you drag this option on your template. The most important thing to note is that these code blocks are limited specifically to HTML, so things such as JavaScript or scripts in general will be sanitized out of the code to ensure that the email goes through when the campaign that contains this code eventually goes out.
- **Apps**: This content block allows you to integrate the template directly into some specific connected apps. This includes things such as Instagram, Calendar Links, and your Google Business Profile if you would like.
- **Product**: If you have a connected store, you can choose to add any product from that store to your template/campaign.

To reiterate, the goal here isn't necessarily to fill out every single content block. The idea is to choose content block types and layouts that you think would be consistently appealing to your audience. When choosing these content blocks, you can leave the default text there if you would like. But what I would recommend editing in the template here is the content you envision being the same every time you use the template in the future. Some common examples of what you might fill out so that it's the same every time you use the template might be the following:

- Logo
- Heading
- Social links
- Buttons:
  - This may be a button you plan on using consistently as a link to the website for your business/organization
- A footer containing legally required content, such as your organization's mailing address:
  - This is provided by default in every template/campaign as it's required to be compliant with CAN-SPAM. It's represented by the merge tags relevant to the audience you end up using the template for, as shown in *Figure 8.6*.

Figure 8.6 – Footer merge tags connected to your Audience Settings

These footer merge tags connect to items you placed in your Audience Settings when you were setting your audience up or are pulled from the current date. Let's take a quick look at them:

- `*|CURRENT_YEAR|*`: This merge tag will populate the current year and can serve as a copyright information for you that updates annually on its own. That way, you don't have to manage it manually.
- `*|LIST:COMPANY|*`: This will populate the name of the business or organization that you set in the settings of your audience when you were setting it up.
- `*|LIST:DESCRIPTION|*`: This inputs the permission reminder found in your audience settings. By default, it is provided by the Mailchimp application and will say **You are receiving this email because you opted in via our website**. This can be edited if you want in the **Required Footer Settings** section discussed in *Chapter 2*.
- `*|HTML:LIST_ADDRESS_HTML|*`: This creates a hyperlinked version of the physical address you input in Audience Settings that can be clicked on to download a **vCard** (`.vcf`) file that the subscriber can add to their address book. Similar to other content you might find in the default footer, things such as a physical address are required to stay in compliance with the CAN-SPAM Act.

Finally, there is, of course, the unsubscribe link. We can usually see it at the bottom of any email, which is similarly a requirement of the CAN-SPAM Act. As a marketing platform that sends emails on your behalf, Mailchimp is required to include it in all email campaigns that go out through the platform. Even if you were to attempt to remove the unsubscribe link, you'd find that once you send a campaign through the platform, the application will still include the link at the bottom to keep any sending through the platform legally in compliance.

So, now that we know a bit more about what goes into a template, let's walk through a quick example.

Let's use one of our previous examples. Our business is a digital bookstore. I like this example because, as you might expect, it would require a balance of text and images. The likely subscribers to my audience are going to be avid readers. This means they'd probably like to be able to skim the email for eye-catching covers, but we could also include a section that's geared to the particular genre they might be interested in.

So, let's say our bookstore predominantly sells fiction, fantasy, science fiction, and history books. Knowing that, perhaps what we want consistently in our templates is a section dedicated to each genre and then an image along with each showing the cover of the featured book, as seen in *Figure 8.7*.

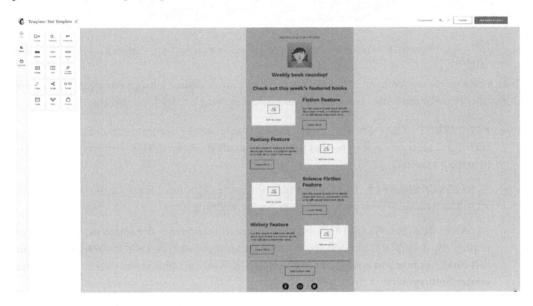

Figure 8.7 – Sample template for a bookstore

Here, you can see that I've created a section for each genre. I haven't removed any of the detailed placeholder text, but I've created a title for each genre. In this example, we want to consistently feature one book from each category, so the category title doesn't need to change. However, in each campaign, we'll be putting in a different book cover for the image and then a different summary or book description under each heading.

Once we're satisfied with the general layout, colors, and aesthetic choices, we can click on **Save Template and Exit** to save the changes we've made and then move on to actually using the template.

Again, the best reason to use the Template Editor is in line with what you will have taken away from each chapter so far. By spending a little more time with one element in your platform, or even one setting, you can streamline future work. In this example, as the owner of a small bookstore, we can spend a little more time on the template for our weekly email to our audience, and then every week, instead of redoing the email layout every time, we can just use the template, change the images and text, and send much more quickly.

So next, let's jump into leveraging the Campaign Editor itself. This is where we will connect specifically to an audience and start editing content in one-off emails.

Using the Campaign Editor

Once you're ready to send a campaign to your audience, you would navigate to the editor using the left-hand menu we've used to access all the products thus far:

1. Click on **Create**.
2. Select the **Design Email** button.

This will take you to the **Campaign Checklist** interface, where you can set the following information:

- **To**: This is the section where you will select the audience that you would like to send this campaign to. Additionally, if you have a saved segment or would like to create a segment, this is where you would use them. We made segments in *Chapter 4*.
- **From**: When you select an audience in the **To** section, this section will be filled out for you with the information you input in Audience Settings. But if you would like, you can edit things such as the name and email address that your audience will see in their inboxes when the campaign is sent out.
- **Subject**: This one probably seems quite straightforward. This is where you would set the subject line that will appear to your audience members in their inboxes when you send the campaign. Additionally, you can set the preview text that appears next to the subject line. In the event that you don't set anything, most email providers, such as Gmail, for example, will just pull the first pieces of text in your campaign to preview here. But Mailchimp provides you with the option to customize it to something more specific to your brand or that you believe might be eye-catching. At the right-hand side of the subject line and preview boxes, you will also see a smiley emoji where you can click and select emojis to add to these lines:
  - A very neat feature of the **Subject** section is that to the right, when you are filling out the field, the Mailchimp platform provides suggestions based on known best practices, as seen in *Figure 8.8*.

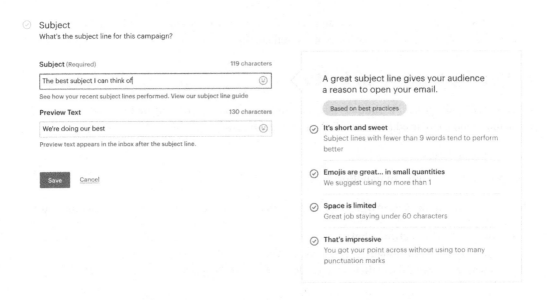

Figure 8.8 – Subject line best practices

- **Content**: This is where we get into the editor itself. Clicking the **Design Email** button here will take you to an editor very similar to the Template Editor we just utilized.

Once you click **Design Email**, the application will take you to the editor, and on the left-hand side, you can choose from the prebuilt templates we saw earlier. There is also a **Saved** section here where you can select the template we edited earlier in this chapter. When you hover your cursor over your desired template, you will be given the option to click on a button that says **Apply** to select the template you will be working on in the campaign, as seen in *Figure 8.9*:

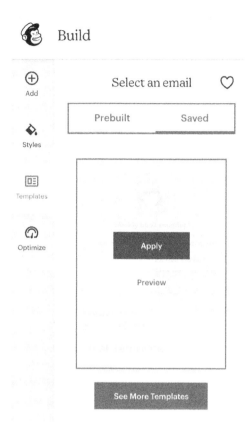

Figure 8.9 – Campaign Editor template options

The Campaign Editor here will look incredibly similar to the Template Editor. There is a menu to the left with the content block options. Similarly, you can select the type of block and then drag it over to the right and drop it where you would like within the layout of the campaign. But because we took the initial first step of creating a template for our bookstore, we can actually get directly to editing the content in the campaign itself. So, for example, if we would like to edit the first set of content from *Figure 8.7*, we would click on the set of text we would like to edit and that will let us type directly into the block. On the left, we will see a menu where we can adjust style items such as the following:

- Text color
- Block background color
- Padding around the block

Along the top of the editing interface, we will be given a menu where we can adjust things such as the following:

- Font type
- Font size
- Style options
- Hyperlink tool
- Text alignment
- Line spacing
- Bullet pointing
- Numbering
- **Merge Tags** drop-down options

We can see both of these menus in *Figure 8.10*.

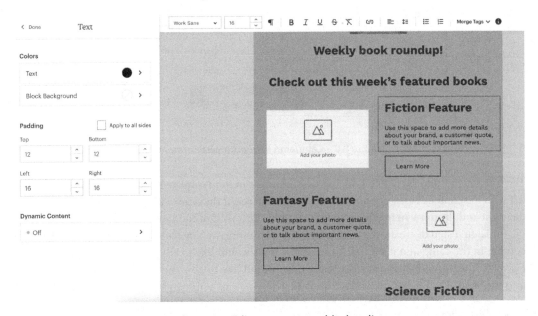

Figure 8.10 – Campaign Editor text content block styling menus

When you've changed the text and edited the styling, you can click on **Done** and that will take you back to the content block menu.

Now, looking at the left-hand menu, you might also see a menu item that's called **Styles**. This is another option that will save us a little time. In this section, we can set things such as the following:

- **Background colors**
- **Fonts**
- **Font sizes**
- **Font colors**
- **Link colors**
- **Pixel height for dividers**
- **Divider style**
- **Divider color**

By setting these in advance, the builder will apply these styles universally to the campaign, and then, as you edit each block, you would only need to change sizes, colors, fonts, and so on for specific lines or words instead of setting all of the style elements from the preceding list manually for each content block.

As we've established, I love a time-saver.

Similar to the text block, editing any of the sections of your campaign is done by clicking on the text, image, or button in the layout. Doing that opens a menu for that content block on the left-hand side, where you can edit the content and styling. For example, for our bookstore, if we would like to edit the button for each book, we would click on the button in the content block and that will open up a menu where we can input the URL we would like the button to hyperlink to. Alternatively, we would highlight the text of the button on the right and change what it says there, as we can see in *Figure 8.11*.

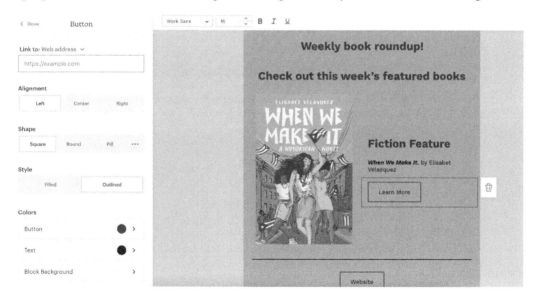

Figure 8.11 – Button content block editing menu

When you've edited all the content in the campaign and you feel good about the layout, design, and content, if you would like, you can preview what the campaign will look like by clicking on the **Preview** button in the upper right. In **Preview** mode, you can send yourself a test email by clicking the **Send a Test Email** button in the upper right or clicking on **Enable live merge tag info** in the menu on the left-hand side.

The latter is a particularly helpful tool if you decide to use audience-specific merge tags, which we went through setting up in *Chapter 3*. When you enable live merge tag info, the application will let you flip through the contacts in your audience to see what the campaign will look like for them specifically when they open the campaign in their inboxes.

When you choose to send yourself a test email, you will see a modal pop up over the interface where you can input email addresses you would like to test with, as seen in *Figure 8.12*:

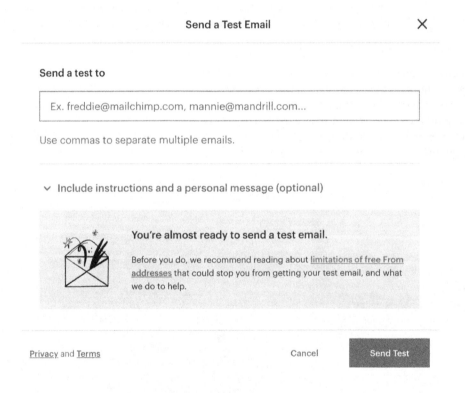

Figure 8.12 – The Send a Test Email pop-up modal

> **Important note about sending Test Campaigns**
>
> If you are using a free domain email address as your **From** email address in the application, it becomes a little more important to send your test to a different email and the same one it will be sent from. As you can't verify a free domain (because while you may own a single email address, you don't own the domain itself), this means that the email address is unverified, because, for example, it's not being sent by Gmail itself. While the email will likely still go through, because Mailchimp goes to great lengths to assist with delivery, the delivery may be noticeably delayed.
>
> More information can be found in the Mailchimp support article *Limitations of Free Email Addresses*, available at `https://eepurl.com/dyil9c`.

If you have your own domain or are looking to buy your own private domain, we will be covering how to add that to your Mailchimp account in *Chapter 9*.

If you like the test campaign in your inbox and think you're ready to send the campaign to your audience, click on **Exit Preview Mode**, and in the Editor, click on **Continue** in the upper right-hand corner.

This will take you back to the Campaign Checklist. Here, if you've removed all the default text from the campaign and filled out all the checklist items, you will see green checkmarks next to each item. Also, you will see, in the upper right-hand corner, that two buttons have become available to you – **Schedule** and **Send** – as seen in *Figure 8.13*:

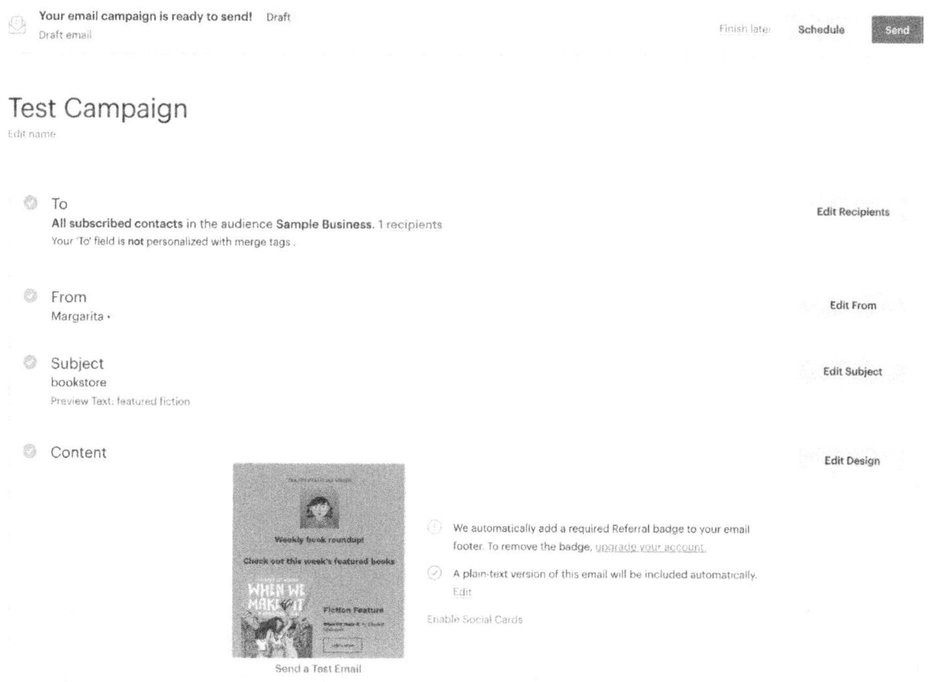

Figure 8.13 – Completed Campaign Checklist

Now that our campaign is designed and ready to go, let's review some of the scheduling options and how to send immediately.

Campaign scheduling

Let's talk a little bit about different types of campaign scheduling. Once you've hit a good stride with designing and filling out your campaigns, you may be in the position of wanting to schedule your campaigns in advance. The Mailchimp application offers three different types of campaign scheduling:

- **Send Time Optimization**: By using this feature, you are leveraging more Mailchimp platform data. Because Mailchimp has millions of users, there is a pretty good chance that the email addresses in your audience are in the audiences of other users. When you use optimization, Mailchimp will calculate the best time for different recipients to receive the campaign within 24 hours of the date you set in the modal seen in *Figure 8.14*. If your account is new and Mailchimp doesn't have data related to a contact on your list, they'll use the scheduled send date you indicate in the schedule setup.

- **Send at a specific time**: This one is fairly straightforward. In this option, you set a specific date and time in the future for the campaign to go out. Keep in mind that the date and time by default correspond to the time zone you set for your account overall.

- **Batch delivery**: If you have a very large audience and you're concerned that there may be too much traffic to a website you've linked in the campaign, you can leverage batch scheduling to break up the audience into a certain number of groups and then separate them by a specific amount of time. That way, your campaign will cascade to the people on your list instead of going to every audience member all at once. This can help to stagger traffic to the site or sites in your campaign.

Let's take a look at the pop-up modal scheduling options offered.

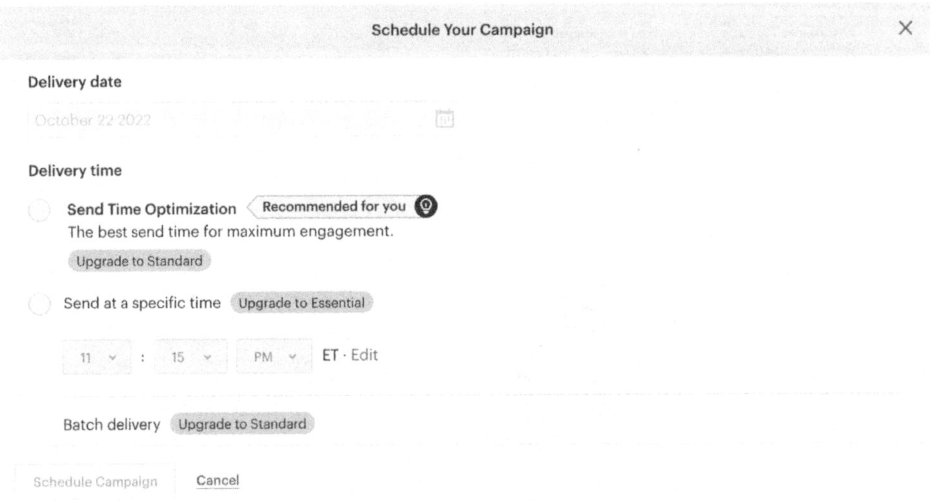

Figure 8.14 – The Schedule Your Campaign modal

> **Important note about scheduling features**
> These campaign scheduling features are not available for Free accounts. Specifically, **Send Time Optimization** and **Batch Delivery** are offered with the **Standard** plan and **Send at a specific time** is made available to Essential account types.

Once you've chosen the scheduling type that works for you, you then click on **Schedule Campaign**, and then you're all set!

Alternatively, of course, as you can see in *Figure 8.13*, if scheduling is not a fit for you, you can also just choose to click on **Send** in the upper right-hand corner. This, as the button implies, will send the campaign to your audience members immediately. A pop-up modal will appear to ask you to confirm that you would like to send the campaign immediately, and when you click on **Send Now**, the campaign will go out! You'll get a confirmation page (*Figure 8.15*) when it's sent out, and then you're done; your first campaign is out there in the wild.

Your email's out there— another job well done

Test Campaign is on its way to **1 subscriber** from the audience, **Sample Business**.

Check email report

Figure 8.15 – Campaign send confirmation

We'll be looking into reports specifically in *Chapter 10*, but if you'd like a little sneak peek, you can click on the **Check email report** button in the confirmation.

So, we've done it. We've set ourselves up to be able to work quickly by creating templates we can reuse over and over. We've also walked through how to edit campaigns, which is at the core of what we're probably looking for from a marketing platform such as Mailchimp. Now that we have an idea of how to build an email strategy, let's go through some examples of how to pair different emails we may want to send with groups/interest categories to give us a starting point to develop our strategy from.

Types of emails to pair with targeted segments

In this particular section, we will be referencing *Chapter 4, Tags, and Segments*. In that chapter, we covered **Groups** and **Segments**, which are the perfect tools to pair with your emails. In this section, we'll go through a couple of examples of businesses and then emails and segments you could pair together when designing and sending your emails. For each example, you'll see context for the business, sample interest groups, and types of emails that may work as a starting point for that type of business.

Digital content creator

A digital content creator would want to get the most number of eyes on their content. Whether it's increasing traffic back to their social media or ensuring opens and clicks to their email so that they have excellent analytics for partnership portfolios, it's important to think about what their goals are. Most digital content creators are looking to achieve an increase in traffic to the content they're creating because many of these entrepreneurs make their living off of selling self-referential merchandise and product/brand partnerships. The name of the game for them is truly eyes on their channels.

Many deliver pitches to brands to persuade them to partner with them and, in doing that, have a brief pitch deck that includes engagement data. This means it can be very powerful for content creators to have concrete engagement data, such as opens and clicks on an email campaign. The main concern for this person would be opens. The focus here should be the choices made around the **Subject** and **Preview text** (see *Figure 8.8*). Also, most content creators are very image-driven, so they'll lean toward a template that features an image toward the top. Additionally, it would be a good idea to link to partnered content further up in the design as well. The main reason for this is that it is generally better to put the content you want the most engagement with further up to capture the attention of people who may just skim your emails in addition to very engaged audience members who will read everything. Some example templates that would suit this, without building a whole template yourself, include **Bold**, **Natural**, and **Gallery** (see *Figure 8.16*).

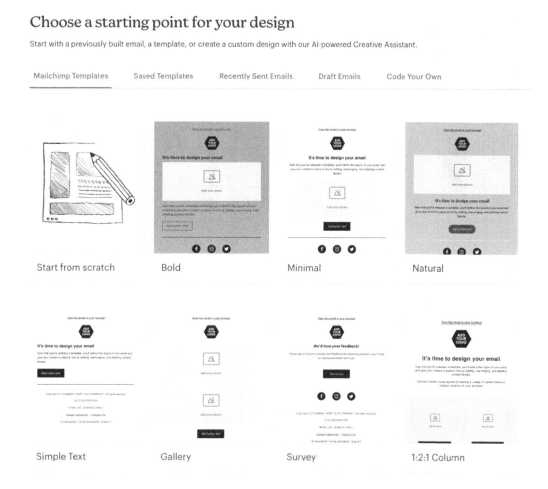

Figure 8.16 – Campaign email templates

Next, let's take a look at a scenario where the user has existing products to sell.

E-commerce marketer

For this user, the clear goal is selling their products. Understanding their goals is always going to be key to their overall business, as well as choices such as their emails. Because an e-commerce business is looking to drive traffic to their products, wherever they live online, the email-related goal isn't going to be just to drive opens, but ideally also to drive clicks to either specific products or their store overall.

Many e-commerce businesses can leverage emails to tease or announce new products or talk to their audience members about products that might be featured or on sale. On the page shown in *Figure 8.16*, you can scroll down and see some template options, such as **New product category**, **New product announcement**, and **Thank you discount**, as seen in *Figure 8.17*.

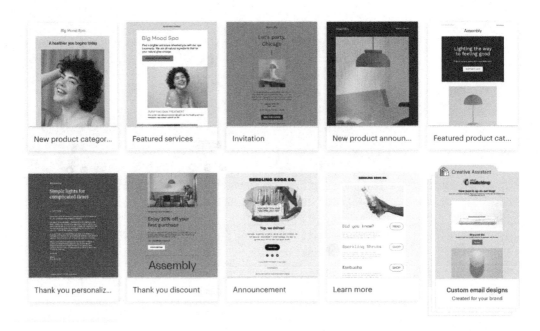

Figure 8.17 – Campaign email templates

Similar to a content creator, purchasing is frequently driven higher by images being prominent toward the top of the email. The core difference you will generally see is that commerce-oriented templates tend to also provide content blocks with information about products and their prices. For example, if you select the **New product category** template, you will see text content blocks (see *Figure 8.18*) with information about the product placed further up in the template.

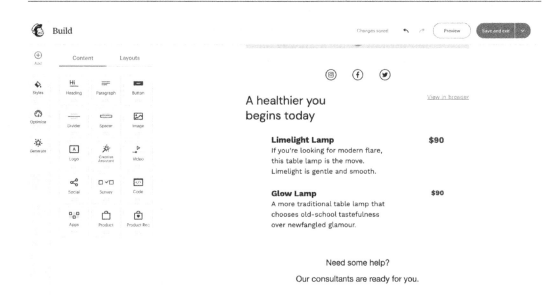

Figure 8.18 – Campaign email editor

The idea with any template or email you're designing is to consider what your business goals are, but additionally, what drives your audience members most. If your business is mostly driven by visual elements, prioritize images further up in your email campaign. If your business is driven by engagement with text (such as if you're an author), then you'll want to prioritize text. You'll generally want to assume that people will skim your email or engage with content further up in your email, so just keep that in mind as you design.

With those examples, let's quickly review what we covered throughout this chapter, and then we'll move on to creating our first website.

Summary

In this chapter, we created at least one consistent template and asked ourselves questions that would assist us in determining what kinds of content are relevant to our specific audience. That way, we can keep some specific elements consistent in our designs. Additionally, we learned how to leverage these templates and consistent pieces in a first campaign. We saw how the Campaign Editor builds on what the Template Editor offers us. These functions essentially build on top of one another, scaling in a way that empowers you to skill up with each step.

Throughout this chapter, perhaps most critically, we learned how to strategize for our audience and the considerations we want to make when designing and setting up our emails in such a way that considers the email services receiving the campaigns and the devices.

As these things can make a difference with respect to how our audience engages with the campaign, as important as the editor itself is, having a strategy for your design, content, and even domain can help to increase your engagement margins in the long run.

In the next chapter, we'll take a look at how we can use the Mailchimp platform to create a domain, or connect one if we already have one, to help with delivery and our branding. We'll also go through how we can use Mailchimp to create our first website!

Further reading

Here are some additional resources to dig further into some of what we covered in this chapter:

- *Limitations of Free Email Addresses*: `https://eepurl.com/dyil9c`
- *Types of Email Templates*: `https://eepurl.com/dyim2z`
- *Create an Email Template*: `https://eepurl.com/dyild9`
- *Templates vs. Campaigns*: `https://eepurl.com/dyim0n`

9
Setting Up Your Marketing Presence with Websites

Now that we have our email campaigns up and running, let's move on to the next best marketing asset you can have – a **website**! It's entirely possible if you've already worked on your business or organization for a while that it might have an online presence such as a Facebook or Instagram account, but a website is the next organic step. It can serve as a hub for information such as the services or products you offer, detailed information about your business, how to contact you, and so on.

In this chapter, we'll be looking at how a domain and website help to create a kind of digital home for your business and can serve as a central home for your brand identity in a way that's visible to your existing audience and people discovering you for the first time.

We'll cover the following:

- Domains – what are they and do you need one?
- Making a website
- Editing settings

Ideally, by the end of this chapter, you'll have a notion of how to use a website to establish a home for your brand on the internet. So, let's start specifically with the question of domains.

What is a domain?

The simplest way to think of a domain is as the address for you and your brand on the internet. Your domain is what people will type into their browser or even search to find you through a search engine such as Google, DuckDuckGo, or Bing. For example, when you log in to your Mailchimp account, you go to `https://mailchimp.com/`, which is their domain.

You also might have noticed a distinction between a private domain and a public email domain. **Public domains** are generally domains that belong to another company, where they provide you with a free email address and they act as your receiving email service provider. Really common examples that you are probably familiar with are domains such as Gmail or Yahoo. These are domains where you may own or have access to a single local address at the domain, but you don't own the domain itself.

The purpose of this distinction is that with a public domain, you can't make changes to the authentication of the domain, and a great many other people have access to or own pieces of the domain. For example, we may both have email addresses at `Gmail.com`, but if you own your own domain, I won't be able to make changes to settings for that domain or have an email address at that domain without you creating one for me. A **private domain** is one that you have purchased and you specifically own and manage. This means that you don't share it with anyone else (except maybe people at your company or organization), but it would not be available to just anybody on the internet.

Do I need a private domain?

Getting straight to the point, I would recommend having one, and I would recommend it for a couple of reasons, which we will go through next.

An additional entry point and sign-up portal

It can act as an additional entry point to your brand where your audience can sign up.

Let's say I encountered your product/brand at a conference or market and I went home and googled what I can remember about your name. Hopefully, I can at least find a social media page, but if you have a website, when I find it, I can skim it to confirm it's really what I'm looking for or has the products I saw. Then, if you have a sign-up form, I can just subscribe there so I don't have to google you or your company again, so you don't have to rely on people being willing and able to search for you every time. This will mean that you have yet an additional item that will come up in a search, but also as a page or set of pages where you can organically grow your audience instead of permanently relying on the audience members you originally imported to your Mailchimp account.

Personalizing your domain settings

You can make adjustments to your domain settings, which you can't access through a public domain.

With a Gmail account, for example, you can edit things such as your domain records. Because the domain needs to work for every Gmail user, Google doesn't allow you to edit the domain in a way that's specific to the platform or platforms you're using. As your marketing efforts grow and you use more tools to automate or streamline your marketing, it will become necessary for you to ensure that your domain is customized to authenticate actions being made by platforms such as Mailchimp. We'll go further into why you would edit your domain later in this chapter.

Improving deliverability

Having a private domain tends to improve your deliverability when sending campaigns through any marketing platform.

As noted in *Chapter 8*, when you send emails using a public domain such as Gmail, because you cannot access things such as the domain records, receiving domains (especially Gmail) take a more critical look at your email campaigns because it knows that you didn't send it through Gmail, but rather through an outside product. This can look suspicious to the receiving email service, which is why it will go through more rigorous filtering and may end up caught in your recipient's spam or junk folders. Because filtering is a combination of factors, such as the content of your email, the URLs you've linked in your content, the frequency with which you've sent emails in the past, how many recipients have marked you as spam on purpose, and your domain records, it's generally advisable to control as many of these factors as you can, and having a private domain is a huge factor.

Having an authentic appearance

Using a private domain makes emails look less suspicious to recipients and firewalls.

When you send using a public domain, applications such as Mailchimp will take extra steps to try and improve your deliverability. Usually, you use a platform such as Mailchimp specifically to create more robust email designs that wouldn't be strictly possible to generate directly using Gmail, for example. However, in order to make sure that the deliverability is good enough to make it worth sending fancier emails and other content, Mailchimp will adjust your sending information to make it a little less likely to get caught in spam filters. However, this means that if your recipient opens the header (where it says who the email is **To** and **From**), they will notice that **From** might look a little different since it shows that it was sent through a platform like Mailchimp. This may be totally fine for you as you start to build your brand, but generally, as you develop your brand and identity more, you want to start removing signs of other brands and the tools that you use to facilitate your marketing. This means that if you eventually want everything, including the full **From email address**, to only refer to your brand, you will need a private domain.

Where do I get one and what if I have one?

If you don't have one and don't really know where to get one, you can do it all inside the Mailchimp platform. Additionally, if you have one, you can add it to your Mailchimp account and get going by adjusting your domain records.

To either go to purchase a new domain or add an existing domain to your Mailchimp account, go to the left-navigation menu, as we have done with all of our other channels thus far. In the menu, we click on **Website**, and then **Domains** from the menu beneath it, as seen in *Figure 9.1*:

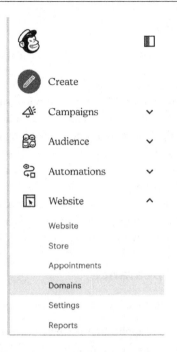

Figure 9.1 – Domains in the Website menu

Right at the top of the **Domains** section, if you haven't added any private domains, you'll see the option to search for the availability of a domain.

> **Note about websites and commerce**
> In order to use a private domain for a website, you would need to purchase the Websites and Commerce Core plan. This will give you access to Websites and Mailchimp-specific Commerce features and grant you the ability to associate domains with them.

Underneath that section, there are two sections called **Email Domains** and **Connected Domains**, as seen in *Figure 9.2*:

Your Mailchimp Custom Domains

Find a new custom domain name for your brand, or manage the exisiting domain(s) you've purchased with Mailchimp.

Have questions? Read how to purchase a domain with Mailchimp.

Email Domains

Your email domains control how your emails are sent through Mailchimp. Verifying and authenticating your domain helps your hard work get to your customers' inboxes.

Public Email Domains

Public domains like Gmail, Yahoo, and Hotmail don't need to be verified or authenticated. Learn more about the limitations of using free email with Mailchimp, and how we can help you make the most of your hard work.

Connected Domains

If you already own a domain from another domain provider, you can connect it to give your landing pages and website a more professional look.

Have questions? Read how to connect your domain or subdomain to Mailchimp.

Figure 9.2 – The Domains page

Let's break down what you would do in each section:

- **Your Mailchimp Custom Domains**: This is where you can see domains you have chosen to purchase from Mailchimp, and you can also use the tool underneath, **Search For New Domain**, to check whether the domain you're interested in is available.
- **Email Domains**: In this section, you can add a domain you already have by clicking on **Add & Verify Domain**. Common providers are places such as GoDaddy, Google, Domain.com, and so on:

- **Public Email Domains**: This also has a sub-section for public domains such as Gmail or Yahoo that you might have already used in previous chapters to send out your emails or even to set up your account.
- **Connected Domains**: In this section, you would add your domain again if you would like it to apply to landing pages or websites moving forward.

Focusing on the first option, if you don't have a private domain, that is where you would click on **Search For New Domain**. When you click on the button, this will take you to an interface where, by default, the application will begin looking for available domain names that roughly match the name of the business you input when creating your account. If you would like, you can of course edit the keyword search, but it'll look something like *Figure 9.3*:

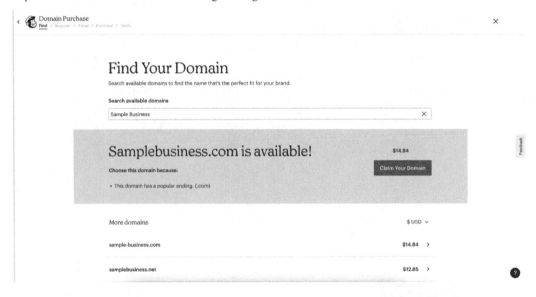

Figure 9.3 – New domain search interface

> **Note about claiming a domain**
>
> You can only claim a private domain that isn't currently purchased or already owned by another person or company. This means that when you search for a specific domain, if it is already owned by someone, it will appear as unavailable. So, in those cases, you'll have to think creatively about your private domain address.

Once you find your domain, you can then purchase it in this interface. Or, if you have your own domain, you can choose the second option from *Figure 9.2*, **Add & Verify Domain**. When you click on the button to add a domain, you'll see a pop-up modal appear, which looks like *Figure 9.4*:

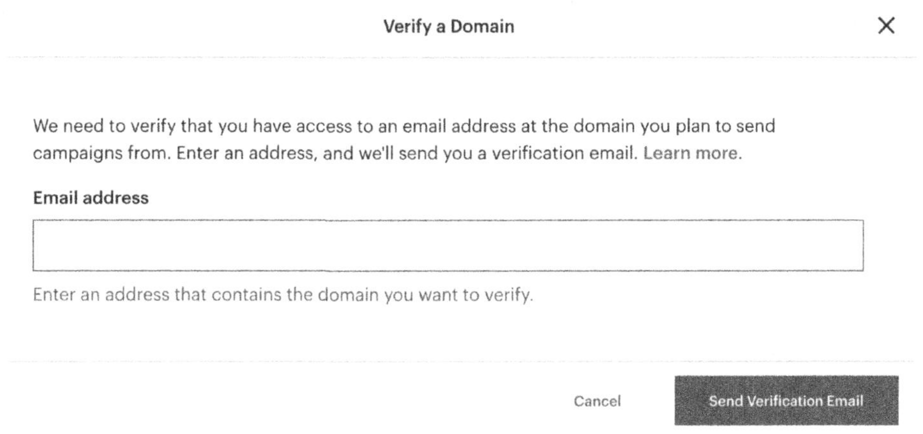

Figure 9.4 – Domain verification modal

Similar to when you created your account, you will always have to verify that you not only have access to the domain but that you also have an email address at the domain. When you enter the address into the field, the application will send you an email and the email will contain an alphanumeric code to input and verify your email address. Once it's verified, you'll see the domain appear on this dashboard and then, if you like, you can add records to your domain to authenticate the domain for sending emails. You can see whether the domain is verified. If it's not authenticated but is on the dashboard, to the right of your domain, there will be a **Start Authentication** button, as seen in *Figure 9.5*.

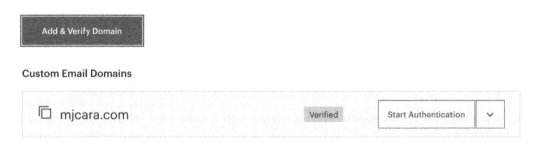

Figure 9.5 – Verified but unauthenticated domain

Authentication is most important if you want your emails to appear to be sent from your private domain. As we discussed in *Chapter 8*, if you want your brand to be consistent, it can be really helpful for both getting through spam filters, but also for making sure that people can identify your brand, to ensure that your emails appear to be sent using a **From** email address from your brand's personal domain.

When you click on **Start Authentication**, you'll see a five-step process appear in this interface, with each step walking you through how to add the right records through your domain provider to ensure Mailchimp can use the domain as an authorized sender.

Let's take a look at these steps:

1. **Start your email authentication process**: In this step, you'll indicate to the application who the domain provider is that you use. This might be a company such as Google Domains, for example.

2. **Go to your domain provider's website**: This will guide you to open your domain provider's website in another window or tab of your web browser. This part is different for each domain provider's interface, but you're looking for the area dedicated to your *domain records*.

    If you need help, check the support pages for your domain provider and search for words such as CNAME or DNS.

3. **Create a CNAME record using Mailchimp info**: These records will be what indicates to your private domain that it's okay for Mailchimp to be an authorized sender on its behalf.

    CNAME records serve as an indication of an authorized sub-domain, which maps back to your domain and allows a service such as Mailchimp to host your content.

    Inside the app itself, here, it will show you the two **CNAME** records you need to create/add to your domain to enable that.

4. **Wait for Mailchimp to check the records**: Depending on your provider, it can take a little while for the provider to make the record available for Mailchimp to validate. Some providers are quicker, but sometimes it can take 24-48 hours for those records to finish propagating.

    The app will send you an email to let you know when it's validated and if you would like, you can click on the **Check Status** button to have it checked again when you happen to be in the app. You can keep sending emails and using the app in the meantime.

5. **Success!**: Once the records are validated (can be detected by an outside service such as Mailchimp), you're all set to send email using your private domain.

Similarly, the final section on this domain page is for applying your private domain to use it for a website, which is ultimately what we're looking to accomplish a first go at in this chapter.

As we saw in *Figure 9.2*, the final section we interact with is **Connected Domains**. Here, we click on **Connect a domain**, which will open a pop-up modal where you input the domain you want to connect, as seen in *Figure 9.6*:

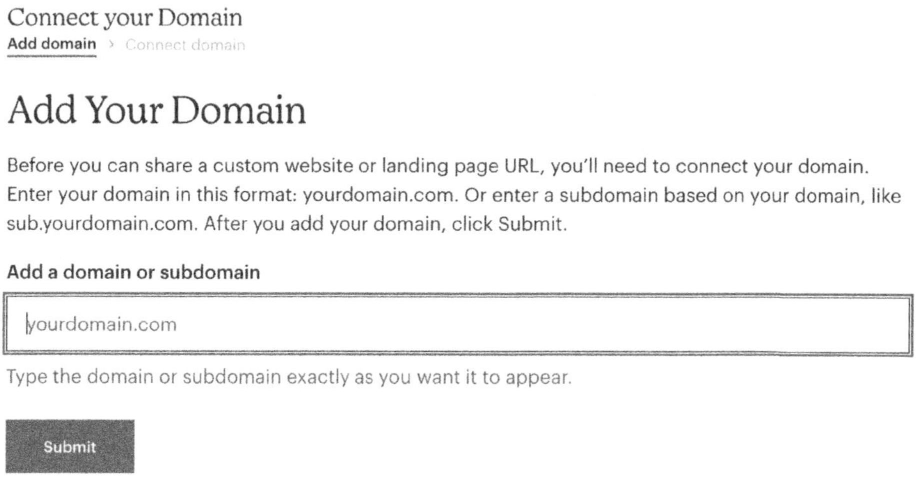

Figure 9.6 – Website-domain connection pop-up

From here, when you click **Submit**, the app will provide you with more information on another **CNAME** record and an **A** record to create with your domain provider, as you did in the previous section. Again, once the records are input, it may take 24-48 hours for the records to propagate, but once the domain is connected, we're ready to use it for our first website. However, you don't need to wait for the domain to finish validating to begin designing your site, so let's take a look at the website builder next.

Making a website

In the same left-hand menu where we found **Domains**, we'll see **Websites**. When we click on it, to start, you will need to put in the name of your website and pick the **Audience** option within your account that you would like the website to be associated with. Because websites can be a point of ingress for people to join your audience, it absolutely is a feature that will be connected to the audience itself to make sure your new visitors as you expand your digital presence can stay in touch.

Once you've named your site and selected the audience, you can then start adding content and designing.

The next interface you'll see is called the **Manage Site** page. Here, you can add **Pages** to your overall site, set **Styles** for the home page and future pages you add, and, critically, if you have customers in California or the EU in particular, you can enable a **Cookie Banner** option to make sure you have informed consent from visitors from there. You can see a screenshot of this page in *Figure 9.7*:

Figure 9.7 –The Managed Site page

Strategically, what you're meant to think about here is what pages are necessary to use to start communicating whatever you would like to build your brand around. Obviously, a home page would be the ideal place to start. For example, maybe you own a restaurant with an event space, and you'd like to start with something catchy on the home page about what kind of food your restaurant serves, its location, its opening hours, and maybe some pictures of the location. But then, maybe you'd like to dedicate an **About** page to information about you, the ownership, and maybe the history of the restaurant and what drove you to want to open it.

This type of story can be engaging for audience members; it's often something that makes your brand feel authentic and accessible. But let's start with the home page. This will be the first page created for you by default, and to access it on the page seen in *Figure 9.7*, you need to hover your cursor over the square and click on the **Edit Page** button. This will take you into what will feel a bit like a larger version of the email editor we used in *Chapter 7*.

When you click on a section of the website template here, you will see a couple of menus appear. In the upper left-hand corner of the section, you will see a **Layout** and **Edit Section** button. On the right-hand side, a menu for the specific section will appear. This will be slightly different per area of the website, but it'll allow you to control things such as the **Background** color, **Color scheme**, and whether you would like the area to be transparent, as you can see in *Figure 9.8*:

Making a website   135

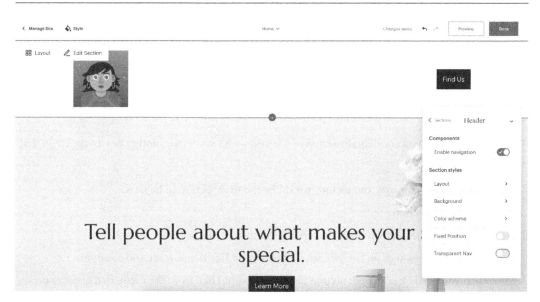

Figure 9.8 – Website section menus on the left and right

When you get into the meat of the website instead of just the header, you will also see that in the **Layout** menu section. Here, you'll have more options for how the content in that area of the page is laid out. You'll have options for where the text sections will be in relation to images. You can also adjust whether the text is laid over an image if you'd like it to be a hero image as your background in that region. We can see how that menu opens up in *Figure 9.9*:

Figure 9.9 – Website Layout menu

You can also delete sections if there are currently more sections within the page than you think are necessary for your purposes. You can remove a section as follows:

1. Hover your cursor over the section you'd like to remove.
2. Click on the section.
3. Click on the trash bin icon in the left-hand menu bar that appears (as you can see in the top left of *Figure 9.9*).
4. You can then click on **Remove Section** in the confirmation pop-up modal.

Additionally, let's say you accidentally removed a section, and you'd like another one back. To do that, follow these steps:

1. Hover your cursor over the section you'd like the new section to be near.
2. Click on the section.
3. You will see a plus sign icon at the top and bottom of that section.
4. Click on the plus sign on the side where you would like the new section to appear.
5. When you do that, select the section layout you would like from the menu that appears on the right-hand side, as seen in *Figure 9.10*.

Figure 9.10 – The Add Section menu

If you like, you can also move the sections up and down. Similar to deleting a section, you do the following:

1. Hover your cursor over the section you'd like to remove.
2. Click on the section.
3. Click on the arrow icon in the left-hand menu bar that appears (as you can see in the top left of *Figure 9.9*).

This will then move the entire section up or down in accordance with the direction the arrow is pointing.

> **Note about sections**
> There are some static sections of a website. For example, all sites tend to have a header, body, and footer. Pieces such as the header and footer are always in the same place on every site, so you cannot move sections above the header in the same way that you can't move sections under the footer.

Once you've replaced the text, images, and links you want on the page, you can preview what it looks like to folks coming to look at your page. To do that, you click on the **Preview** button in the upper right-hand corner of the editor. In the preview mode, you will see a small computer icon and a cellphone/mobile icon at the top so that you can toggle between these options to preview what the page looks like on those types of devices. If you're happy with how the page looks as a starting point, you can then click on **Exit Preview** and then **Done**.

This will take you back to the **Managed Site** page, where you can then choose whether you would like another page for your site, as seen in *Figure 9.7*. If you decide to add another page, when you click on the **Add Page** option, it will direct you to a menu where you can choose the type of page you would like to add, as seen in *Figure 9.11*:

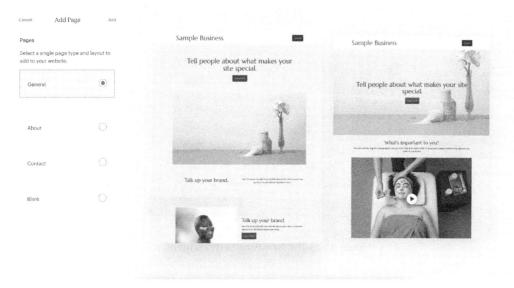

Figure 9.11 – Add Page options

You'll be given two layout options per page type, as you can see in the preceding. Do the following when you're ready to choose one:

1. Hover your cursor over the layout you prefer.
2. Click on **Add Page**.

This will automatically take you to the website builder we just worked through and you can edit, add, or remove elements, as you did on the previous page. The one difference when adding a page to your website versus editing the home page for it is that you will be prompted initially to fill out some of the settings for this page. You'll be prompted to make a couple of decisions (in the **Settings** menu in *Figure 9.12*):

I. Name the page itself.

II. Choose whether you would like to set it to the new home page or add it to the website navigation.

III. Input a lowercase path for the **URL Path** field.

IV. Set how you would like the domain/URL to appear in search results.

V. Set how you would like previews of the page to appear on social media.

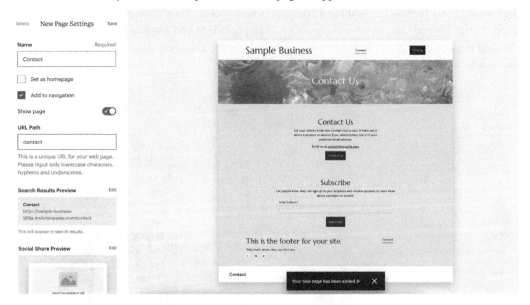

Figure 9.12 – The New Page Settings menu

Once you feel good about your pages as a starting point, you can publish your site. To navigate there from the page editor, you click on **Done** in the upper right-hand corner and then **Publish** in the next interface. When you click on **Publish**, Mailchimp will push your website live and then send you back to the **Website** overview. You'll see a little tag that indicates the website is published, and, underneath that, if you have enabled tracking for the website, you'll see stats about the pages, as seen in *Figure 9.13*:

Figure 9.13 – Website Overview page

With that, you've set up your website. It's live and available for you to link in your campaigns and share the URL on your social media and will act as the home for your business or organization on the internet. Next, let's take a look at how you can edit the settings for your new website as needed.

Editing settings

If you would like to adjust your tracking types or other settings, you can do that at any time.

For example, let's say that you didn't have a private domain to use when you first set up your website, but down the line, you have decided you really want that personal branding and have purchased your own domain. Once you've added it to your account, as we walked through earlier in this chapter, you can add it here too!

Do the following:

1. Click on **Settings**, either in the **Website** overview you can see in *Figure 9.13* or the left-hand navigation menu.
2. Click on **Edit** in the **Domain** field.
3. Select the radio button next to **Use a custom domain**.
4. Choose **Private domain** from the drop-down menu.
5. Click on **Save**.

Additional things you can edit in the settings include the following:

- **Site title**
- **Site icon**
- **Domain**
- **Pop-up form**
- **Site tracking**
- **Site status**

Really, at the end of the day, as noted earlier in this chapter, if your goal is to use the website as yet another entry point for your audience as a means of furthering your brand, then the most important piece is making sure you have forms at least on the home page. From this **Settings** page, you can enable a pop-up form if you would like, but you may have noticed in the editor when you worked on the website that you can add embedded sign-up forms from there too, as you can see in the listed options in *Figure 9.10* by clicking on **Subscribe**.

This **Settings** page is quite flexible. You can edit these items as needed and as your brand evolves. Things such as the given **Site title** may need to be tweaked a little as you adjust your brand to suit your audience.

Summary

In this chapter, we walked through setting up and boosting a more consistent marketing presence in the form of a website with its own domain, which can serve as a home and face of your brand on the internet. This helps us increase our brand presence and identity. Specifically, we learned things such as how to understand the benefits of using a private domain and determined why you might want to select a hosted option versus a public domain. Additionally, we walked through how to do that through Mailchimp or another domain host depending on whether you already have one to work with.

We also learned how to create a website within Mailchimp; the different types of layouts; how to edit, remove, and add them; and how establishing this type of presence online will help us grow our audience while supporting our brand.

Next up, we'll move on to refining our understanding of what reports and analytics can offer us with respect to understanding our audience, as well as how we can then think about interpreting these reports to inform other choices we make on our platforms as we eventually look ahead toward automation.

Further reading

About Your Website in Mailchimp: `https://eepurl.com/gIY5xX`

Part 4:
Refine and Automate

This section is where we will begin exploring some of the channels. Here is where you will expand your understanding of how your audience members interact with your basic channels, and you will learn how to grow your automation utilization so that the Mailchimp app will do more of the marketing work for you!

This section has the following chapters:

- Chapter 10, Understanding Reports and Analytics
- Chapter 11, Implementing A/B Testing and Multivariate Testing
- Chapter 12, Strategies for Automating Using the Customer Journey Builder
- Chapter 13, Setting Up a Mailchimp E-Commerce Store

10
Understanding Reports and Analytics

I believe that the best marketing strategies are refined over time. As you get to know your audience a little better or even as the audience grows, you might find that what keeps people engaged over time might change. And the best way to adjust and pivot is to look at the data that your platforms are giving you. I'm a fairly data-driven person, meaning that I like to accumulate and slice my data to extrapolate what an ideal next step or experiment might be.

This can be a bit of a double-edged sword in the sense that I used to get decision paralysis; faced with so many options and possibilities, I would overthink and overanalyze every data point. In this chapter, I'd like to help you cut through the noise, look at your data holistically, and help make sure you're not stuck obsessing where I might have obsessed in the past.

We'll be going over the following topics:

- The types of information that are accessible in Mailchimp's reporting
- How you can use or interpret email campaign reports
- Expanded/advanced reporting features

Now, because Mailchimp is an all-in-one platform, this means that there are lots of features available within the platform and, therefore, plenty of different types of reports for those features. As we go through the types of information that the platform can give you, it's important to keep in mind that not all of these will be immediately applicable to you. We'll start with some of the core features and channels that you're most likely to have come to Mailchimp for before digging into some of the more niche pieces of data. So first, let's review what kinds of information exist within Mailchimp's reporting.

Technical requirements

Some features, such as **Comparative Reports**, are more advanced reporting features, so to access these, you will need to be on a Premium plan or using the Mailchimp Pro add-on. The **Comparative**

Reports feature is not available with Mailchimp's Free or Standard plans. Additionally, if you have not yet sent a campaign, you should at the very least send yourself a campaign so that you can see a campaign report in your account to follow along.

The types of information that are accessible in Mailchimp's reporting

If you're not new to Mailchimp, the reporting you're most likely familiar with is **Campaign** reporting. Mailchimp was first known for its marketing email channel and still is to some extent, though it offers a lot more now. But, because it was the first and certainly the most well-known channel in the product, when they log into their accounts, lots of Mailchimp users click on **Campaigns** in the left-hand navigation menu instinctively, as shown in *Figure 10.1*:

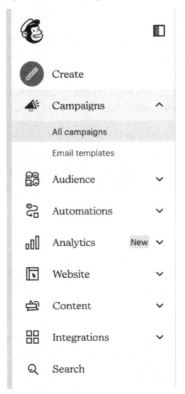

Figure 10.1 – Campaigns menu and submenu

This takes you right to the top of the **Campaigns** list, which is where you can see all the campaigns drafted and sent for a particular audience in your account. And specifically, when we are looking at the sent campaigns, we can see that some basic, at-a-glance stats appear to give us a little taste of how that campaign did.

The platform will serve up the percentage of opens, clicks, and revenue, and a button called **View Report**, which will take us to the fuller report for the campaign, as shown in *Figure 10.2*:

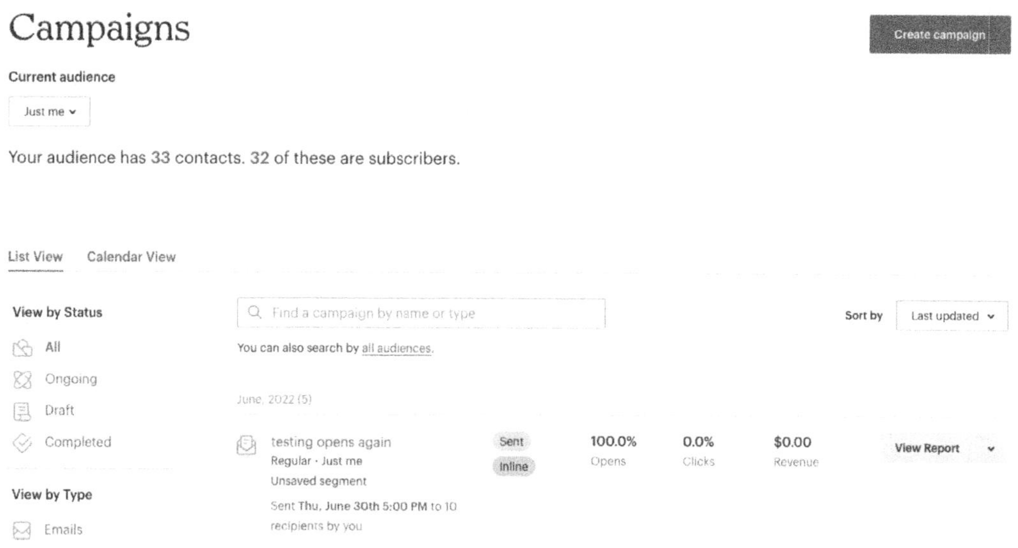

Figure 10.2 – Campaigns list page and a sent campaign

> **Note about some reported stats**
>
> Because the platform is used for so many different types of businesses and organizations, not all of the stats that appear on the **Campaigns** List page or the report are going to be 100% relevant to you. As we can see in *Figure 10.2*, **Revenue**, for example, shows **$0.00**. But this campaign did not have any e-commerce connections and was not attempting to get the audience to purchase from the campaign, so we should expect to see a $0 value reflected here.

So, if we click on the **View Report** button for any campaign that's been sent to an audience, we'll be directed to the full report for that specific campaign.

Now, I'd like to break up reviewing the information available to you by discussing each of the pages of the report, as opposed to listing all of the available numbers and stats spread across the entirety of the report. That being said, if at any point in the future you would like a list of these stats all in one place, you can check out the article from Mailchimp's knowledge base linked in the *Further reading* section at the end of this chapter, called *About Email Campaign Reports*.

So first up, we'll start with the **Overview** page, since it's likely to be the one you look at the most frequently. Here, we can see some basic information listed for us right at the top under the menu, as shown in *Figure 10.3*:

146 Understanding Reports and Analytics

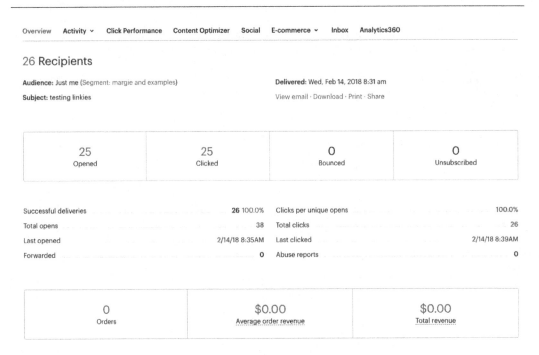

Figure 10.3 – Campaigns Report page for a single sent campaign

Between the report menu and our most critical stats for an email, we see the following:

- Number of **Recipients**: This is a clickable link that goes to a list of all of the people in your audience to whom you sent the campaign.
- **Audience**: This is the name of the specific audience in your account that this campaign was sent to. If you sent it to a saved segment, you will see that represented in parentheses next to the audience.
- **Subject**: This is the subject line that the members of your audience saw in their inboxes when you sent them the campaign.
- **Delivered**: This is the specific time you sent the campaign out to your list. It will provide you with not just the date but also the specific time.

  The timezone is based on the timezone set by you in your account settings.

Then you'll have a few basic options listed under the delivery time. These are all fairly straightforward and, while they don't provide any additional data, they do represent some options for socializing the report within your organization if the marketing stats are relevant to more than just you. We have the following options:

- **View email**: This is a quick link to glance at the preview of the campaign in case you need a quick reminder of what your audience saw in their inboxes when they opened your email.

- **Download**: This will start the download of a .CSV file, which you can open in Microsoft Excel or Google Sheets if you want to just grab the raw data and share it with some coworkers, or if you need to generate some quick data for another person in your organization.
- **Print**: This will create a quick, printable version of the report, which you can then choose to save as a PDF to share with your colleagues, or you can print it out to share – whichever works best for you.
- **Share**: This feature allows you to send a custom link to an email address and set a desired password for accessing the report online. It's a neat feature because you don't have to add the person to your account as a user, but you can still share the results of your marketing efforts if you want or need to.

These pieces of information are really centered on helping you ensure that you're reviewing the right campaign. Because your sending volume can change over time, you generally want to be sure you're checking out the right campaign results before digging too far into the data in the report itself.

This brings us to the next section: the core table and its associated stats. We can also see this represented in *Figure 10.3* as the four horizontal boxes and the eight pieces of information listed underneath these boxes. In the four horizontal boxes, we see the four pieces of information you'll probably get the most use out of:

- **Opened**: This is the total number of unique individuals in your audience that opened your campaign email.
- **Clicked**: This is the total number of audience members who clicked a link in your campaign email.
- **Bounced**: You may remember this term from *Chapter 3*. This is the term used when the email for a specific audience member was not successfully received. There is a myriad of reasons that a particular email address may not have received it successfully, and they break down into two categories:
  - **Hard bounces**: These are permanent reasons that the email address won't work. It can be an email address that doesn't exist, is misspelled, or, for some reason, receiving has been blocked. These will typically be cleaned from your audience for you to prevent bad email addresses from inflating your audience costs and damaging your sending reputation.
  - **Soft bounces**: These are temporary reasons that the email address cannot receive emails. The reasons here are more varied. For example, there could be a quota set for how many emails can come in at a time on the receiving end, maybe the server is down, or maybe there's a firewall with requirements you don't meet. In these cases, the Mailchimp app will still try to send the campaign again.
- **Unsubscribed**: These are audience members who clicked on the **Unsubscribe** link in your campaign and chose to opt out of future emails.

With respect to which are the most critical here, I think biasing toward **Opened** and **Clicked** is the best. These two are the best higher-level stats to indicate how your campaign is performing. The reason we should think of these as the most important is that they're the best insight into the percentage of your audience members that are actually looking at the campaign.

> Note about Bounced and Unsubscribed stats
>
> Common questions about the other two stats here – **Bounced** and **Unsubscribed** – tend to center on how you can prevent them from happening. The reality here (especially for **Bounced** email addresses) is that unless you are using the Mailchimp platform for communication internal to a company or organization, you may have limited control over receiving firewalls. If you are using the platform for internal communication, you should work with your IT department to ensure you're authenticated, as covered in *Chapter 9*.

Why opens and clicks?

General stats overview

You may have noticed in your account (or if you haven't sent a campaign yet, you may notice in *Figure 10.3*) that there are additional *opens* and *clicks* stats listed under the four horizontal featured data points. There are a further eight data points, including **Total opens** and **Total clicks**. You may wonder, though, why these sometimes appear different from the highlighted opens and clicks. The answer is to provide some more nuance to the way you might analyze your report and the behavior of your audience.

The differences are as follows:

- **Opened**: This provides us with *unique* opens. This means that if I am a member of your audience and I open the campaign email three times, I would only account for one of these unique opens.
- **Total opens**: This is the precise number of times the campaign email has been opened and the assets of the campaign loaded. So, if I opened it three times as a member of your audience, it would include all three opens in this number.

Similarly, we find the same two stats for clicks:

- **Clicked**: This provides you with the *unique* number of times the audience members clicked on links you might have placed within the campaign email. Now, because your campaign may have multiple links, this will be the total number of unique clicks per link. So, if you have three links in the campaign email and I, as your audience member, click on each link, this will count as three unique clicks.

- **Total clicks**: Total clicks, similar to total opens, will tell us the total number of clicks, regardless of whether it was the first click or the third click by a single audience member. So if I, as your audience member, click on the first link two times and the others once, then I will account for four total clicks on the campaign.

What I really like about the nuance of having both of these *opens* and *clicks* stats available to you is that it can be a really informative way of understanding or analyzing which links or content might be the most engaging. For example, as you review and compare your reports, you might see that links attached to an image may see more activity or callbacks over time. Or links toward the top of the campaign email might see more clicks than those lower down.

Let's drill down through the other data points available on the **Overview** page of the report, and then we can talk through some other ways to think about and analyze that data:

- **Successful deliveries**: This is the number of audience members in your recipient list who were confirmed to have received the email (meaning that Mailchimp's servers were able to receive a confirmation from the receiving email server that it was at least initially accepted into their server).

- **Last opened**: This is the last time that someone in the audience was confirmed as having opened the campaign.

- **Forwarded**: This is fairly unique to Mailchimp. This isn't a reference to the forwarding function within every email provider itself, but rather Mailchimp offers a unique forward-to-a-friend feature that you can add to your campaigns if you want to encourage your current audience members to forward their emails to friends, family, colleagues, and so on.

    I'll include some information on this feature in the *Further reading* section, but it can be added when you're designing your campaign as a kind of call-to-action.

- **Clicks per unique opens**: This is a percentage-related stat, and it shows you the percentage of audience members who opened and also clicked on a link in your campaign.

    This is a nice one to pair generally with your general clicks and opens. It can be a good barometer for increased engagement. For example, if your opens and clicks are staying inside the same ~10% range campaign over campaign, but you're seeing an increase in **Clicks per unique opens** as you move the placement of links and other calls-to-action, this is a really positive sign that you're getting a better handle of what additional steps drive your audience members to engage with you more deeply.

- **Last clicked**: This is the last time that anyone in the audience was confirmed to have clicked on any tracked link in the campaign.

- **Abuse reports**: This is the number of audience members who indicated to their email providers that the campaign was spam/abuse. When this is reported to Mailchimp by a third party such as Gmail, for example, the platform will take the necessary steps to remove the address from your subscribed contacts and ensure that they do not keep receiving campaigns, and also that they don't further impact your future sending reputation.

- **Orders**: This is specific to e-commerce, but if you have either an e-commerce integration connected or are using Mailchimp's e-commerce store, then when you send a campaign in which audience members can buy from a campaign (or initiate a purchase from that campaign), then the Mailchimp app will count that as an order that the specific campaign was able to net for you.
- **Average order revenue**: Similarly, this is also an e-commerce statistic and will provide us with the average value of the orders placed/associated with the specific campaign.
- **Total revenue**: This is e-commerce-related as well and provides us with the total amount of money that people spent with you through the campaign.

> **Note about e-commerce stats**
>
> These are largely dependent on query strings from the campaign itself. For example, when I click on a campaign sent through a marketing platform such as Mailchimp, the platform adds a string of characters to the end of the URL I entered. This is generally unique to each campaign, and when the audience member clicks on a link, it will persist at the end of their URL and allow us some minor insight into what actions the audience member is taking until their cart is created. In the event that these queries and cookies are wiped from the URL, the information may not be fully comprehensive, but as long as the email address from the purchase is the same, for most integrated commerce platforms, you'll at least have their purchase information in their audience profile.

Then, continuing to scroll down, we have a couple of other core sections; the first you'll see is the **Content Optimizer** section. This is fairly new to the *Reporting and Analytics* feature set for the Mailchimp platform and it is designed to help you better understand how your audience views the balance of your campaign. We can see a sample of the **Content Optimizer** section in *Figure 10.4*:

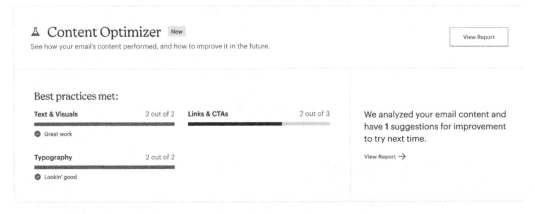

Figure 10.4 – Content Optimizer section for a single sent campaign

That being said, because it's a separate reporting set, we'll come back to this in the *Advanced features* section. I'd like to finish walking through the **Overview** page of the report first.

Click performance interface

Following the **Content Optimizer** section, you'll then see the **Click performance** section. This one is really just a visual representation of some of the click information we've already reviewed together. It'll show you a brief view of the campaign you sent on the right-hand side and then, on the left, you'll see a list of the top links clicked within your campaign. This usually will just display the top handful of links that performed, but then if you would like to dig in further, you have the option of clicking on either **View All Links** or the **View Click Map** option, which will show you how all the links performed. You can see a sample of this section in *Figure 10.5*:

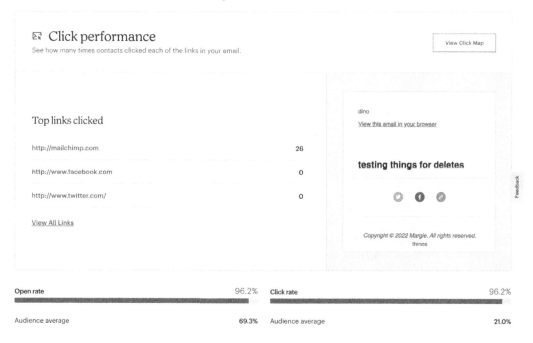

Figure 10.5 – Click performance section for a single sent campaign

My favorite thing that this little section adds is the visual information related to the percentages of open and click rates compared to their audience averages. This will let you know how this one specific campaign performs against the average of your overall campaigns sent to this specific audience. You can use this information to help you decide whether the choices you made for the positions of these links in this campaign were better than average, which will help you decide whether you need to work on refining your link positions.

Predicted Demographics interface

Next on the **Overview** page, you'll see **Predicted Demographics**, which gives you some demographic predictions about the audience that interacted with your campaign. This is a pretty neat data tool that leverages behavioral analytics from Mailchimp directly to predict some gender and age range information about the members of your audience. As you can see in *Figure 10.6*, the report will provide you with the predicted distribution of Gender for your Recipients and the Age Ranges of those Recipients. Additionally, if you would like, you also have the option to see how this predicted information is distributed across **Opens** and **Clicks**.

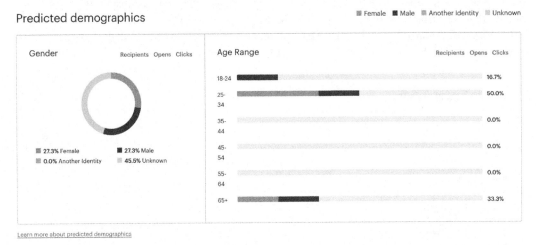

Figure 10.6 – Predicted demographics section for a single sent campaign

This information isn't meant to be precise. As the word *predicted* implies, this information is based on analysis done by Mailchimp over the years of the observed behavior of recipients with campaigns they receive. Taking that information, the platform uses it to attempt to predict distributions of gender and age.

This can be helpful in the context of targeting your campaigns. Over time, as you learn more about your audience members, this type of information (in addition to the opens and clicks information we saw in the previous part of the campaign) can be used to create segments. As we covered in *Chapter 4, Tags, and Segments*, targeting your campaigns and refining them to be more specific to your audience can help to drive up engagement with your campaigns.

The next couple of sections here are really geared more toward understanding the immediate performance of the campaign and, in my opinion, provide slightly more surface-level information, but it's not necessarily particularly helpful for informing your choices in the long run. These sections are as follows:

- **24-hour performance**: This is fairly straightforward. It's really only helpful for understanding the first 24 hours of engagement with your campaign. This is when the majority of your engagement will occur, but it's largely just a graphical representation of the data you've already seen further up in the report.

- **Subscribers with most opens**: Again, a very descriptive name for this data point. It serves as a list of the most engaged recipients of the campaign. This may be interesting data if your recipient list is quite small, but for larger campaign sends, this data is perhaps interesting but not necessarily helpful for providing you with an analytic data point to adjust or inform your strategy in the long run.
- **Social performance**: This provides a high-level view of whether the campaign performed well in a shared Facebook post or Tweet. For these to populate data, you have to be integrated with Facebook and Twitter.
- **Top locations by opens**: This will show you what regions your recipients live in. When possible, Mailchimp will review the IP address that recipients are using when interacting with your campaign, and then, using that IP address, it will extrapolate their approximate region.

And that's the **Overview** page, which, frankly, is pretty meaty and provides you with the majority of the information you might use to inform your choices as you build and send campaigns in the future. So let's talk about how you can choose to use this information.

How you can use and interpret these reports

I'm of the opinion that how you choose to interpret the data tends to dictate the choices you make as a result. Maybe most importantly, as with your overall marketing journey, we should be thinking of the data in campaign reports as just a piece of your overall analytic performance. It can be quite tempting, particularly earlier in your marketing efforts, to hyper-fixate on the performance of a single campaign, but really, we should be thinking of it as a single reference point and then leverage that data to make different decisions.

The goal in better understanding the performance of your channels is to help inform how you experiment with things such as your segments, content (such as your text and images), and even variables such as send time. Small adjustments over time can really help you better dial in what most appeals to your audience.

As discussed in the previous section where we reviewed the **Overview** page, the most important data points for you to compare over time are the two higher-level metrics: opens and clicks. Depending on how many campaigns you've sent thus far, things such as the relative rate of opens and clicks won't necessarily be super informative up-front. For example, if we look at *Figure 10.7*, we will see that this campaign didn't perform particularly well. The campaign went to eight people and didn't receive any opens or clicks:

154　Understanding Reports and Analytics

Figure 10.7 – Campaigns Report page for a single sent campaign

So if I was looking at this, I might be wondering, *why didn't my campaign get opened? Could the subject line have been more engaging or specific to my audience?*

Part of designing your marketing strategy is thinking about each campaign and channel as an opportunity for experimentation. So, the next step here would be to choose sets of variables you want to experiment with. If, for example, we saw a performance like in *Figure 10.7*, I would want to start with variables such as how firewalls might be seeing my email (as discussed in the previous chapter when we talked about domains) and the items people see in their inboxes before they even click to open the campaign. So, we can consider experimenting with the following:

- Domain authentication
- Subject Line
- From Email Address
- From Name
- Preview Text
- Send Time

I would recommend picking one or two of these at a time; that way, you can narrow down what is most effective in driving your audience to open your campaigns. If you were to change all the variables at once, it'll be more difficult to know which specifically your audience is most responding to.

Once you've chosen your variables, think of it like any other experiment. You'll form a general hypothesis around why the change you're making is the right one, and design your next campaign such that you make those changes to the Subject Line, for example. Then, when you run your next campaign, you'll look at the subsequent report as your next data point. In this example, we were experimenting with increasing opens specifically, so that's the stat you'd be looking at predominantly in the second report. If you see an increase, then you know you're moving in the right direction.

Similarly, if you were seeing satisfactory opens but you're looking to impact your clicks within the campaign, you might look at changing variables such as the following:

- Changing link locations:
  - If you predominantly linked text previously, maybe you want to add more images and link those
  - Make sure the most important links to you appear further up in the campaign
  - Ensure the same URL is linked more than once; perhaps linking text and an image
- Adjusting text-to-image ratios:
  - If your previous campaign was text heavy, perhaps your next iteration should use more images to draw attention to the text near it and house your links

The goal here is really to help you better understand your audience over time and make sure that you're able to leverage the data your audience is passively communicating to you to inform future choices. From here, you can also begin to add more data to your analytic constellation as you learn more about your audience and dial in your strategy. For example, information such as **Top locations by opens** might be of interest to you if you have a growing audience outside of your region. If my business is based in Argentina but I start seeing a growing interest in Brazil for my business, knowing that these locations are appearing in my campaign report might prompt me to start developing products or content specific to a Portuguese-speaking audience. It could even inform segments you use in the future. If that audience grew sufficiently, you may want to run campaigns just for this segment of your audience.

Once you have a handle on how you can compare reports over time to help you understand your audience, you might even want to expand into leveraging some of the additional reporting features. Platforms such as Mailchimp offer lots of features, channels, and other tools; it's all a matter of finding out which will be of service to you for where you are in your marketing journey. So, let's take a look at some of the advanced features available to you in reporting.

Expanded/advanced reporting features

While you can find the vast majority of your bread-and-butter report-related data points on the **Overview** page, as you start to get more sophisticated with how you think about your audience as a whole, you may want to start leveraging some of the advanced features available within the platform. The first I want to go back to is **Content Optimizer**.

> **Note about access to Content Optimizer**
> Due to this being a more advanced reporting feature, to access this, you will need to be on a Standard Marketing plan or higher. It is not available through Mailchimp's Free plan.

As I noted earlier in this chapter, this is a relatively new feature to the reporting section of the platform but, particularly as you grow your experimentation muscle, it can be a really handy tool. In *Figure 10.8*, we can see an example of the initial analysis of the content of a campaign on the **Overview** page of the report. But as I alluded to earlier, we can see a slightly more robust analysis of text and visuals in a fuller report by clicking on **View Report**.

Figure 10.8 – Content Optimizer section for a single sent campaign

The neat thing about this tool is that it will compare your campaign, the text, and the inclusion of images against Mailchimp's known best practices for you. It'll then make suggestions for you, and you can use this information to inform the subsequent variables you want to experiment with to drive better performance. This can be really helpful, particularly if you're not sure where to start in choosing what variables to adjust from one campaign to another. For example, if I clicked on the **Content Optimizer** report and saw the information in *Figure 10.9* at the top of the report, it would leave me with one pretty clear starting point for my next campaign:

Expanded/advanced reporting features   157

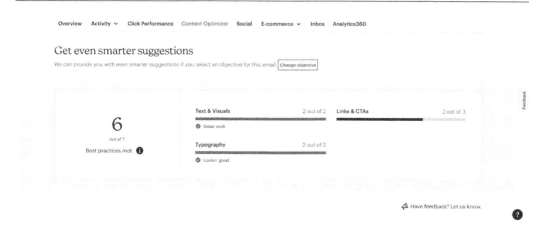

Figure 10.9 – Top of Content Optimizer report

Seeing this, I know that, based on broader best practices, my campaign had a good number of **Text & Visuals** and met the **Typography** standards, but maybe needed work in the **Links & CTAs** category. So I would want to check out the suggestions in that section of the **Content Optimizer** report most specifically. There, I see the suggestions shown in *Figure 10.10*:

Figure 10.10 – CTA and link suggestion section for a Content Optimizer report

Here, we can see clearly that upon reviewing my campaign, the app was unable to find any **calls to action** (**CTAs**). This is a really great call out for the platform to make to me. CTAs (essentially, asking the audience member to engage in some specific way) can be a really tangible way of driving engagement with your audience and even directing them to a website or purchase, depending on what your goal is. Things such as **Click here** or **Buy now** buttons or links might be a good first step to take to drive that engagement.

Speaking generally, **Content Optimizer** is positioned to provide and analyze the following three categories per campaign:

- **Text & Visuals**: This looks at the total number of visuals and the average heading length of your text
- **Typography**: This look at the average heading font size and consistency
- **Links & CTAs**: This looks at total links, total CTAs, and total social links to see whether you're encouraging your audience to take additional steps to engage with you

Additionally, you can even set specific objectives for **Content Optimizer** to narrow in on. At the top of the report, you have the option of adjusting the report to a specific goal; the options are shown in *Figure 10.11*:

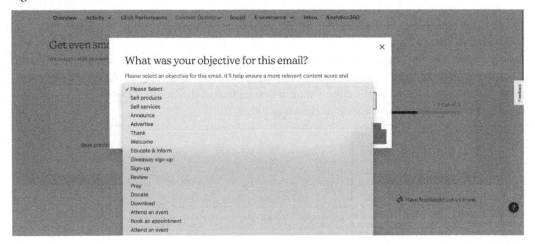

Figure 10.11 – Content Optimizer objective drop-down menu

If, for example, this was a **Welcome** campaign, where I wanted to thank my audience members for signing up to my audience at a conference or event, I would select that as the objective, and I'll see the report change its analysis to better analyze against content usually seen in welcome campaigns. With that adjustment to my goal, I'll see that different standards appear to me, as shown in *Figure 10.12*:

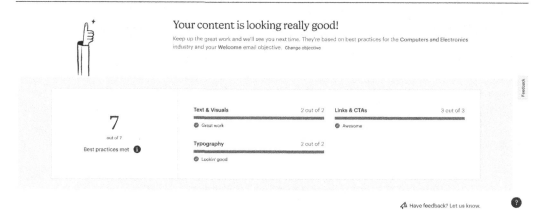

Figure 10.12 – Content Optimizer report for a Welcome email objective

The reason for this is that as it's in response to an action the audience already took (joining my audience), there isn't the expectation that I would be requesting another immediate CTA so soon, I may just be providing links to resources, but I wouldn't be expected to be pushing quite so hard.

Now that we have a sense of how we can use **Content Optimizer**, let's talk about another really neat advanced reporting feature. Next, I would like to talk about **Comparative Reporting**.

Comparative Reports

Comparative Reports is a neat feature set if you're interested in having Mailchimp do the comparison of two campaign reports for you. In the previous section of this chapter, we discussed comparing two campaign reports to help you direct the experimenting you do with content and format in your campaigns. The Comparative Reports feature does what it sounds like it does. You can choose two campaigns and have Mailchimp generate a report for you that compares stats to stats.

Specifically, because you always want to be using the most recent data possible, you can compare any two email campaigns within the last 18 months. The thing I particularly like about this feature, though, is that you can schedule what the feature calls a **Snapshot** to run either daily or weekly. This is great because as you look forward to scaling and thus automating parts of your marketing effort, this serves to make sure that you can stay connected and informed about decisions you make with your marketing, but it also takes some of the work of comparing your campaigns and audience segment performance off of your shoulders.

So let's take a look at how to access this feature. When logged into your account, follow these steps:

1. Go to the left navigation menu as you have to find all the features thus far.
2. Click on **Analytics**.
3. Click on **Reports**.

4. Click on **Create Comparative Report** in the upper-right corner, as shown in *Figure 10.13*:

Figure 10.13 – Create Comparative Report button on the Reports page

From there, you will be given a menu to input the audience and criteria by which you'd like to filter campaigns, as shown in *Figure 10.14*. Then, you can click on the campaigns you'd like to compare and run the report.

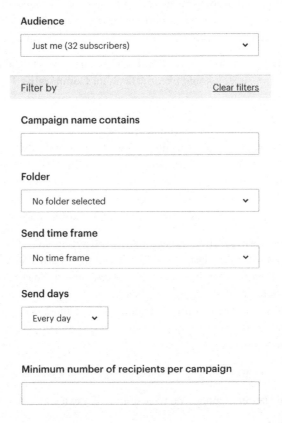

Figure 10.14 – Audience and Filter menu for Comparative Report

It'll take some time to run, so you can click on **Save and Exit** and go about additional work. When the comparison report is ready, you'll receive a notification. Once it's complete, you can find it (and any other comparative reports you've run) by following these steps:

1. Click on **Analytics** in the left navigation menu.
2. Click on **Reports**.
3. Click on **Comparative**.
4. Click on the specific report you're looking for.

When the report is finalized, the app will offer you a Snapshot, as we referenced earlier, which will offer you some similar stats to a single campaign's report **Overview** page, but it'll obviously provide you a comparison of those stats for multiple campaigns. The Snapshot will provide you with the following:

- Baseline calculation
- Performance over time
- Table comparing send dates, total sends (audience members), open rate, click rate, unsubs, bounces, and abuse reports

Additionally, if you need to provide the report to someone else, you can also download a CSV of the data to import into another data analytics platform or product (if you work at a larger company and maybe your boss just wants an Excel file, for example). Or, you can use the **Share Latest Snapshot** option and email your colleague a copy of the report directly.

One last neat feature is that you can also edit the reports if you would like. You can add segments to your reports to see how different people in your audience respond to campaigns over time. If that's something you wanted to add to a report, you would navigate to the report itself and follow these steps:

1. Click on **Edit Report**.
2. Click on **Campaigns Filters**.
3. Compare **# Campaigns**.
4. Click on **Add Segment to Report**.

And that will provide you with a segmenting interface that should look quite familiar based on your previous work with segments in an earlier chapter. We can see the segmenting interface in *Figure 10.15*:

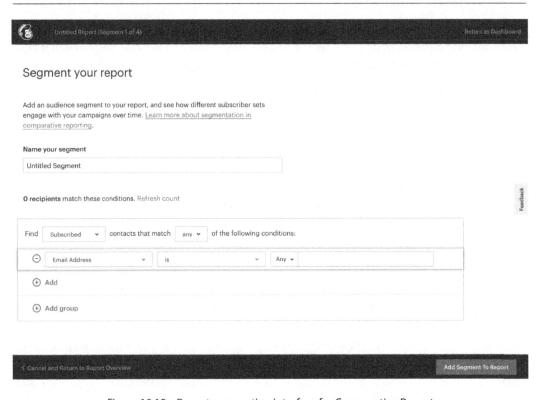

Figure 10.15 – Report segmenting interface for Comparative Report

Once you've made the segment you'd like to focus on, click on **Add Segment to Report** and let the report run again. When the segment is added and the analysis is ready, the performance of the segment will appear in the report under the baseline. That way, you can see how the people in that segment performed against the broader audience itself if you would like.

The intrinsic benefit to the **Comparative Report** feature is really centered on your ability to schedule the report and have the Mailchimp platform do the work of running the analysis for you and delivering it in a tidy, single report to you to then read over and action. It removes the need for you to do the comparison alone, which, in the long run, saves you time to focus on strategizing your next move. If there's a comparative report you ran that you quite like, in the **Comparative** section of **Reports**, you would click on the arrow button to the right of the **Edit Report** button and select **Schedule Report** from the drop-down menu. This will open a popover modal, as shown in *Figure 10.16*, where you can choose the frequency and time for the report to run:

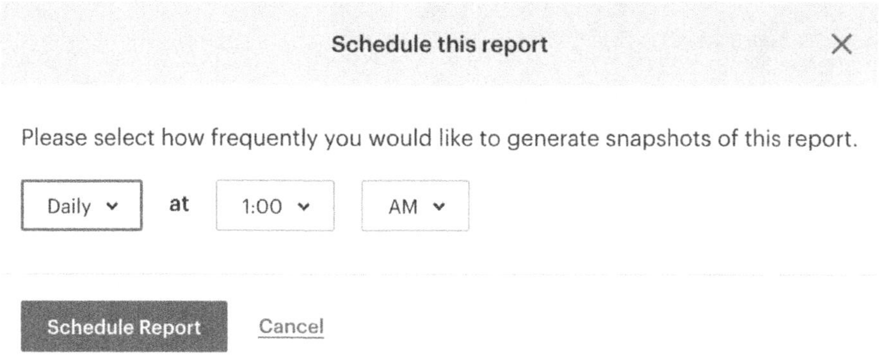

Figure 10.16 – Scheduling modal for a comparative report

This is really where you maximize the utility of this feature. By scheduling it, you take this load off you and let Mailchimp handle it.

Summary

In this chapter, we reviewed all the campaign reporting features and how they could be leveraged to better understand your audience members. We went over some of the basic definitions of what you can find in the reports and what stats were available to you. More importantly, though, we talked a bit about how you could actually leverage that information over time and think of your reporting data as part of an overall story – similar to how we're thinking of your marketing as a journey as well. Data helps you paint a story about your audience and how they engage with you. Then we dug a bit deeper into some advanced features of Mailchimp's platform that help to do some of the heavy lifting for you, such as reviewing the common variables inside your campaign (CTAs, for example). We also looked at how to automate the comparison of campaigns.

Next, in the same vein of experimenting with content to drive engagement, we'll be looking at some campaign experimentation features that allow you to run your own experiments efficiently with the platform.

Further reading

- *About Email Campaign Reports*: https://eepurl.com/dyij5L
- *Share a Campaign Report*: https://eepurl.com/dyimI9
- *Download a Campaign Report*: https://eepurl.com/dyilvL
- *Soft vs. Hard Bounces*: https://eepurl.com/dyimM1
- *Add the Forward to a Friend Link*: https://eepurl.com/dyikGP
- *About Predicted Demographics*: https://eepurl.com/dyikgz

11
Implementing A/B and Multivariate Testing

It must be obvious by now that I love experimenting. At the heart of being a product manager, particularly if you're both the marketer and product manager for a small business, is a willingness to experiment. What a product manager should do best is take available data about their own audience and the market more broadly and design experiments around informed hypotheses to drive interest and engagement.

To this end, in this chapter, we'll be going over two very neat tools that empower you to experiment with your audience and the campaigns they receive. They allow you to design these experiments and let Mailchimp handle executing and crunching the numbers.

We'll be going over the following topics:

- Why experiment with engagement?
- Multivariate options and what elements you can experiment with
- How do you take information from the results to better understand your audience?

So, let's talk about that first point immediately!

Why experiment with engagement?

The core benefit of experimenting is to better understand your audience. By ensuring you understand why your audience engages with you, you can be sure that you are designing content in your various channels that actually appeals to them. It's also key if you have lingering concerns about your stats in your reporting, such as opens and clicks.

Keep in mind, you will always see a variance in your stats. This is completely normal. Some businesses have a peak season around the winter holidays, for example. So, they should expect that outside of that season, the open and click rates should be a little lower. Even non-profit organizations have peak seasons, such as around Giving Tuesday and typically closest to their largest events. That being said, experimentation can be a really useful tool for determining how you can drive the best possible engagement for the different seasons that are relevant to your organization.

As we touched on in the previous chapter, choosing your variables depends on what you're trying to impact. Like with any experiment, the design strategy varies, for example, if you're trying to influence whether people open an email campaign. You'd want to focus on playing around with variables that are visible *before* your audience even sees the content of the email. This would include variables such as the following:

- Subject line
- From name
- Send time

These are variables that impact when an audience member sees the email in their inbox and, of course, what you're telling them about yourself and how you're positioning the content of the email. How are you enticing your audience to engage?

And then, of course, if you're looking to influence clicks inside of your email campaign, you'd be looking to experiment with the content of that email itself.

Driving stats such as opens and clicks increases engagement with your content, which is really at the center of why folks such as us leverage marketing automation platforms. This is ultimately the goal because engagement is at the crux of success for your business or organization. If you're marketing specific products, you can't sell them if your audience isn't aware of the products themselves. If you're a non-profit organization trying to fundraise and bring awareness to a particular cause, you can't accomplish that without driving opens for your emails so that your audience can actually learn about your latest efforts.

Now, with a sense of why we want to engage in experimentation, let's take a look at the two features within Mailchimp to handle the process for you.

Multivariate options and what elements you can experiment with

There are two features within Mailchimp that will handle experimentation for you:

- **A/B Testing**
- **Multivariate Testing**

> **Note about accessing these features**
>
> Both of these are paid features within the Mailchimp platform; they're just available at different price points. **A/B Testing** is available with the **Essentials** and **Standard** plans and **Multivariate Testing** is only available to those with a **Premium** account, or **Pro** add-on if you have an older account.

The core differences between the two features are that, as the name implies, A/B Testing only allows you to test one variable at a time, whereas Multivariate Testing allows you to mix and match up to three variables at once. The variables that they both allow you to experiment with are as follows:

- Subject line
- From name
- Content
- Send time

There are a couple of consistent items between the two of them. To see which of these variate features is available for your paid account, when logged in to your Mailchimp account, click on the **Create** button in the left-hand navigation menu, and when you're directed to the **Create** page, click on the **Email** option in the menu as opposed to selecting one of the central options, as seen in *Figure 11.1*:

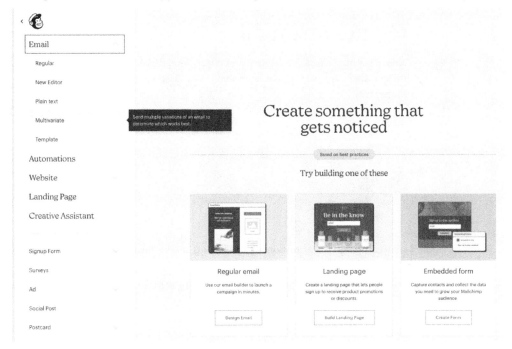

Figure 11.1 – Email menu in the Create interface

Now, depending on which paid plan type you have, you'll only see one of the options in this menu. That's because if you have access to Multivariate Testing, you have the option of experimenting with just one variable like with A/B Testing, so having both would be redundant.

When you start your campaign, you'll be asked to name it, regardless of which feature you have access to. The only difference will be how many versions of your campaign the platform indicates you'll be able to make. We can see a comparison in *Figure 11.2*:

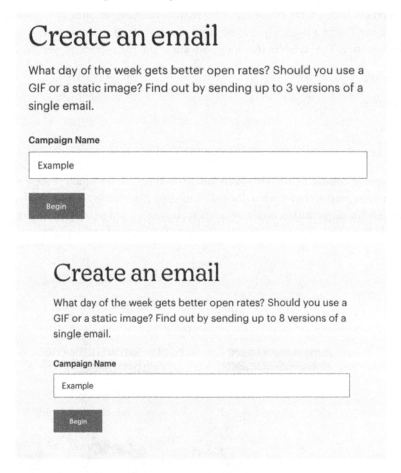

Figure 11.2 – Campaign Name option for A/B Testing and Multivariate Testing

Similarly, the subsequent experiment design page will have most of the same options, just with different thresholds and options for combining variables. You'll be asked to choose the following:

- Variable:
  - This is where you would tell the platform what you would like to test.

- **A/B Testing**: With this feature, you would select a single variable, but you can choose whether you would like to compare two or three versions.

- **Multivariate Testing**: With this feature, you would select up to three variables at once and up to eight versions:

  - For example, you might want to test four different subject lines and four different from names. This would be eight total combinations/versions.

- Percentage of recipients:

  - Here, you would tell the platform what percentage of the recipients in the audience you selected should be experimented with. You may only want to experiment with 50% of your audience, for example, in which case you would indicate here that you only want to use a specific percentage of your audience for the experiment.

- How the winner is determined:

  - This is where you get to define what successful experimentation looks like. For example, if we're trying to drive an increase in the open rate and, thus, that's why we're experimenting with the subject line, we would want to set the winner based on the open rate. You'll have the option to select from the following (also seen in *Figure 11.3*):

    - By click rate
    - By open rate
    - By total revenue
    - Manual selection

  - Additionally, you'll be able to set how long you would like to give your audience to interact with the experiment. So that way, if you want to know what the open rate is within the first several hours of the email being in their inbox, you can set a specific threshold. You'll have the option to choose to have the app determine the winner after hours or days.

  - Alternatively, if you'd like, you can tell the platform you'd like to choose the winner yourself after a manual review.

How should we determine a winning combination?
By open rate
after
4
hours
By click rate
By open rate
By total revenue
Manual selection

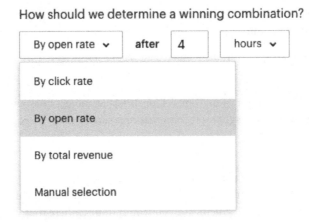

Figure 11.3 – Winning combination criteria menu

Once you've set your variables, audience percentage, and how winners are determined, you'll move on in the builder to actually inputting your experimental variables. For example, if you chose to try and design an A/B Test to drive up the open rate and you've chosen to experiment with the subject line, you'll be given 2-3 fields (depending on the number of versions you want to test) when you go to fill out information about the subject of the email, as seen in *Figure 11.4*.

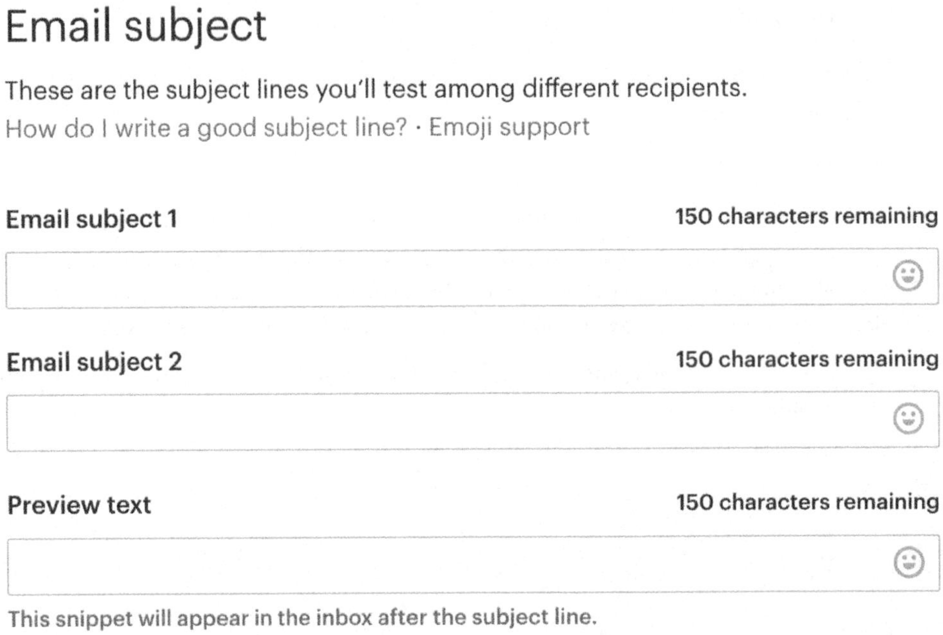

Email subject
These are the subject lines you'll test among different recipients.
How do I write a good subject line? · Emoji support
Email subject 1
150 characters remaining
Email subject 2
150 characters remaining
Preview text
150 characters remaining
This snippet will appear in the inbox after the subject line.

Figure 11.4 – Email subject menu for experimental variable input

This is where you would input the two versions, for example, that you want your audience to see.

Let's say, for this example, I have an audience of 5,000 subscribers and I choose to experiment with all 5,000 recipients. If I want to compare two different subject lines, this means that each subject line will be sent to 2,500 people. Then, if I tell the app that I would like to know which performs the best based on the open rate within the first five hours the email campaign is out, the feature will automatically inform me which subject line performed the best among its respective 2,500 audience members.

> **Note about audience selection**
>
> Because the focus of these features is to understand the efficacy of the selected variables to impact a specific goal, such as increasing the open rate, the app will randomly assign audience members for you to one of the versions being experimented with. It is not possible to assign specific audience members to receive a specific version you're experimenting with using this feature.

Similarly, if you would only like to experiment with a smaller percentage of your audience, you absolutely can, just keeping in mind that this means a reduced pool in the preceding example. For example, if you have 5,000 subscribers in your audience and you'd only like to experiment with 50%, this means that if you're experimenting with two subject lines, each subject line will be sent to 1,250 audience members. The percentage is relevant to the number of people in your audience that will be experimented on, not the number that will receive each variant.

Once you've set your experimental design, you'll proceed to design your email campaign as you would any other campaign. You'll make decisions about text and image content and design it. Once you feel good about the content, you can then send it as you would any other email; you can send it immediately or schedule it (see *Chapter 8*).

With the experiments sent, you'll then have a report that you can review to understand which of your experiments will provide you with the best results. Let's take a look at how to make sure you can understand that and translate it into choices for future email campaigns.

How do you take information from the results to better understand your audience?

As with any channel, you'll have a report available to you with information such as opens and clicks. To access it, you would do the following:

1. Click on **Campaigns** in the left navigation menu.
2. Click on **All Campaigns** from the sub-menu.
3. Click on the **View Report** button for the sent A/B Testing or Multivariate Testing email.

If you have gone through *Chapter 10*, the top of the report will look very familiar to you. You'll have stats available such as the following:

- **Recipients total**
- **Audience name**
- **Open rate**
- **Click rate**
- **List average**

Also, you'll have some new stats, such as the following:

- **Percentage tested on**
- **Variable tested**
- **Recipients per combination**
- **Winning metric**

You can see a sample in *Figure 11.5*:

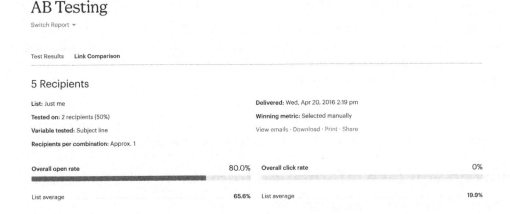

Figure 11.5 – A/B Testing report results

But what makes these reports different is the table underneath this section that will show you a comparison of the variables tested/the different versions that were sent to your audience. It'll provide you with the following information:

- **Subject line** – this is where you will see the variable you're testing
- **Open rate**
- **Click rate**

- Sales
- Sends
- Unsubs
- Abuse
- View Report

If you'd like to watch the progression of the open rates, for example, you would scroll down to the table and see something along the lines of what you can see in *Figure 11.6*:

Combination results

Combo ↑	Subject line	Open rate	Click rate	Sales	Sends	Unsubs	Abuse	
1	example1	16.7% ± 11.5%	0.0% ± 0.0%	$0.00	6	0	0	View repo
2	example2	0.0% ± 0.0%	0.0% ± 0.0%	$0.00	6	0	0	View repo

Figure 11.6 – Combination results report table

There, you can see that the first subject line is currently performing better than the second combo. If you want to see the full report, you can click on **View report** on the right. Depending on the amount of time you selected when setting up the test, you'll need to give it some time to determine the winner from the sent variables. When the winner is selected, you will then have more information in the table you have in your account about which of the subject lines, for example, most spoke to your audience.

With that information, you can then iterate the subject line of your next campaign email. For example, let's say that you were testing subject lines and were curious about whether your audience would be more likely to respond to a subject line with emojis. So, maybe your two combos would look something like this:

- **Subject line 1**: Boots on sale!
- **Subject line 2**: Boots on sale! 😍 👢

Or maybe you want to understand whether multiple emojis or longer, funny text-based subject lines perform the best and you're using Multivariate Testing and want to experiment with the following:

- **Subject line 1**: Boots on sale!
- **Subject line 2**: Boots on sale! 😍 👢
- **Subject line 3**: 😍 Check out this sale on boots!
- **Subject line 4**: New boot goofin'! Sale on boots!
- **Subject line 5**: Check out this sale on boots, bestie 💁 👢

> **Note about emojis**
> Mailchimp has some interesting stats and information about the use of emojis in subject lines. If you'd like to check that out, you can find the article *Mailchimp's Most Popular Subject Line Emojis* linked in the *Further reading* section at the end of this chapter.

Our goal in these examples would be to see whether emojis in the subject line and/or longer, catchy text would tempt the audience receiving these campaigns to open and check out the extended content. For example, if *Subject line 2* performed the best of the preceding five subject lines, we would have learned that the audience prefers something shorter but did engage with the emojis. Then, in the future, maybe we would want to experiment just with shorter subject lines with a couple of emojis to see whether there's a sweet spot for the number of emojis used. Or, we can just go straight into using this format in normal email campaigns – whatever you feel comfortable with as a next step. It really all depends on whether you feel you've learned what you set out to learn about your audience.

The goal, as I've said before, is really just to learn what most engages your audience and keeps them coming back. Because at the end of the day, the goal of a marketing automation platform is to make sure you're optimizing your marketing efforts and getting the most you possibly can out of engagement with your audience. With that said, let's review what we've learned in this chapter.

Summary

In this chapter, we learned how the Mailchimp platform could help you take your experimentation to the next level and how to let it handle the number crunching for you. The whole goal is to empower you to better understand your audience and what helps you drive your business forward in that way. We reviewed some theory and the general reasons we should view our marketing as something worth experimenting with. From there, we walked through all the variables you could choose from, which ones could be combined, which features give you access to these experimental designs, and, most importantly, how to choose variables based on the impact you were looking for.

Finally, and probably most importantly, we learned how to check out these results and interpret them to better inform future experiments and iterate on future email campaigns. In the next chapter, you can bring those lessons into automating your campaigns with Classic Automations and the Customer Journey Builder. That way, you can take another step toward letting the Mailchimp platform do some of the heavy lifting and sending for you.

Further reading

- *About Email Campaign Reports*: https://eepurl.com/dyij5L
- *Share a Campaign Report*: https://eepurl.com/dyimI9
- *Download a Campaign Report*: https://eepurl.com/dyilvL
- *Soft vs. Hard Bounces*: https://eepurl.com/dyimM1
- *Add the Forward to a Friend Link*: https://eepurl.com/dyikGP
- *About Predicted Demographics*: https://eepurl.com/dyikgz
- *Mailchimp's Most Popular Subject Line Emojis*: https://mailchimp.com/resources/mailchimps-most-popular-subject-line-emojis/

12
Strategies for Automating Using the Customer Journey Builder

Mailchimp is a marketing automation platform. We've covered quite a bit thus far related to the marketing channel features available and even talked a bit about channels such as **websites** that can stand alone and represent your brand and products, and funnel visitors to your audience if you'd like. But to really tap into the power of automation with the platform, we'll be looking at the **Classic Automation** and **Customer Journey Builder** features.

In this chapter, we will cover the following key topics:

- The basics of automation and events
- The types of automation, journeys, and their logic
- Common use cases and recipes
- Setting up a Classic Automation or the Customer Journey Builder

So let's review some of the theory behind how these types of automation features function and what kind of events we should consider when considering leveraging them.

Technical requirements

Due to there being a previous iteration of Mailchimp's automation suite, some features such as **Classic Automation** can only be accessed with an account that has previously used or drafted one. Alternatively, the newer automation feature is called **Customer Journeys** in your account. To access these features, you will need an **Essentials** plan or higher. Throughout this chapter, unless otherwise indicated, *automation* will refer to both products as they both, in essence, look to accomplish the task of removing manual processes from your to-do list.

The basics of automation and events

The central benefit of automation is to let the platform you're using perform the repetitive tasks you currently manually carry out, leaving you to focus on other things to support your business. For example, if you find yourself sending a monthly welcome email to people who are new to your business that month, why not let the platform do that for you? The content of your welcome emails to new subscribers is likely to be pretty consistent, so setting up a single welcome email or email series would save you a great deal of time. You could even schedule it to send more frequently than once a month; immediately or with a defined delay, whatever works for you. In that scenario, you reap the benefit of engaging your new audience members more quickly without an investment of time.

Like a lot of things we've talked about, the idea is that this kind of feature can save you time following some up-front investment of effort. But with this feature, you can start to add extra functionality and integrate automatic actions based on what your audience does.

Some core journey or automation-specific words and phrases we should know going into this chapter are the following:

- **Events**: This is the term that will be used to refer to things that audience members do when interacting with your channels that trigger the automation. It is the behavior that you want the application to monitor for.
- **Triggers**: This is how the subscriber to your business is moved through the automation or journey pathways. These are the conditions you'll set that tell the application what actions you want it to take when it detects the behavior you're interested in.
- **Queue**: This is perhaps the most literal term. It's the list of audience members who have met the set conditions to receive the campaigns set up by an automation or journey but are waiting to receive the email based on the delay you've set.
- **Journey point**: These are interaction points within the Customer Journey Builder where you have mapped out a specific condition or behavior that you're expecting from an audience member before they proceed to receive more campaigns in a series.
- **Action**: You can program these additional actions into your automation and customer journeys. These are tasks you would like the Mailchimp platform to execute for you when an audience member reaches a given point in their journey or workflow. For example, you may want a specific tag to be added to a person's profile when they reach a certain point so that you can segment these audience members later, as described in *Chapter 4*.

With this language in mind, the two most important terms that I'd like to focus on are **events** and **triggers**. These are important to keep in mind throughout the chapter because even if you're only automating around a single audience member's behavior, the simplest automation will need one event and one trigger.

Before you jump into the building and design, the basics here consist of a couple of questions you need to answer:

- What do I want to automate?
- What behavior from my audience do I want this automation to be based on?

With question number one, we're really focusing on what kind of campaigns you perform manually and repetitively. The most common example, and the one we talked about earlier in this chapter, is welcome emails or series. But another example of something you might want to automate is a follow-up email if an audience member purchases something and you have that information in their user profile.

We'll cover this more in *Chapter 14*, but for example, if you are using an e-commerce platform and use it for listing your products and even sending things such as order confirmations and shipping notifications, if you integrate your commerce platform with Mailchimp, you can sync information about the purchase to the subscriber's profile. From there, there are various options for e-commerce-based events, but let's say you just want to send a follow-up to anyone who purchases anything from your store.

You can choose to identify that as the behavior you want to focus on, and then presumably, what you would want to automate would be, at minimum, the follow-up email itself. But you can also automate actions. So you might want to consider that once the email or series of emails is sent, is there something you want the platform to do with the contact? Should they be removed from your audience? Should their profile be tagged to indicate they're part of a new segment? These are all things you can have the automation or journey take on for you.

Types of automation, journeys, and their logic

So when we talk about logic as it relates to either automation or journeys, we're talking about how we think about the design of the overall flow and what we expect the automation or journey to do for us. In line with much of what we've already discussed, we can almost think of it as a type of experimental design. When thinking about what to automate in any marketing platform, consider the logic as *cause and effect*:

Cause: Why something happens

Effect: What happens as a result

A new person signs up for your newsletter on your website, *so they're added to your audience.*

A new contact is added to the audience, *so they're sent a welcome email campaign.*

A person purchases a book from your store, *so their purchase information is synced back to your audience's contact data.*

Your store syncs information about a purchase back to your audience, *so they're sent a follow-up email about other items they can purchase.*

With this in mind, you'll want to focus your planning on what behavior from your audience should trigger a journey or automation (cause and effect). Then, once you've determined what behaviors you want to focus on, you'll need to determine what happens when the platform detects that behavior.

The core logic here is that some behavior **triggers** the automation or journey.

> **A reminder of the definition of a trigger**
> This is the way the subscriber to your audience is moved through the automation or journey pathways. These are the conditions you'll set that tell the application what actions you want it to take when it detects the behavior you're interested in.

With that foundation, let's take a closer look at how we can apply this logic and some common use cases for when to use specific triggers.

Common use cases and recipes

Triggers can be grouped conceptually into families of behavior or logic. These include the following:

- Audience/contact activity
- E-commerce activity
- Date-based events and data
- Marketing channel activity
- Integration and API events

Each of these is the broader conceptual group that you should think about when considering what you're doing manually (or that you're not doing at all because it would be too much work) that you could let the platform handle for you.

And I want to pause here and really emphasize this question:

What are you not doing because it's too difficult and time-consuming?

This is the powerful point of automating some of the tasks that Mailchimp can undertake for you. It's obviously wonderful if you can automate tasks you may have already been doing manually as discussed in some of the earlier examples in this chapter, but if you can create more contact points with your contacts, you create more opportunities to engage them with your content or for them to check out your products.

This is the fine line you walk as a marketer:

How do you optimize the amount of contact your business or brand has with your contacts without becoming too spammy?

The benefit of partnering with more automated experimentation, as covered in *Chapter 11*, with email campaign automation is that you can take learnings into the automation you design in either Classic Automation or Customer Journeys. You can refine the volume of contacts through the Classic Automation or Customer Journeys while taking the learnings from your testing to ensure that your outreach is as effective as possible.

So let's take a quick look at examples of use cases of the types of behaviors and logic that fall into each of the preceding families or categories before we move on to building a sample automation. You can find a full list of all available starting points for Customer Journeys linked in the *Further reading* section at the end of the chapter, but I want to provide a sample of the kinds of behaviors that might fall into each family.

Audience/contact activity

These are probably the most common behavior that people use or even think of when building their automation in a marketing platform. These encompass behaviors such as signing up for your audience, being assigned to a specific group, or being tagged (as covered in *Chapter 4*), data is added to a specific audience field, or they click a link on your Mailchimp website. These are really the bread and butter of marketing automation. Let's take a look at some examples.

An example using sign-up behavior:

1. *Person A* goes to your website where you have an embedded sign-up form.
2. They sign up using their email address.
3. Mailchimp adds them to your audience.
4. Customer Journey **triggers**, based on the **sign-up action**.

An example using tagging behavior:

1. At a conference, you collect contact information for people who would like to receive your newsletter.
2. You import these contacts with the `2023EXPO` tag.
3. Mailchimp adds them to your audience and adds the tag to their contact profile.
4. Customer Journey **triggers** based on the **Tag added** action.

An example using leaving audience group behavior:

1. This audience has groups for options related to contact frequency: **Weekly**, **Monthly**, and **Quarterly**.
2. *Person A* is a member of the group in your **Weekly** group but they opt to update their preferences from the **Update Preferences** link at the footer of your email.
3. *Person A* switches to **Monthly** and deselects **Weekly** in their contact preferences and saves.

4. Mailchimp updates their subscriber contact profile and moves them from the **Weekly** group to the **Monthly** group.
5. Customer Journey **triggers** based on the **Leaves audience group** action.

Audience and contact activity is probably one of the larger subsets of automation event options, so really play around with them as your audience grows and begins to engage with your content more and more.

E-commerce activity

While not the number one for frequency of use, e-commerce related emails are perhaps the ones people think of most when thinking of automated emails. If asked how they use the internet, a great many people think of online shopping. And because so many of us have been online for so long, we have specific expectations around what is normal behavior when we interact with commerce brands in particular.

What do I mean by that? Well, when I'm shopping online, let's say I'm going ahead and purchasing something from a business. We all expect roughly the same general steps in the experience:

1. I peruse the website for the product I'm looking for.
2. I add the product to my cart.
3. I fill out my contact information.
4. I input my payment information.
5. I confirm my billing information.
6. I place the order.
7. The site displays a success message of some kind.
8. I receive an order confirmation to the email address I input when filling out my contact information.

The last behavior is surprisingly critical.

For most people doing their online shopping, if they place an order online and the website doesn't indicate to them that there would be some reason they should expect a delay in receiving an emailed copy of their order confirmation, then most people would be a little surprised if they opened up their email and saw no sign of confirmation within a minute or two.

This is such a common automation that we, as consumers, don't really think about how ubiquitous it is until it's not there. Typically, there aren't a bunch of employees at that business individually sending out order confirmations. Most commonly, these are triggered by automation either from the platform the company is using to manage its online store or from marketing automation platforms such as Mailchimp that the company is using to run its marketing channels.

So let's go through a couple of examples of e-commerce behaviors that can serve to drive automation.

An example of automation using the purchase of any product:

1. *Person A* purchases a pair of shoes from your online shoe store.
2. They confirm their purchase.
3. Your e-commerce platform sends the purchase data to Mailchimp.
4. Mailchimp updates their subscriber contact profile with information about the product and purchase.
5. A Customer Journey **triggers** based on the **Buys any product** action.

An example using the behavior where a contact abandons their cart:

1. *Person A* is shopping on your site.
2. They add a product to their cart and keep shopping.
3. They start the checkout process and input their contact information, but do not proceed.
4. Your e-commerce platform categorizes their cart as abandoned after a while.
5. The e-commerce platform sends the cart information to Mailchimp.
6. A Customer Journey **triggers** based on the **Abandons cart action**.

> **A note about e-commerce automation and journeys**
>
> Marketing and spam-related laws around contacting people are slightly different when looking at e-commerce. The expectation of customers when making a purchase online is to receive order notifications and shipping information, so we differentiate between **subscribed** and **transactional** contacts as noted in *Chapter 2*.
>
> So some of this automation such as abandoned carts, order notifications, shipping confirmations, cancellation confirmations, order invoices, and refund notifications cannot be combined with other starting points because they apply to both transactional and subscribed contacts. Unless the contact specifically opts in, you cannot send marketing content to transactional contacts. These are, as the name implies, one-off situations based exclusively on one transaction. This is why you will see in some examples that I will note that a subscriber's contact profile is updated.

Date-based events and data

When setting up a form or audience, you can use date-based fields. For example, when people are signing up, you can ask for their birthday, or maybe you run a wedding business, so you request their wedding date. These are examples of date-based information you might want to use to re-engage your subscribers. These are good opportunities to celebrate with your contacts and bring them back to your content.

An example using a birthday:

1. *Person A* signs up for your audience through a form in January and provides their birthday, which is in May.
2. Mailchimp adds them to your audience.
3. In May, a Customer Journey **triggers** based on the **Birthday** action, offering a birthday discount on a product or service.

An example using a recurring date:

1. *Person A* reaches out through my wedding photography site subscribes to my audience, providing their wedding date if they have it.
2. Mailchimp adds them to your audience.
3. *Person A* hires me to be their wedding photographer.
4. At their anniversary, a Customer Journey triggers based on the **Recurring Date** action, offering them a discount on an anniversary shoot.

Marketing channel activity

These can be great for scaling up or down your email campaigns or tailoring the content based on how your contacts engage with other one-off campaigns. These are **triggers** predominantly based on how your subscribed contacts are or are not engaging with your email campaigns.

An example of when a specific email campaign is opened:

1. *Person A* receives email *campaign A* on Saturday.
2. *Person A* opens the email on Sunday.
3. A customer journey **triggers** based on the **opens email** action.

An example of when any link is clicked in a campaign email:

1. *Person A* receives email *campaign A*.
2. *Person A* clicks on any link within the campaign.
3. A customer journey **triggers** based on the **clicks any email link** action.

Integration and API events

The great thing about the API is that it is largely capable of doing most of the things you can do within the web app itself. With this family of starting points, you'll have access to some triggers specific to integrations such as Zapier or Eventbrite. Or, you or a developer can create a **trigger** based on whatever you would like on your end by using the **Customer Journeys API trigger**.

An example of when a ticket is purchased on Eventbrite:

1. *Person A* buys a ticket to your event on your Eventbrite landing page.
2. Eventbrite sends the contact's data to Mailchimp.
3. Mailchimp updates their subscriber contact profile.
4. A Customer Journey **triggers** based on the **Purchases any Eventbrite ticket** action.

With those use cases reviewed per category, we can move on to what the interface looks like when we're building automation on the Mailchimp platform.

Setting up a Classic Automation or Customer Journey Builder

As noted at the beginning of this chapter, whether you have access to both **Classic Automation** or **Customer Journeys** will largely depend on the age of your account and whether you have attempted to build a **Classic Automation** in the past. That being said, there are some practical advantages to leveraging **Customer Journeys** even if you have access to **Classic Automations**. The main one is that you'll have access to what is generally referred to as **branching logic**.

Branching logic is where you can set actions for two different occurrences. It's also commonly referred to as an *if/else* rule. Whatever you call it, it's a conditional statement that accounts for whether something is true or not true and then takes two different actions depending on the outcome: true or false. If we were to put an example together in a statement, it might look something like this:

If *Person A* **does open** *Campaign X*, then they will receive *Customer Journey email 1*. Else, if *Person B* **does not open** *Campaign X*, then they will be removed from the *Customer Journey*.

This type of map allows you to create various options and program actions you want the Mailchimp platform to take for you. Let's walk through building a welcome series of emails with multiple actions for Mailchimp to take on for us.

For this example, let's assume I run a small bookstore, and when people sign up for my audience through my Mailchimp website, I'd like to set up a sequence of automation with information about me and my business. So as I build out my map inside Mailchimp, I will need to consider the following points:

- How many emails would I like to have in this series?
- How much time would I like to have between each email campaign?
- Can I use branches to better target my audience?

Let's get started. When logged into your Mailchimp account, follow these steps:

1. Click on **Automation** in the left-hand navigation menu.
2. Click on **Overview** from the sub-menu.

This will take you to the main page containing information about your recent journeys and an overview of some of the popular options for pre-built journeys (these are like templates but for customer journeys instead of a single campaign) as seen in *Figure 12.1*:

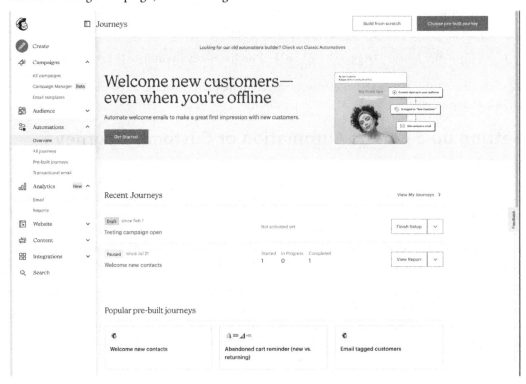

Figure 12.1 – The Customer Journey Overview page

If you would like to build a **Classic Automation**, click on **Check out Classic Automations** at the top of the screen. Or, if you would like to build a newer **Customer Journey**, click on the **Build from scratch** button. Both options are shown in *Figure 12.2*:

Figure 12.2 – A zoom-in on the buttons for drafting a Classic Automation or Customer Journey

We're going to focus on building a **Customer Journey** automation simply because the **Classic Automations** will have many of the same options for starting points, delays, and post-sending actions. The core difference is that you can use the aforementioned branching logic in **Customer Journey** automation and you will not have the same option in **Classic Automations**.

So, to draft and begin to edit your **Customer Journey**, take the following steps:

1. Click on **Build from scratch** in the upper right-hand corner of the screen.
2. Input a name for the journey (this is only seen inside your account, not displayed to contacts in your audience).
3. Select the audience you would like to connect to this journey.
4. Click on the **Start Building** button.

This will take you to a very clean interface where you can choose the starting point for your journey. These refer to what we discussed in the previous section, but in this interface, you click on **Choose A Starting Point**, and a popover modal will appear where you can check out all of the available starting triggers for a journey, as seen in *Figure 12.3*:

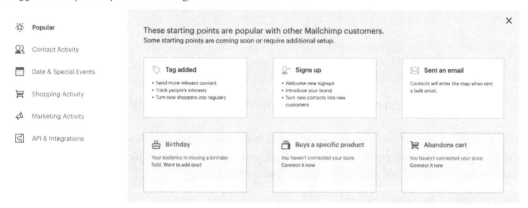

Figure 12.3 – Customer Journey starting points popover modal

As you can see, the options are grouped into families of triggers/behaviors, so you can peruse your options.

As noted, for this example, we're interested in creating a welcome series, so one of the popular options from the popover modal works for us; **Signs up**. For each starting point, you are given a bit more information about the possible use and application of each starting point. For the **Signs up** starting point, we see the following text:

- **Welcome new signups**
- **Introduce your brand**
- **Turn new contacts into new customers**

Once we've clicked on this option, the modal will ask us to confirm if we would like to include contacts that are imported to the list in the future. You can choose to enable that, and once you make your choice, you can click on **Save Starting Point** in the lower right-hand corner of the modal, as seen in *Figure 12.4*:

Figure 12.4 – The Signs up starting point settings modal

This will take us to where we can start building our map. You will see a block with a dotted line outline that says **Add a journey point**, and this is where you can add your first item that occurs after our starting point. You can add one of two things, **Rules** or **Actions**.

Rules are defined as the following:

- If/Else
- Percentage split
- Wait for trigger
- Time delay

Actions are defined as the following:

- **Send email**
- **Send email with a survey**
- **Group/Ungroup**
- **Tag/Untag**

- **Unsubscribe**
- **Update contact**
- **Archive contact**

For my example bookstore, I know my signup form is linked from the homepage of my store's website. So when someone signs up, I want the first email to go to them immediately, and to thank them for signing up, I want to offer them a 10% discount code. So my ideal first journey point would be **Send email**.

When I click on that option, it will automatically send me to a familiar email builder screen where I can start setting my **To & From** email address, **Subject**, and **Schedule**, and I can head straight into building my email campaign as I would any other campaign, as seen in *Figure 12.5*:

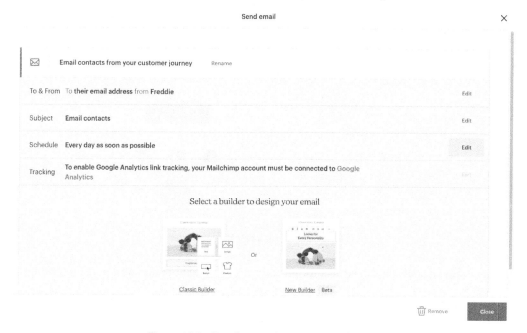

Figure 12.5 – Email campaign setup interface

When navigating the email builder, you'll be popped into the interface you'll be familiar with from *Chapter 8*, as seen in *Figure 12.6*:

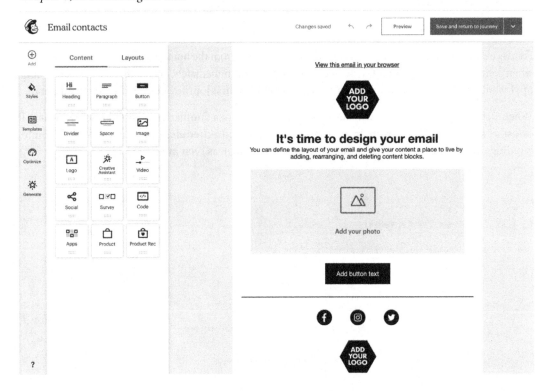

Figure 12.6 – Email campaign builder

For our example bookstore, the driver for this first email would be to accomplish the following:

- Welcome new contacts to your audience and brand.
- Link to your store.

    You can also encourage foot traffic by featuring the physical address if you have a brick-and-mortar location.

- Provide a discount code.

    These typically need to be set up in your e-commerce platform in advance, but then you can input the text of the code here.

Once you've finished designing the first email, click on the **Save and return to journey** button in the upper right-hand corner. This will take you back to where you were building your journey map. Now, if I wanted to add more emails to make this a sequence to try and build a relationship with the contacts that opened their emails, I would want to consider how much time I want to leave between the first and second contact points. For example, I would want the second contact to be about a day or a week away. The reason is, if I want to build out an abandoned cart journey later down the line, that should typically be sent to my contact within the same day to try and capitalize on the existing engagement point.

So next in my journey builder, if you hover your cursor over a plus sign, you'll see a clickable block appear with text indicating you can **Add a journey point**, as seen in *Figure 12.7*:

Figure 12.7 – An Add a journey point block

To add the desired delay, when you click this block, you would then click on **Time delay** from the open menu, allowing you to choose the delay that works for you. You'll have a text block to enter the desired number, and then you can choose the integer from a drop-down menu with the following options:

- **Days**
- **Hours**
- **Weeks**

Once you've made your selection, click on **Save**, as seen in *Figure 12.8*:

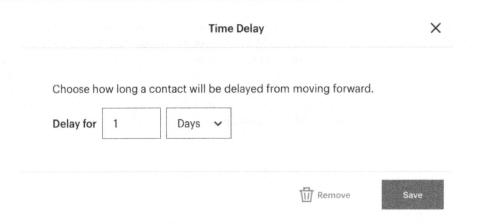

Figure 12.8 – The Time Delay modal

From there, let's say I want to have the rest of the sequence with classic book suggestions and information about my business go to the contacts who open the first email, but I want to send a final email to people who didn't open the first email about their coupon. I would do the following:

1. Hover my cursor over the plus sign following **Time delay**.
2. Click on **Add a journey point**.
3. Select **If/Else** from the menu.
4. Select the name of the first email in my journey from the campaign drop-down list (*Figure 12.9*).
5. Click on the **Save** button:

Figure 12.9 – The If/Else settings modal

This will give us our first branching path. One branch will be for contacts who opened the first email, and the other will be for people who did not open the first email. This will let us create an email for each scenario and determine what we would like the journey to do with contacts in each branch.

So let's say I want the welcome series to be three emails. I add those emails into the first **Yes** branch we just created that takes the first email opened as indicating interest. That will look like *Figure 12.10*:

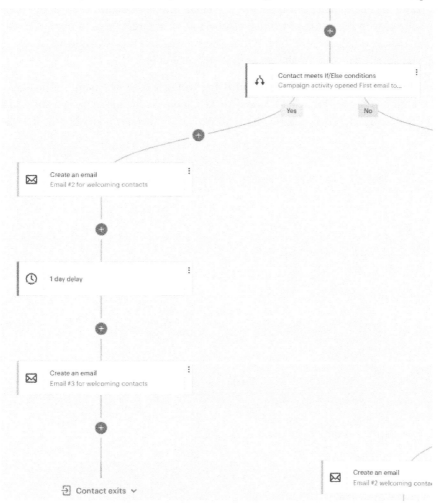

Figure 12.10 – The Yes branch

Then, I want to make sure going forward that I know which contacts didn't engage with the first welcome and the follow-up. So I want to tag those contacts. In the **No** branch, I'm going to do the following:

1. Create a follow-up email with the coupon code again.
2. Add another 1 day **Time delay** after it.
3. Add an **If/Else** condition branching based on whether the follow-up email was opened.

And here again, I'll get to refine what happens at this second branch. Since my goal is to identify the people who didn't engage at all, I want to focus on something different for the **No** branch here. For contacts that didn't open the first or the follow-up email, I want to tag them so that in the future, if they don't engage with my future individual campaigns, I can target them to try and re-engage at a future point and eventually archive them if they never engage, so that my audience stays mostly full of people who are at least occasionally engaged with my content.

So, in this branch, I'll **Add a journey point** called **Tag/Untag** and create a name for that tag as we did in *Chapter 4*. And in the **Yes** branch, I'll largely make it look like the initial branch and add a second and third email with 1 day delays between them. We can see this secondary branch in *Figure 12.11*:

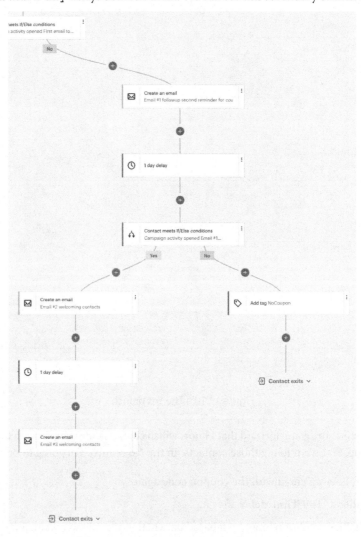

Figure 12.11 – First No branch

Once you're ready to go, you can click on **Continue** in the upper right-hand corner and click on **Turn On** to kick it off. Keep in mind this will apply to contacts as they join from the point that the journey is turned on and will not work retroactively. However, you can, of course, edit the journey map in the future if you would like by opening the journey and clicking on the three dots that appear on the right-hand edge of every journey point, and selecting **Edit** from the menu that appears (*Figure 12.12*):

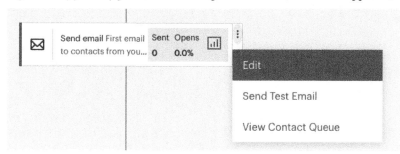

Figure 12.12 – Journey point Edit option

Additionally, as you can see, you'll see stats per email in this interface as well. However, if you would like, you can also click on the **View Report** option in the upper right-hand corner of the journey page. This will provide you with the info you'll have seen in the **Analytics and Reporting** chapter.

Now that we have a notion of how to build automation, you can jump right into letting the Mailchimp platform handle the stuff you found too time-consuming to pursue, or you can let it pick up smaller daily tasks such as sending order confirmations and shipping confirmations.

Summary

In this chapter, we learned how the Mailchimp platform can help automate and expand how you stay in touch with your subscribed and transactional contacts and how you can leverage those opportunities to increase and drive engagement with them. We reviewed the many families of triggers and starting points that can be automated and their various possible applications. Finally, and most importantly, we talked about how we could roll all of these things together and practically apply this new skill together with some of the functionality we've previously covered, such as tagging.

In the next chapter, we will dive into leveraging Mailchimp Stores to build your digital market footprint.

Further reading

- *About Customer Journeys*: `https://eepurl.com/g-DRsD`
- *About Classic Automations*: `https://eepurl.com/dyijXf`
- *All the Starting Points*: `https://eepurl.com/g-DTjr`
- *Use If/Else Rules*: `https://eepurl.com/hNFAPj`

13
Setting Up a Mailchimp E-Commerce Store

If you're a brick-and-mortar store, the last 3 years during the pandemic probably required you to get creative quickly with how you kept in touch with your customers and, especially, how you sold products to your customers. Even now, with our habits changing again and people trying to find their own semblance of normality, businesses are still learning this lesson and trying to increase the number of ways they keep their products available and at the forefront of their audience's consciousness.

This is where a platform that gives you the ability to not just display your products but also make a sale can come in handy. This chapter and the next will focus on these concepts. If you're a business without a method of selling products digitally and you already use Mailchimp or are considering it, you can start in this chapter on Mailchimp stores. If you already use a specific e-commerce platform, you can check out the next chapter on shopping integrations to connect your platform to Mailchimp's, allowing you to combine the two efforts, make your marketing channels more robust, and leverage your existing commerce data.

In this chapter, we'll be covering the following topics:

- What is an e-commerce feature?
- Setting up a Mailchimp store
- The expansion of a contact dataset to include commerce/purchasing data
- Setting up automations specific to e-commerce

Technical requirements

The **Mailchimp Store** feature uses Stripe to process payments to your store. So, a prerequisite for this feature is to create a Stripe account so that you can connect it to your Mailchimp account. Additionally, keep in mind that there will be associated transaction and processing fees. For more information on creating one if you would like to move forward, you can see more information about Stripe specifically on the following website: `https://dashboard.stripe.com/register`.

First, let's talk briefly about how we think of and define e-commerce and what is available on the Mailchimp platform.

What is a commerce feature?

When we think about online commerce specifically, we're referring to the natural commercial extension of a website. It's the piece of your digital footprint that actually allows you to create a revenue stream. Frequently, your other channels such as emails and even social footprints are ways of funneling your audience to your content, services, or physical goods. However, an e-commerce store itself functions as both a channel to show off your brand to your audience, as well as a way of actually taking in revenue.

In the event that you already have an e-commerce platform, you can proceed right to *Chapter 14*, to connect your existing store. The Mailchimp platform itself can be connected to a myriad of third-party applications, and frequently when people come to Mailchimp to expand their marketing efforts, particularly e-commerce business owners and entrepreneurs, they may already be leveraging one of the following popular e-commerce platforms:

- Shopify
- WooCommerce
- Magento

In the event that you are leveraging one of these, or you would like to integrate with another e-commerce platform, *Chapter 14* dives into an example of connecting a Shopify integration to funnel your commerce data to Mailchimp. This style of data movement through an integration, built by leveraging the Mailchimp API and Webhooks, will be fairly similar for all integrations and will look quite familiar should you decide to develop your own integration using Mailchimp's API.

However, if you're a brick-and-mortar/physical store or service provider with no existing e-commerce store, Mailchimp stores can be a simple way to dip your toes into the e-commerce space. Additionally, if you're already using a physical *Stripe Terminal* point-of-sale device or mobile app when selling your products, you're already prepared to use the Mailchimp store feature, as Stripe is the transaction processor for this as well.

Generally, when people think of e-commerce features, even simply in the context of doing their own shopping online, they think of things such as the following:

- **Shopping pages**:
  - **Product listings**: This is where you would see a list of all available products and services
  - **Product details**: This is the in-depth information about a specific product that's displayed in its listing
  - **Product images**: One or more images displaying the specific product in the product details

- **Checkout**:
  - **Shopping cart**: This is the list of products selected by a single shopper on a website
  - **Checkout**: This is the interface to list items in the cart and associated fees, such as shipping, and initiate payment processing
- **Order and shipping**:
  - **Shipping**: This is the interface to select shipping options
  - **Order confirmation**: This is a review and summary of the order after the payment has been processed

Now, let's set up our Mailchimp store to start selling our products.

Setting up a Mailchimp store

Now, creating a store in Mailchimp will be quite familiar to you if you read the chapter on creating a website earlier in this book. This is because, fundamentally, a store is a specific type of website. So when you have logged into your Mailchimp account, to start this process you do the following:

1. Click on **Website** in the left-hand navigation menu.
2. Click on **Store** from the submenu that appears (*Figure 13.1*).

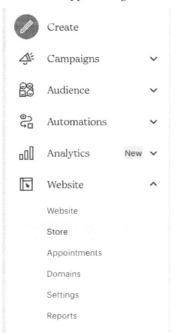

Figure 13.1 – The left-hand navigation Website submenu

If you've never attempted to create a store with Mailchimp, the **Stores** page provides you with only one option when you click on it – the **Start Your Store** button. This will take you directly into a builder, and as with every other channel, you start by naming your channel – in this case, providing the business name for the store, as shown in *Figure 13.2*.

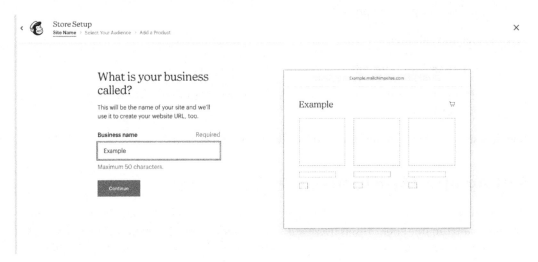

Figure 13.2 – The Site Name builder step

Once you've named your business as it will appear on your store, the next page of the builder will ask you to choose the audience in your account that you would like to connect your store to. This will be the audience you want the purchase and subscriber data from any contacts who purchase through your store to be logged to. Finally, in the last step of this builder, you'll walk through adding your first product.

As with the other two pages of the builder, you will see an example rendered for you on the right as you go along. You will have the following fields to fill out (*Figure 13.3*):

- **Product name**
- **Price**
- **Product description**
- A product image
- The tax-exempt status of the product

Now let's add your first product:

Figure 13.3 – The adding a product builder step

You'll then see a success message and will be provided with the option to continue adding products to your store or continue setting up your store. Personally, I would recommend finishing your store setup, the reason being that if you're short on time, you can always come back to add more products slowly over time, but the sooner you get any products live on your store for purchases to start, the sooner you can begin turning over some revenue from the store.

When you opt to finish the store setup, there will be three core tasks you have to complete:

1. Verifying your address.
2. Setting up shipping.
3. Completing the payment processing setup.

The first of these should be pretty easy. The app will just provide you with a **Confirm Address** button, and if it's not the right address for your business, you'll click on **Edit** (*Figure 13.4*).

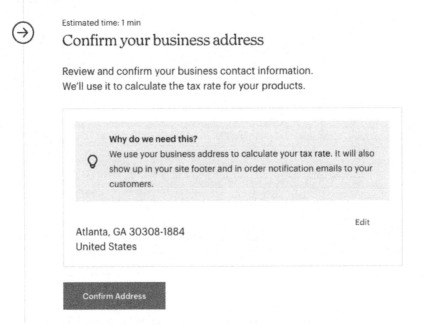

Figure 13.4 – The Confirm your business address setup step

Similarly, the **Stores** dashboard will automatically advance you to the next step to finish the setup of your store. Next is setting up the shipping options for your store, as shown in *Figure 13.5*:

Setting up a Mailchimp store

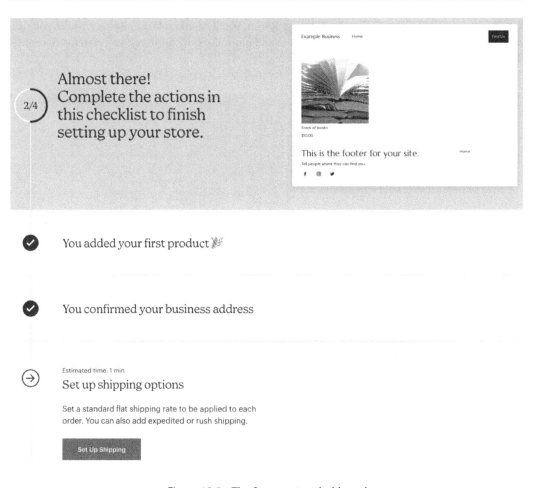

Figure 13.5 – The Stores setup dashboard

When you click on **Set Up Shipping**, you'll be taken to an interface where you can set up at least one basic shipping option, but you'll also be able to see things such as the following:

- The ability to set up free shipping if you'd like to conditionally offer that
- Customize rates per additional item to account for large packages
- Tips on how to manage your shipping

When you create and save at least one shipping option, you'll be taken to an interface where you can see the one option you've created, and a button to add more shipping options if you plan to offer more than one, as seen in *Figure 13.6*.

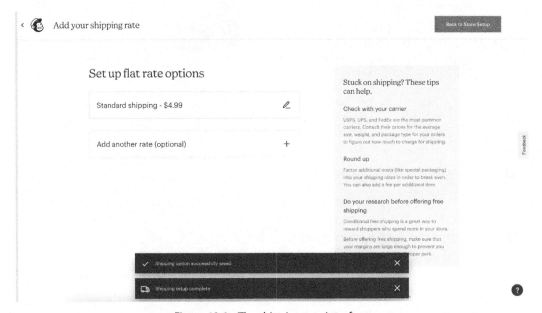

Figure 13.6 – The shipping rate interface

Once you've added the shipping rates you want available, you can click on **Back to Store Setup** in the upper-right-hand corner, which will take you back to the **Store** dashboard where you can complete the final step to set up your store – connecting Stripe to process your payments.

To start this final step, click on **Connect Stripe**. From there, you will be taken to an interface to connect your Mailchimp account to your Stripe account.

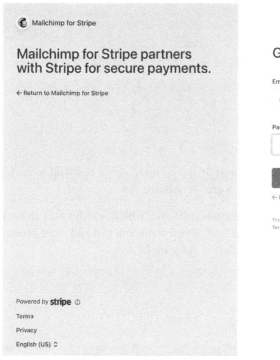

Figure 13.7 – The Mailchimp for Stripe connection interface

You'll then be asked the following:

- Business location (country)
- Type of business
- Your legal name
- Email address
- Date of birth
- Phone number
- Industry
- Product description
- Bank service information to receive payouts:
  - Routing number
  - Account number

- Public details for invoices:
  - Statement descriptor
  - Shortened descriptor
  - Customer support phone number
  - Customer support address
- Optional climate commitment

Once you've set up or confirmed the details of your Stripe account, you'll be asked to review the information you input, and then you can click on **Agree & Submit**.

From there, Stripe will have to confirm the information you input, which usually takes about 10–15 minutes. However, you don't have to sit there and wait. If you want, you can add more products or personalize your store website while you wait, as shown in *Figure 13.8*.

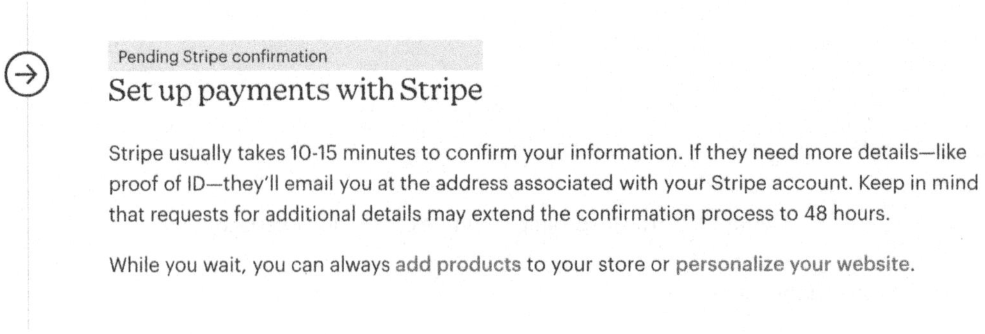

Figure 13.8 – The Pending Stripe confirmation message on the Store dashboard

You can click on either **add products** or **personalize your website** in this interface. The **add products** option will take you back to the interface you'll be familiar with to add a single product from the initial building of the store, and **personalize your website** will take you to a page that looks quite similar to the website builder we walked through in *Chapter 9*, as shown in *Figure 13.9*. Using and editing it is identical to building a website. You'll have the list of pages on the site on the left, and then you can choose the specific pages on the right.

Setting up a Mailchimp store

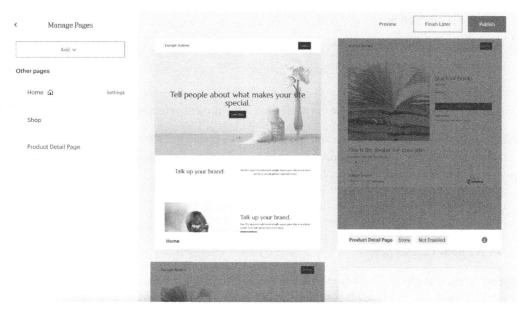

Figure 13.9 – The Manage Pages interface for a store

Once you've made the edits you want, you can then click on **Publish** in the upper-right-hand corner and your store is all set!

Another possible step in your setup would depend on whether you want to set up a service with yourself as the product. If your products are all physical products, you're all done. However, if you sell services such as in-person or Zoom consultations, massages, haircuts, and so on, you can set up appointments that you can then publish as a listing page for your store and site.

You can customize your service options and create one-on-one services as well as group services that multiple people can attend. To create a service, when logged into your account, do the following:

1. Click on **Website** from the left-hand navigation menu.
2. Select **Appointments** from the submenu.
3. Click on the **Add A Service** button.

This will take you to the appointment builder. Here, you will do the following:

1. Choose the service type:
   - One-on-one
   - Group
2. Give the service a name.

3. Input a description.
4. Set the appointment duration.
5. Set the appointment price.
6. Create a service URL.
7. Select whether you would like to enable SMS appointment-related messages.

When you've input the information and made the relevant selections for the service option you're creating, click on the **Continue** button at the bottom of the page. In the following interface, you then choose what type of appointment service you're offering:

- An **In Person** service
- A **Virtual** service
- A **Phone Call** service

When you make a selection, you can then fill out more details about the meeting. For example, if you select **In Person**, you can then fill out **Location information**, as shown in *Figure 13.10*.

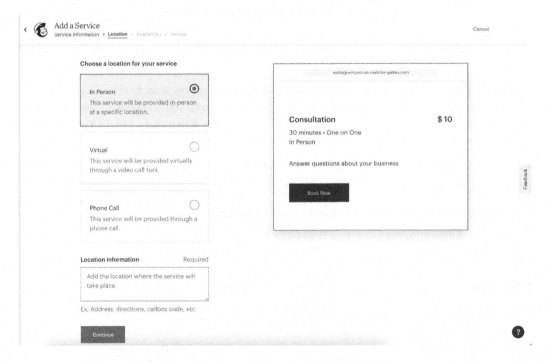

Figure 13.10 – The Location step of the appointment builder

In the next step, you'll set the availability for these appointments. By default, the time slots will be enabled Monday through Friday from 9a.m. to 5p.m.. Each day can be enabled or disabled by utilizing the toggle to the right end of each block, and you can edit the time by clicking on the pencil icon to edit the specific day of the week. You can see an example of these blocks in *Figure 13.11*.

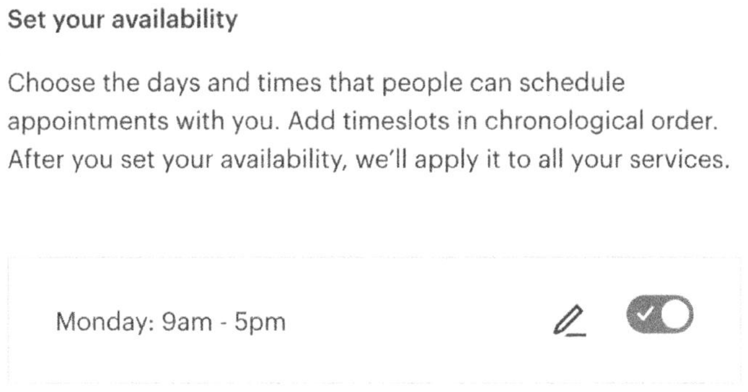

Figure 13.11 – The availability block

Additionally, toward the bottom of the availability section, you can edit the time increment if you want – from 30 minutes to 60 and vice versa. Once you've made the edits you want, click **Continue** at the bottom and review all of your selections. If you're happy with the review, you can then click on **Publish Service on Website**. This will publish your service to its own listing page, and you're all set to start accepting appointments.

Once you have the store set up and/or appointments posted, you should be able to see purchase/commerce data in your account as people begin shopping in your store.

The expansion of a contact dataset to include commerce/purchasing data

As you promote your store and products using your other marketing channels, you will eventually see that you have revenue data associated with your store reports and in the profiles of your subscribed contacts. If you read the previous chapters, you'll be generally familiar with these areas of the platform, but it is valuable to note places where you can use this purchase and revenue data to better understand your contacts and leverage the information you're collecting.

So, let's highlight a couple of places where this e-commerce data will appear and tools that can leverage it:

- **Contact table**:

    If you recall, you can check out every contact for a particular audience by doing the following:

    I.   Click on **Audience** from the left-hand navigation menu.

    II. Click on **All contacts** from the submenu.

    III. Find the **Revenue** column.

    IV. Scroll down to see the contact member you want (*Figure 13.10*).

Figure 13.10 – Contact table revenue view

- **Contact profile page**:

    From the preceding steps, you can actually go one level further and see additional details about the specific purchases that contributed to the revenue listed in the table. To do that, follow the same steps as previously and then do the following:

    I.   Click on the email address of the specific contact.

    II. Scroll down to the **Activity Feed** section.

    III. Select **E-Commerce** from the **Activity Type** dropdown (*Figure 13.11*).

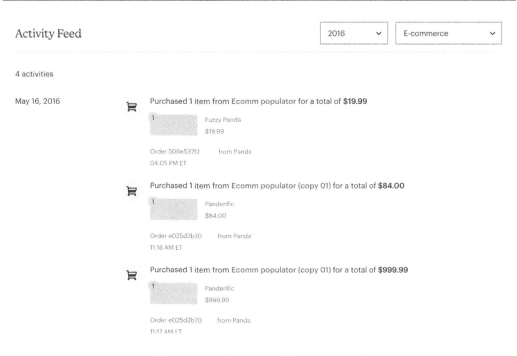

Figure 13.11 – Contact profile Activity Feed

- **Campaign Overview**

    As we covered in *Chapter 10*, you can also see **Revenue** for a specific campaign, at a glance, from the primary **Campaign Overview** page. To get there, when logged into your account, do the following:

    I. Click on **Campaign** in the left-hand navigation menu.

    II. Select **All Campaigns** from the submenu.

    III. After **Opens** and **Clicks**, you will also see **Revenue** for each sent campaign listed there (*Figure 13.12*).

Figure 13.12 – An analytics overview for a specific campaign in Campaign Overview

- **A single campaign report:**

  You can also see more detailed information in a report for a specific campaign, by following the previous steps and doing the following:

  I. Click on **View Report**.
  II. Select the **E-Commerce** menu.
  III. Select **Product Activity** or **Order History**:

  - **Product Activity** will show you which specific products sold from the campaign
  - **Order History** will show you who made those purchases from the campaign

With these places where you can visualize **Revenue** data, you can also, of course, leverage it to better understand your contacts, as we discussed in *Chapter 4*. As we covered in that chapter, any data brought into your account through integration or created through your contacts interacting with your various channels is something that you can segment data on, to better target your future campaigns and drive up engagement with those contacts.

To create a segment, follow these steps:

1. Click on **Audience** in the left-hand navigation menu.
2. Select **All contacts** from the submenu.
3. Select **New Segment**.
4. Select **Regular** or **Advanced Segment** from the drop-down menu.

E-commerce data will be available to you using either regular or advanced segments. You'll have commerce-related options to segment, based on the activity dropdown, such as the following:

- **Amount spent in total**
- **Amount spent on a single order**
- **Average amount spent per order**
- **Products purchased**
- **Purchase activity**
- **Purchase date**
- **Store ordered from**
- **Total number of orders**
- **Vendor Purchased**

The neat thing about integrations and leveraging more channels within the platform is that your segmenting options grow as more data arrives from other platforms and channels. So, for example, if I wanted to segment based on a specific product purchased, then I would choose the following when in the segmenting interface – **Products purchased | is | [name of product]**.

An example is shown in *Figure 13.3*:

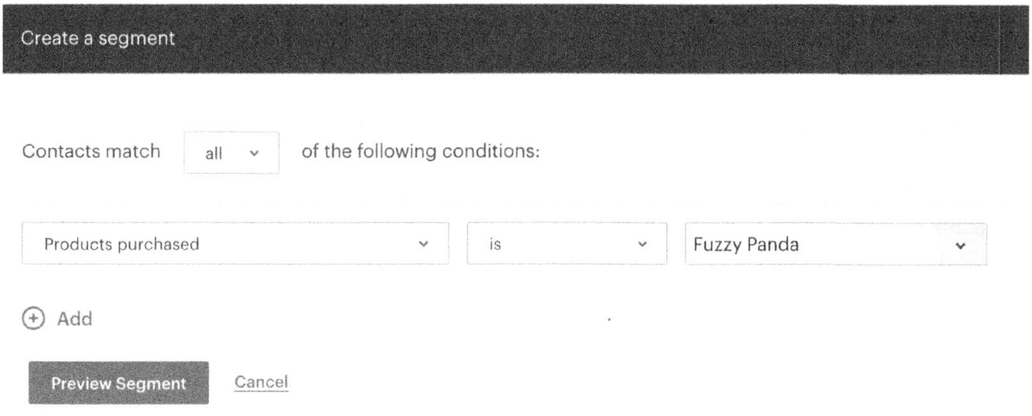

Figure 13.13 – An example of a Products purchased segment

This type of targeting will enable you to segment your email campaigns and recommend new products to people who have bought similar products in the past. Alternatively, you can add filters to your **Customer Journeys** to refine and funnel your automated audiences through the branches of your automation. Next, let's take some time to talk more specifically about those e-commerce-specific Customer Journeys that I mentioned in the previous chapter.

Setting up automations specific to e-commerce

As noted in *Chapter 12*, there is a selection of **Customer Journey** options that are specific to e-commerce. These can largely be thought of as falling into two categories:

- **Transactional journeys**: These automations are specifically for people and instances where only one email or communication is expected – for example, an **Order Confirmation** when they make a purchase in your store. These are transactional because even if the contact has not subscribed to your audience, you're allowed to reach out to them to provide them with information following a purchase.

- **Subscriber journeys**: These automations are exclusively for contacts that have subscribed to your audience and include options such as following up when the contact buys any product.

When you have an active store in your account or connect an e-commerce platform (which will be covered next, in *Chapter 14*), you'll have additional options to choose from as starting points when building your **Customer Journeys**. To check them out, when logged into your account, do the following:

1. Click on **Automations** in the left-hand navigation menu.
2. Select **Pre-built journeys** from the submenu.
3. Click on **Topics**.
4. Select **Ecommerce** from the drop-down menu that appears.

These are particularly interesting because they're combinations pre-designed by Mailchimp for you. They frequently include not only the starting point chosen for you but also things such as pre-selected segmented filters/conditions. It contains options such as abandoned cart reminders, repeat customer automations, and targeting based on customers who have shown interest in a specific product. You can see this interface and some of those pre-built options in *Figure 13.14*.

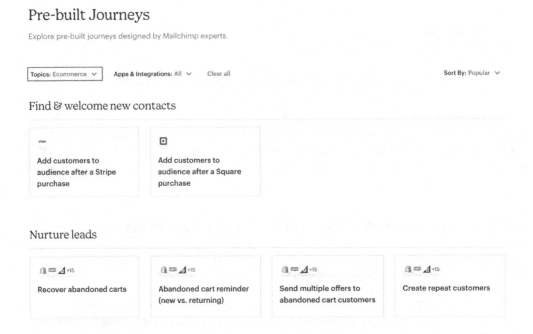

Figure 13.14 – Pre-built Journeys filtered for e-commerce

You can also just build a **Customer Journey** from scratch if you want. To do that, when logged into your Mailchimp account, do the following:

1. Click on **Automations** from the left-hand navigation menu.
2. Select **Overview** from the submenu.
3. Click on the **Build from scratch** button in the upper-right-hand corner.
4. Input a **Name**.
5. Select an audience from the **Audience** drop-down menu.
6. Click on **Start Building**.
7. Click on **Choose A Starting Point**.
8. Select **Shopping Activity** (*Figure 13.15*).

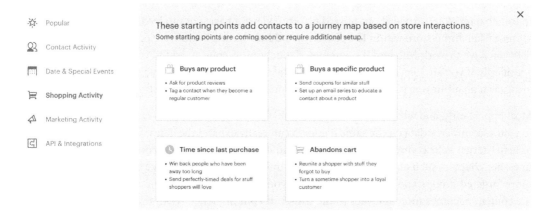

Figure 13.15 – Shopping Activity starting points

Where we see a little deviation is in the transactional journeys. If your e-commerce data comes from a platform other than Mailchimp via integration, you can add a starting point for a **Customer Journey**. For a Mailchimp store, as we saw in this chapter, you do the following:

1. Click on **Websites** in the left-hand navigation menu.
2. Select **Store** from the submenu.
3. Click on **Manage Store Settings** in the upper-right-hand corner.
4. Click on **Order notification emails**.

This will take you directly to the building interface, where you can choose to edit the **Order confirmation**, **Shipping confirmation**, or **Tracking information** emails that are sent out with each purchase from your store.

When you choose one of these emails, the editor will be just like the email editor we already covered in *Chapter 8*. You can largely edit the aesthetics of the emails, although some of the content can't be changed extensively. Because these are largely transactional, meaning they're going to reach more than just your subscribed contacts, the amount of marketing content they should contain needs to be slightly more limited to ensure that it's compliant with most anti-spam laws. However, you can, of course, edit things such as the aesthetics and designs of the emails.

This helps you to make sure that even your transactional, automated emails for purchases align with your brand. Unifying your communication channels, including small touchpoints such as transactional emails following a purchase, can really help to ensure your branding is cohesive as well as effective. We'll continue to cover how to make your e-commerce branding more cohesive in the next chapter, *Shopping Integrations*.

Summary

In this chapter, you learned about how Mailchimp views a basic commerce feature set, how you can set up a Mailchimp store within the platform, and how having commerce data can help expand the data you have to work with and the automated touchpoints you can add to your marketing universe. Specifically, if you are someone with a limited digital footprint for your products or services, Mailchimp brings you an all-in-one platform to get those products online and in front of your audience.

Most importantly, and what we'll continue to build on in the next chapter, we saw how having access to your e-commerce data on the same platform can really expand the dataset you have to work with, to better target your communications to your audiences and drive engagement. As we talked about in earlier chapters such as *Chapter 4*, when you understand your audience and can separate it into more targeted groups and segments of people, you can drive engagement and even revenue up as the content becomes more relevant to the subset of your audience. With that said, let's move on to connecting shopping integrations to build on that e-commerce-related dataset, for those of you who already leverage another digital commerce platform and want to stick with it but still want to reap the benefits of having access to your existing and future data on your marketing platform.

Further reading

- *About Your Mailchimp Store*: `https://eepurl.com/hvFhND`
- *Connect or Disconnect Stripe*: `https://eepurl.com/haCZ5H`
- *All the Starting Points*: `https://eepurl.com/g-DTjr`
- *Create Order Notifications for Your Connected Store*: `https://eepurl.com/dyillH`
- *Create an Abandoned Cart Customer Journey Map*: `https://eepurl.com/h_u0qD`

Part 5: Get Smarter and Connect

This section explores how to expand your Mailchimp dataset by leveraging integrations in the wider ecosystem. These chapters will cover integrations as well as use cases, showing you how to orchestrate everything throughout the book as an overarching strategic marketing story.

This section has the following chapters:

- *Chapter 14, E-Commerce Integrations*
- *Chapter 15, Form and Survey Integrations*
- *Chapter 16, CRM and Connectivity Integrations*
- *Chapter 17, Use Cases and Real-World Examples*

14
E-Commerce Integrations

In the previous chapter, *Chapter 13*, we covered how to set up a store in the Mailchimp application if you don't already have an existing e-commerce footprint. In this chapter, however, if you are already using another shopping or e-commerce platform, we'll go over some of the benefits of connecting that platform to your Mailchimp account and what some of the most common and popular integrations are.

In this chapter, we'll go over the following:

- Featured commerce integrations
- The movement of information between platforms
- How to expand your marketing efforts with your commerce data

Before we get too far ahead of ourselves, I want to be sure to clarify what we mean by **integration** within the context of Mailchimp. **Integration** here is used to refer to an application serving as an intermediary to pass data from one platform to another. These integrations can be developed by Mailchimp or another developer (for example, possibly the other platform you're looking to integrate), but fundamentally, you can think of them as a bridge that helps to ensure that your two separate platforms share the information you want in both places.

First, we'll go over what those featured integrations are, as they're typically the most common external platforms you may already use.

Technical requirements

In order to leverage integration with another platform, you will need the login information for that other platform. Mailchimp will not be able to connect with another application without the credentials for your account with that other software, so keep in mind that you should have that other account and its credentials available to you before starting.

Additionally, it's generally good practice to create a backup of the audience for which you plan on syncing any integration. This is just a precaution, but you can see the steps for exporting contacts in *Chapter 3*.

Featured commerce integrations

When you're logged into your Mailchimp account, you can see a highlight of some of the most common integrations for different purposes by doing the following:

1. Click on **Integrations** in the left-hand navigation menu.
2. Click on **Discover** in the sub-menu.

This will take you to an interface where you can see some options at a single glance, as seen in *Figure 14.1*:

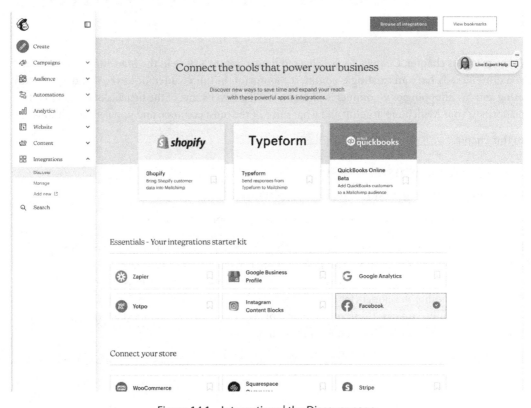

Figure 14.1 – Integrations | the Discover page

On this page, you'll see three featured integrations at the top and then a sub-section. For this chapter, we're interested in the section you can see in *Figure 14.1* called **Connect your store**. Between the top featured integrations and the specific store section, we can see the following e-commerce/shopping platforms:

- Shopify
- WooCommerce
- Squarespace Commerce

- Stripe
- BigCommerce
- Magento
- Square

These are the primary integrations people tend to leverage outside of Mailchimp most frequently, so we will focus on a couple of these throughout this chapter to demonstrate typical integration flows and how to leverage these connections.

> **A note about available integrations**
>
> If you do not see an integration available to you on this first page for whatever e-commerce platform you use outside of Mailchimp, this does not mean that one doesn't exist. In the upper-right-hand corner of *Figure 14.1*, you will see a **Browse all integrations** button. It is possible that one exists for you, it may just not be one of the most popular options and therefore may not be featured on this dashboard, but you can check for one specific to the platform you use in that directory.

For most of these integrations, we can think of the connection of integrations as consisting of the following overarching phases:

1. **Installation**: Because integration is an application that sits between Mailchimp and another application, you will need to install it to begin leveraging the connection.
2. **Authentication**: This is where you log in to your e-commerce platform to allow the integration to pass information from your e-commerce platform to your Mailchimp account.
3. **Setup**: This phase is where you configure the integration and indicate where within Mailchimp the data should be directed to.
4. **Syncing**: This phase is more passive and is where the integration will start syncing data (based on the parameters from the setup) from your e-commerce platform to your Mailchimp account.

So, let's go through with an example integration connection from the featured integrations dashboard from *Figure 14.1*. Since it's the most common, we'll go through a Shopify connection process.

As a reminder, to get to the dashboard and start the connection, when logged into your Mailchimp account, do the following:

1. Click on **Integrations** in the left-hand navigation menu.
2. Click on **Discover** in the sub-menu.
3. Click on **Shopify**.
4. Click on **Connect A New Site**.

5. Click on **Add app**.

This will take you to the page where you log into your Shopify account. Once you've logged in to your Shopify account, you will then have to click on the **Install app** button to confirm that you're allowing access to your Shopify account to pass information from one platform to the other (*Figure 14.2*):

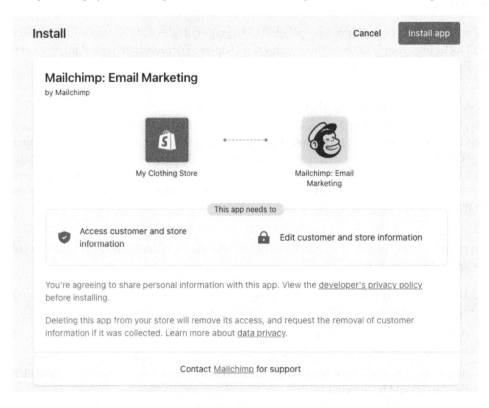

Figure 14.2 – The Install app button in Shopify

This will take you to the installer on the Shopify side. You'll go through three steps there:

1. **Before installing:** This is a checklist of notes related to the access level needed to complete the installation and to the templates available to you.
2. **Connect**: This section is where you will select the Mailchimp account you would like to connect to. Each Shopify store can only be connected to one Mailchimp account.
3. **Sync**: This step is where you will select the audience in your Mailchimp account so that contacts and their data can be synced to allow you access to their data and leverage it in your marketing.

> **Notes about potential redundancies**
>
> If you have used Shopify or other shopping platforms that provide some kind of automated email (for example, a welcome email) for a long time and you would like to use the data from these platforms with Mailchimp, you will need to remember to disable automated emails of this kind in your e-commerce application first. Then, you can build a series in Mailchimp. Shopify, for example, provides guidance on where you can find those here: `https://help.shopify.com/en/manual/promoting-marketing/create-marketing/create-marketing-automations`.

The *Sync* step is where you'll do most of the setup and mapping of data from Shopify to Mailchimp. You can optionally adjust the following:

- **App Settings**:
  - Here, you can choose to enable double opt-in for your Mailchimp audience, which is where people signing up to your audience must confirm in an email that they would like to opt in to receive email marketing from you. Enabling it here will change the setting in your Mailchimp account.
  - The second option here is if you would like to enable the integration to also pass contact information back to Shopify. This means that whenever people subscribe to your audience on the Mailchimp side, they will also be synced to your Shopify account, even if they haven't made a purchase yet.

- **Merge Tag Mapper**:
  - In this optional section, you can choose to connect the dots between your Mailchimp merge tags (*Chapter 3*) and the fields in your Shopify contacts. By default, the first name, last name, and email address are done for you because those are the minimum needed to identify subscribers, but you can add more if you like – the customer's address, for example, as seen in *Figure 14.3*.

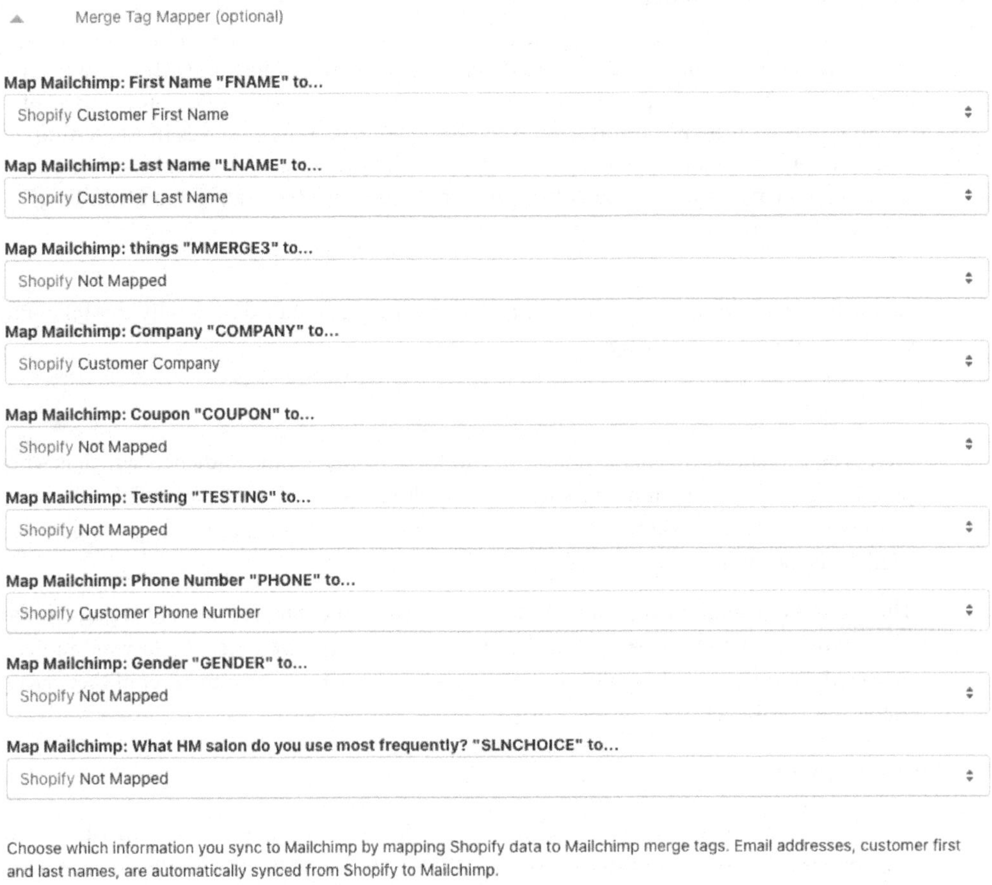

E-Commerce Integrations

> ▲ Merge Tag Mapper (optional)
>
> **Map Mailchimp: First Name "FNAME" to...**
> Shopify Customer First Name
>
> **Map Mailchimp: Last Name "LNAME" to...**
> Shopify Customer Last Name
>
> **Map Mailchimp: things "MMERGE3" to...**
> Shopify Not Mapped
>
> **Map Mailchimp: Company "COMPANY" to...**
> Shopify Customer Company
>
> **Map Mailchimp: Coupon "COUPON" to...**
> Shopify Not Mapped
>
> **Map Mailchimp: Testing "TESTING" to...**
> Shopify Not Mapped
>
> **Map Mailchimp: Phone Number "PHONE" to...**
> Shopify Customer Phone Number
>
> **Map Mailchimp: Gender "GENDER" to...**
> Shopify Not Mapped
>
> **Map Mailchimp: What HM salon do you use most frequently? "SLNCHOICE" to...**
> Shopify Not Mapped
>
> Choose which information you sync to Mailchimp by mapping Shopify data to Mailchimp merge tags. Email addresses, customer first and last names, are automatically synced from Shopify to Mailchimp.

Figure 14.3 – The Merge Tag Mapper step in the Shopify integration setup

- **Shopify Customer Tag Mapper**:

    In this section, you can create tags for customers as they move from Shopify to Mailchimp only. This will not create tagging in Shopify but rather applies a tag to be used in Mailchimp (you can find more information on tags in *Chapter 4*).

- **Tags & Groups:**

    In this section, you can create criteria to dictate when a tag is applied to a contact that is passed over to your Mailchimp audience. For example, if you would like anyone who purchases a specific product to be tagged with a particular phrase, such as **VIP** maybe, then you can build a rule to indicate that when that contact is synced after purchase, that tag should be added (*Figure 14.4*).

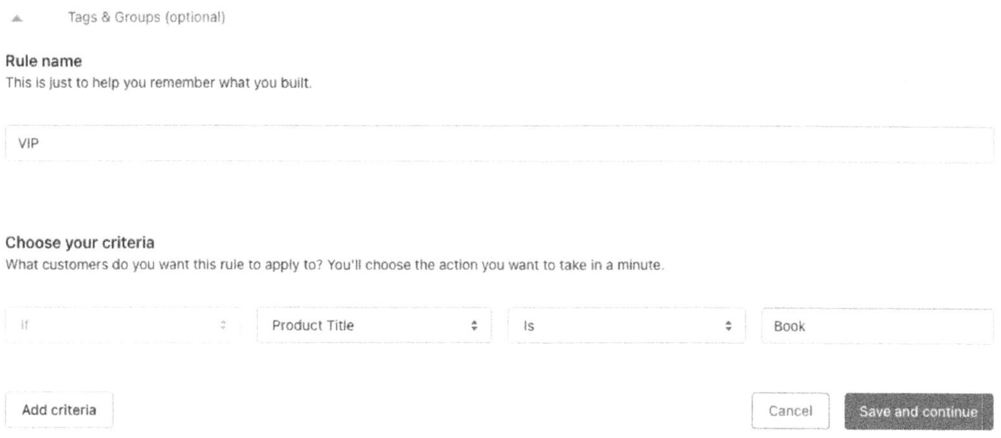

Figure 14.4 – The Tags & Groups step in the Shopify integration setup

In *Figure 14.5*, you can see all these options together:

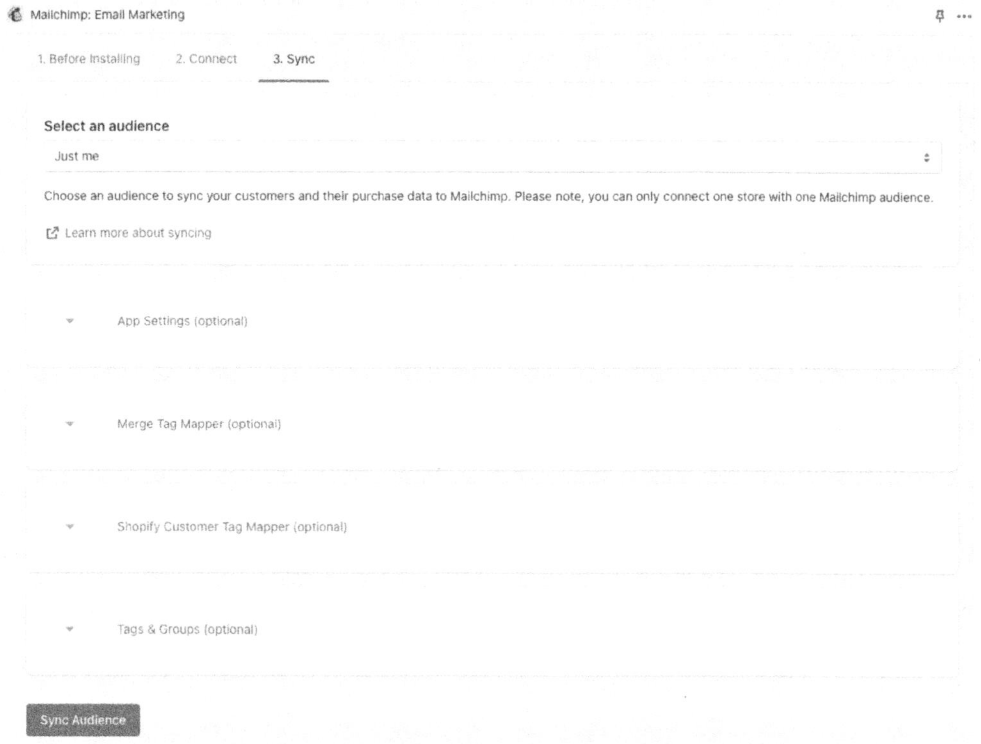

Figure 14.5 – The Sync page in the Shopify integration setup

The most important of these four sections and the most beneficial to you is the **Merge Tag Mapper** section. In this section, you can take steps to draw a connection and map the contact information from Shopify to Mailchimp. In this section, you will see the name of the field in Mailchimp listed above a drop-down menu for the fields in Shopify. This is where you will have the opportunity to indicate to the integration what information does or doesn't match between Shopify and Mailchimp, as seen in *Figure 14.6*.

Figure 14.6 – The Merge Tag Mapper section in the Shopify integration setup

Once you've made the selections you'd like in these settings, you'll click on the **Sync Audience** button at the bottom. This will then initiate a sync, as seen in *Figure 14.7*:

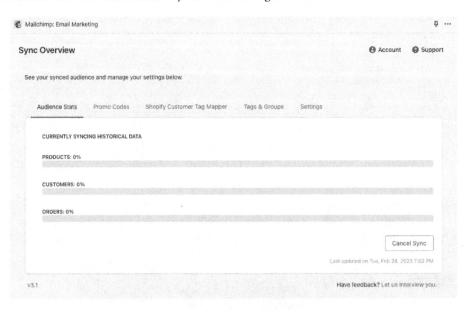

Figure 14.7 – Sync Overview in Shopify integration

Once the sync is complete, you will be able to see confirmation in the Mailchimp application of the connected Shopify integration. To see it, when logged into your Mailchimp account, you would do the following:

1. Click on **Integrations** from in the left-hand navigation menu.
2. Click on **Manage** in the sub-menu.
3. Click on **Manage your sites** at the top.

Here, you'll be able to see at a glance the audience that the integration is connected to and the features you have available to enable for the store and your customers. You'll be able to enable the following:

- A pop-up form for your site
- An abandoned cart email to encourage customers to complete their purchases
- A product retargeting email, which is an automated email that encourages people who view products on your site to purchase them
- Order notifications to send your customers receipts for their purchases
- Data processing restriction features, which you can enable if you have customers in California, for example, whose data you need to handle differently

By connecting this type of integration, you can really maximize the way you leverage your data and utilize both your e-commerce and Mailchimp platforms. Next, let's go through how information is passed from one platform to another through connected integration.

Movement of information between these platforms

The process for connecting these types of integrations is roughly the same for a great many of them. They are initiated through the **Integrations** page. There, you will select the integration for your shopping platform and proceed through the connection/authentication process.

What can be most useful to understand is how information is passed back and forth between the platforms. When you authenticate an integration, it enables that integration to act per the settings when you start the sync of the application. After that initial sync from the setup, generally, integrations will then send information about contacts and subscribers as they complete purchases or abandon carts when logged into their accounts with the store.

So, let's go through an example. Let's say for the purposes of this example, I am the following:

- A customer purchasing something from your store
- A first-time buyer
- I have never completed a purchase

I browse your website and choose to purchase a green t-shirt. I add that shirt to my cart and proceed to checkout. There, I will add my shipping information and my billing information. Then, I will be given the option to subscribe to receive future marketing and information from you once I complete the purchase.

If I *do* **opt in**, data will be synced to Mailchimp as **subscribed**.

If I *do not* **opt in**, data will be synced to Mailchimp as **transactional**.

Based on that decision, how the contact is passed over to Mailchimp will dictate what types of automation are available to use with those contacts:

- For transactional contacts:
  - Abandoned cart notifications
  - Order notifications
  - Shipping confirmations
  - Tracking information
- For subscribed contacts:
  - All of the previous
  - Welcome series
  - Post-purchase customer journeys
  - All other customer journeys

> **Note about synced contacts**
>
> Some information in your e-commerce platform is more specific to the work you will be doing over there, so you may have data on things such as whether you need to collect tax for that contact present in their profile in Shopify, but not within their contact profile in Mailchimp.

The movement of data from one platform to the other, after the initial sync, is based on actions your customers take, as we saw in the example. As I, the customer in that scenario, made choices during my shopping experience, that dictated what information about me was moved between the two applications.

Additionally, as I make purchases from your store, data about those products and what the purchase entailed will be synced back to Mailchimp as well. As we saw in *Chapter 13*, you will be able to see a contact profile page for a specific customer and which products they purchased when looking at their profile by doing the following:

1. Click on the email address of the specific contact.

2. You will notice **Average order value** at the top of the contact profile.
3. Scroll down to the **Activity Feed** section.
4. Select **E-Commerce** from the **Activity Type** dropdown (*Figure 14.8*).

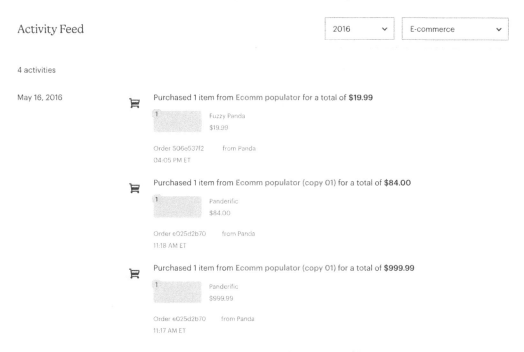

Figure 14.8 – Activity Feed contact profile

The great thing about this movement of data to Mailchimp is it really expands the dataset you have to work with when we think about refining your marketing channels, so let's go through how this type of integration impacts the data in your Mailchimp account.

How to expand your marketing efforts with your commerce data

Ultimately, the best use of many of these integrations is to help make sure that as people purchase items through your store, you can continue to contact those people who are interested in following your business. Keeping these people in your marketing funnel helps to increase the possible revenue you can achieve by marketing to them. In previous chapters, we talked about how we can use data to better target your contacts. By narrowing the scope of your marketing to be more specific to what your subscribers are genuinely interested in, you will see more engagement over time. This is equally true for commerce data.

For example, if you are an e-commerce store with a brick-and-mortar location, it can be helpful to know what zip code your contacts live in. That way, you can target marketing about events at your store specifically to people who are in your area and able to come to them. Similarly, with the e-commerce data available to you within Mailchimp, you can leverage segmenting from *Chapter 4, Tags, and Segments*, to focus on e-commerce data points as a mechanism for targeting your marketing for your contacts. These segmenting options become available as data is synced over from your e-commerce platform. These options include the following:

- **Total number of orders**
- **Average number of Products per order**
- **Total number of orders**
- **Products purchased**
- **Purchase activity**
- **Purchase date**
- **Average amount spent per order**
- **Amount spent on a single order**
- **Amount spent in total**

This wealth of e-commerce data, paired with the data that you accumulate over time through your Mailchimp forms and website, means that you can increase the nuance of your marketing efforts. As your marketing channels and communications become tailored to your audience, you'll see an increase in engagement and revenue, which is likely the reason why you sought out a marketing automation platform.

Summary

In this chapter, we learned where you can go within the Mailchimp application to connect your e-commerce platform in the event that you already sell products online through another application. Walking through an example integration connection, we then got to the really important part, which is *why* you would want to connect Mailchimp to your e-commerce platform to begin with. We went through how the data about your contacts, their purchases, and their products moves from one place to the next, and from there, we went over some of the uses of that data inside your Mailchimp account.

The greatest benefit of an all-in-one marketing platform such as Mailchimp, and the reason you should integrate it with your other platforms and applications whenever possible, is that the more data you have about your contacts at your disposal, the more well tailored and harmonized your marketing will be for the people you want to engage with. In the next two chapters, we'll expand to talk a bit more about additional types of integrations you might consider using (if you are not already) and how to connect them.

Further reading

- *About Integrations*: https://eepurl.com/dyij1l
- *Connect or Disconnect Mailchimp for Shopify*: https://eepurl.com/dNIM8U
- *Manage User Levels in Your Account*: https://eepurl.com/dyimdf
- *All the Segmenting Options*: https://eepurl.com/dyikND
- *Segment an Audience by Purchase Activity*: https://eepurl.com/dyimBn
- *View or Export Your Contacts*: https://eepurl.com/dyinqP

15
Form and Survey Integrations

In the previous chapter, *Chapter 14*, we started talking about integrations and the benefits of connecting other applications and platforms to your Mailchimp account.

In this chapter, we'll be going over the following:

- Using form and survey integrations to build your audience
- How to find the right integration and connect it

As we saw in the e-commerce integration chapter (*Chapter 14*), we will go through how you can find integrations for existing forms or websites to connect to your Mailchimp account. That way, you can leverage any related traffic in your marketing efforts in Mailchimp. Even better, when you use applications that connect your forms and surveys, you can use those to grow your audience. We covered the types of forms offered *inside* the Mailchimp application in *Chapter 6*. In this chapter, we will be looking at some of the most popular integrations in the event that you're already using another website builder *outside* of Mailchimp.

Technical requirements

In order to leverage integration with another platform, you will need the login information for that other platform. Mailchimp will not be able to connect with another application without the credentials for your account with that application. So, keep in mind that you should have that other account and its credentials available to you before starting.

Form and survey integrations can be a really great option for using embedded and pop-up forms on a website you might already use outside of Mailchimp. Let's take a look at where you can find some of these integrations and how to leverage them.

Using form and survey integrations to build your audience

When you're logged into your Mailchimp account, you can see a highlight of some of the most common integrations for different purposes by doing the following:

1. Click on **Integrations** in the left-hand navigation menu.
2. Click on **Discover** in the sub-menu.

This will take you to an interface where you can see some options at a single glance, as seen in *Figure 15.1*.

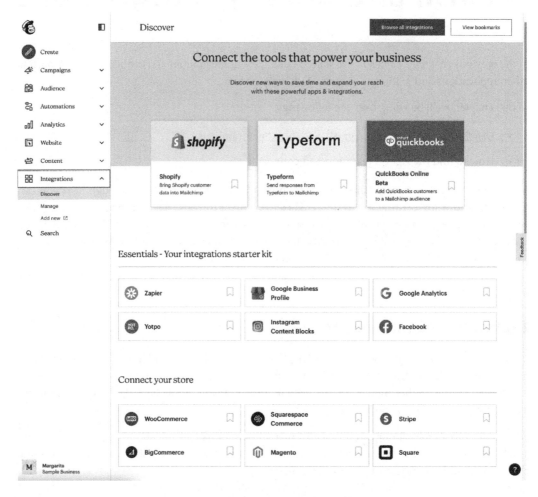

Figure 15.1 – Discover integrations page

On this page, you'll see featured integrations at the top and then there are a number of popular integrations. Let's take a look at some of these integrations and what kinds of forms and funnels into your audience they offer:

- **Typeform**: Typeform is a company that offers some great, simple forms and surveys. If your organization is already leveraging Typeform to run surveys or to create forms for people to sign up for your content, you can connect this integration to send answers to your forms to a specified audience in Mailchimp.
- **Mailmunch**: This is a fairly popular option for pop-up and sign-up widgets that can be built in a visual builder like Mailchimp's. It's compatible with WordPress, Shopify, Squarespace, Weebly, and Wix, to name just a few platforms.
- **SurveyMonkey**: One of the better-known survey form applications, this is a great integration to use if you have an existing SurveyMonkey account to collect feedback and information from your audience.

Those are the primary integrations displayed on the **Discover** dashboard in the Mailchimp application, but if you're a user of another application, you can investigate whether it's available in the larger directory. When logged into your Mailchimp account, do the following:

1. Click on **Integrations** in the left-hand navigation menu.
2. Click on **Discover** in the sub-menu.
3. Click on the **Browse all integrations** button in the upper right-hand corner (*Figure 15.2*).

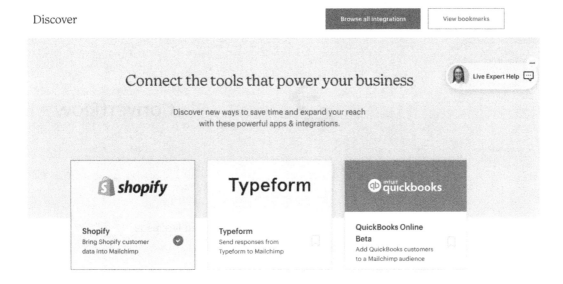

Figure 15.2 – Discover integrations page

This will take you to the broader **Connect Apps & Integrations** marketplace on Mailchimp's website. Along the left-hand side, there is a **Category** panel where you can filter the types of integrations, and there is a **Forms & Surveys** option. This will give you a fuller list of integrations that offer form and survey applications that can be integrated with your Mailchimp account. Similarly, you can use the search bar at the top to look for integration with a particular application. You can see both the **Category** menu and the **Search** bar in *Figure 15.3*.

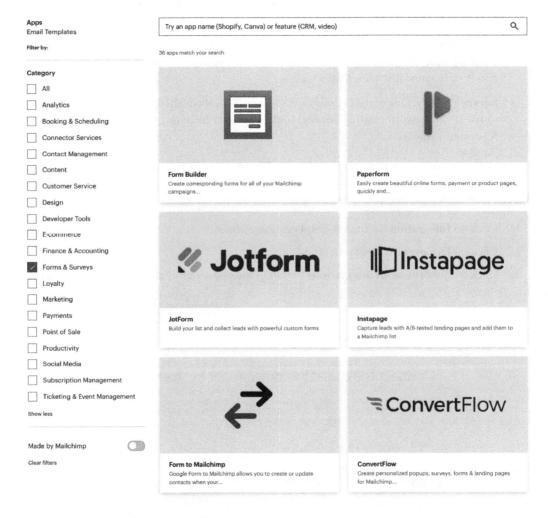

Figure 15.3 – Connect apps and integrations marketplace page

I think of these types of integrations as being grouped together into two types:

- **Website integrations**: These integrations connect your existing website, which may house contact information for subscribers already, with your Mailchimp audience.
- **Form & survey add-on integrations**: These integrations help with the creation of the form or survey itself and the connection to your audience in your Mailchimp account.

The goal with any of these form and survey integrations is to funnel people into your audience in one place or another. Even if you have channels on disparate platforms (for example, maybe you manage your email and automation channels through Mailchimp and your website and e-commerce through different platforms), you want to be able to use at least one as your *source of truth* – one platform that houses the majority of the context and contact information about your audience.

By leveraging integrations on your website or adding on forms and surveys, you're expanding your sales and marketing funnel. As a reminder, in *Chapter 6*, we touched on the conceptual sales funnel (*Figure 15.4*).

Figure 15.4 – Traditional conceptual sales funnel

By adding forms and surveys, you're expanding the number of people who have the opportunity in the **Consideration** portion of the funnel to opt in to follow along with your audience. Because funnels are never 100%, meaning that not all of the people who enter at the top of the funnel will decide that they'd like to subscribe, you want to make sure that you increase the number of opportunities they have to make a choice about your content, brand, or products.

So, leveraging the search bar at the top of *Figure 15.3*, you can search for an integration that pairs up with your website specifically. For example, if you are already using Squarespace to host your website, you can type Squarespace into the **Search** bar and you'll see integrations for the two types of websites Squarespace offers, as seen in *Figure 15.5*.

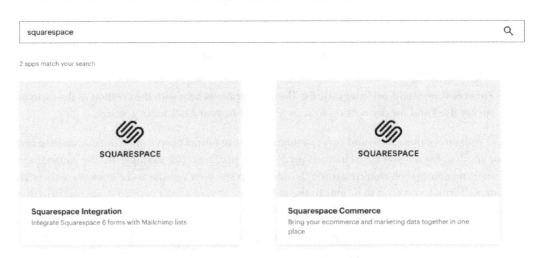

Figure 15.5 – Squarespace integration results

If I were a Squarespace website user, I could click on the **Squarespace Integration** option, which is an integration developed by Squarespace specifically to help you create forms for your Squarespace site and connect those form fields directly to your Mailchimp audience fields.

Additionally, there are some integrations for applications such as Zapier. Zapier is a really great application to use as a bridge between thousands of other apps. It allows you to connect two platforms that may not already have native integration. There are so many options in the broader digital marketing and e-commerce platform marketplace that applications such as Zapier are really great for filling in those gaps where connections between all applications might not already exist. We'll cover Zapier as a connectivity app in *Chapter 16*.

Now that we have a sense of what kinds of integrations exist for leveraging forms and surveys, whether you have a website that has its own integration or need integration for a website that doesn't have its own integration, let's dive further into how to find those integrations and walk through some examples of what connecting an integration might entail.

How to find the right integration and connect it

As we covered earlier in this chapter, let's walk through the steps to reach the **Integrations** interface. When you're logged into your Mailchimp account, you can reach the dashboard by doing the following:

1. Click on **Integrations** in the left-hand navigation menu.
2. Click on **Discover** in the sub-menu.

This will take you to the **Discover** interface in *Figure 15.6*:

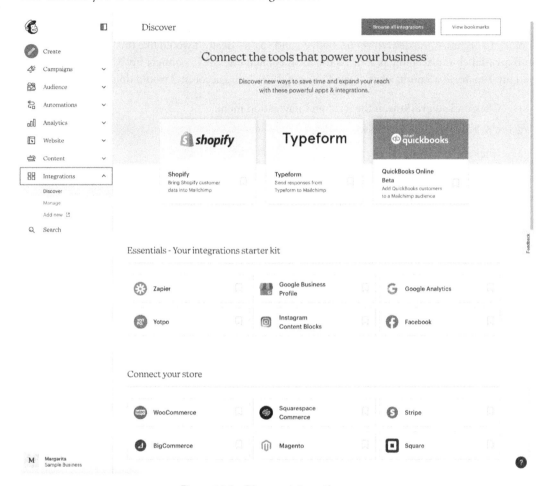

Figure 15.6 – Discover integrations page

On this page, you can select any of these integrations if they correspond to an application you use outside of Mailchimp. Or, alternatively, if you don't see an integration on the main page there, you can search for one by clicking on **Browse all integrations** in the upper right-hand corner.

When you find an integration, you can click on the block that corresponds to the integration and that will take you to a page for the integration itself. The page for that specific integration will provide a description of the application you're integrating with and, most importantly, the page will give you context on what the integration will do for you. Let's check out an example.

For the purposes of this example, let's say I'm an event planner. When I am conducting an intake for a project, I use a standard form I made using Typeform to collect not just the contact information for my client but also some details about what they're looking for. Details such as what size event they're looking to organize, the desired venue, budget, and so on. Ideally, I would like this information to go into my Mailchimp account as soon as the form is filled out. So, to connect my Mailchimp account and my Typeform account, when logged into my Mailchimp account, I would do the following:

1. Click on **Integrations** in the left-hand navigation menu.
2. Click on **Discover** in the sub-menu.
3. Click on **Typeform**.
4. Click on **Get Started**.
5. Click on **Grow your Mailchimp contact audience**.
6. Click on **Use this integration**.
7. Log into my Typeform account (*Figure 15.7*).

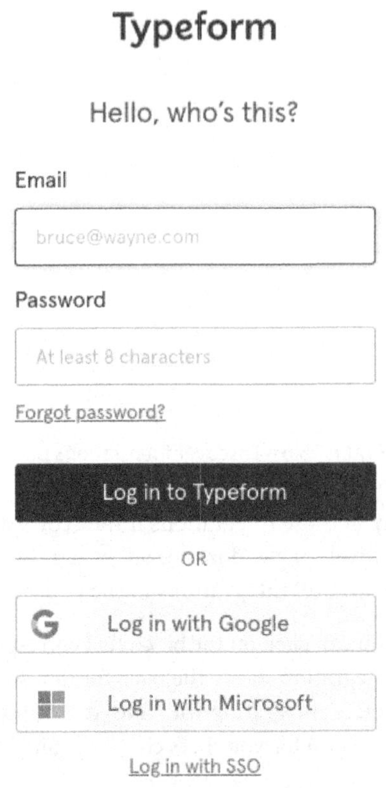

Typeform

Hello, who's this?

Email

bruce@wayne.com

Password

At least 8 characters

Forgot password?

Log in to Typeform

———— OR ————

G Log in with Google

▦ Log in with Microsoft

Log in with SSO

Figure 15.7 – Typeform integration login page

Once you log in to your Typeform account, you will be shown a drop-down menu of the existing forms in your account that you can select from, as seen in *Figure 15.8*. And then you can click on **Connect**.

Figure 15.8 – Typeform connection page

When you've selected a form and clicked **Connect**, it will take you to a page where you will confirm that you authorize data to be transmitted by the integration when a response is submitted to the Typeform form. When you click on **Authenticate**, it will pop up a window where you will log in to your Mailchimp account, as seen in *Figure 15.9*:

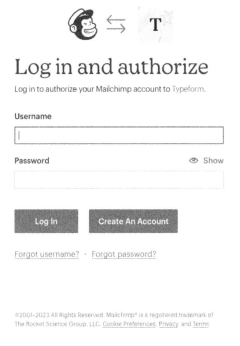

Figure 15.9 – Typeform Mailchimp integration authentication

When you log in here, you will then click on **Allow** to move on to setting up the audience in your Mailchimp account. Next, you'll select the name of the audience you'd like the data to go to and then, finally, you'll map the questions in your form to a field in your Mailchimp audience (*Figure 15.10*).

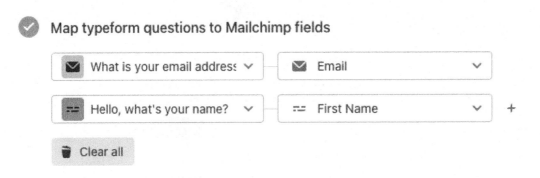

Figure 15.10 – Audience mapping step

When you're done, you can click **Save** and this will complete the connection. From that point forward, as people fill out your form, information will be passed over to your audience in Mailchimp and you can confirm that the integration is connected to your Mailchimp account by looking at the **Integration Discover** page, where you will see a check mark on the Typeform integration card, as seen in *Figure 15.11*:

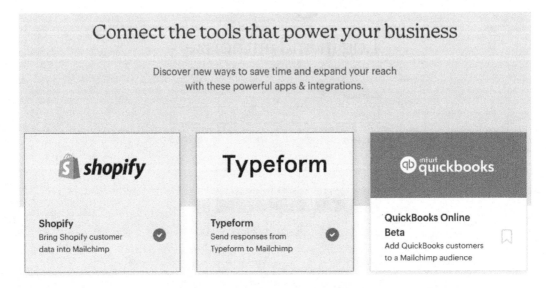

Figure 15.11 – Integration Discover page

Connecting integrations will largely follow the same pattern:

1. Choose the integration.
2. Authenticate the integration.
3. Set up the integration mapping (how data is handled from one app to another).
4. Syncing.

Generally, from that point forward, the integration will handle the movement of data in alignment with the settings and mappings. But, keeping that in mind, you'll largely be focusing on looking for an integration that either bridges the two applications you're already using (Mailchimp plus another platform) or an integration that augments or creates a form or survey in a specific aesthetic you feel you can't achieve within Mailchimp.

Summary

In this chapter, you learned where you can go within the Mailchimp application to connect your existing website platform in the event that you're already hosting your website through another application, and how to find an integration that will augment that website with additional forms or surveys. We reviewed all the various ways in the Mailchimp application you can find available integrations to help you connect your existing digital presence with your Mailchimp account. Additionally, we walked through how to search for a specific integration when you have one in mind and how to connect that integration.

In the next chapter, we'll move on to reviewing integrations for **Customer Relationship Management** (**CRM**), to get your customer data married to your Mailchimp account.

Further reading

- *About Integrations*: `https://eepurl.com/dyij1l`
- *Connect or Disconnect Mailchimp for Shopify*: `https://eepurl.com/dNIM8U`
- *Manage User Levels in Your Account*: `https://eepurl.com/dyimdf`
- *Zapier Integration*: `https://mailchimp.com/integrations/zapier/`

16
CRM and Connectivity Integrations

Up to this point, we've covered two really big categories of integrations you may need: e-commerce integrations and form or survey integrations. In this chapter, I'd like to tackle the next big category of integration people use most commonly: integrations to connect your existing **customer relationship management system** (referred to as a **CRM** from this point onward) with your Mailchimp account and general connectivity integrations. Central to your Mailchimp account, and digital marketing more broadly, is how you leverage and access your data. If you have already used a CRM, you should know that better than those who may just be starting their marketing journey.

In this chapter, we'll be going over the following topics:

- Popular CRM and connectivity integrations and why to connect them
- What the various integration paths are and how to find and use them
- Understanding where data is present when syncing is initiated and whether it unlocks any advanced features

As in the other integration chapters, I want to be sure to clarify what we mean by **integration** within the context of Mailchimp. Integration here is being used to refer to some application serving as an intermediary to pass data from one platform to the other. These integrations can be developed by Mailchimp or another developer (for example, possibly the other platform you're looking to integrate), but fundamentally, you can think of them as a bridge that helps to ensure that your two separate platforms are sharing the information you want in both places.

Technical requirements

In order to leverage integration with another platform, you will need the login information for that other platform. Mailchimp will not be able to connect with another application without the credentials for your account with that other software. So, keep in mind that you should have that other account and its credentials available to you before starting.

Additionally, it's generally good practice to create a backup of the audience you plan on syncing any integration to. This is just a precaution, but you can see the steps for exporting contacts in *Chapter 3*.

Popular CRM and connectivity integrations and why to connect them

CRM software is generally utilized to maintain information about a business's sales, transactions, accounting, and other operational data so that it's centrally accessible. From a growth standpoint, CRMs are designed to help you to conceptualize your engagement funnel with customers. If you think about your overall customer ecosystem, somewhere in your funnel there might be people who are prospective clients of yours. Let's say we sell a physical product in wholesale quantities, and there are people who have reached out to us expressing an interest in carrying our product on their website or in a physical store.

These types of contacts may exist in our CRM as a prospect, but would not be in our marketing funnel currently because they have not provided consent to receive marketing (for email marketing, you must receive consent to abide by CAN-SPAM and other anti-spam laws). However, as we work with them as a wholesale customer, we may eventually receive consent, and in our CRM, I may mark them as a customer instead of a prospect. When that shift happens in my CRM, we'd like to make sure that their data moves from our CRM to our Mailchimp account to ensure that they're included in our marketing emails and other channels.

Doing that and having integrations connecting the different platforms we're using helps to ensure that we're maximizing our opportunities to market to the appropriate contacts. Additionally, by leveraging integration to manage that process, we are not in the position of needing to manually copy contacts from one application to another and can focus our efforts on other parts of our business. This type of automation of what might have previously been small, manual data management really empowers us to maximize the audiences and touchpoints we may be cultivating across more than just one platform.

So, to view available integrations, when you're logged in to your Mailchimp account, you can see a highlight of some of the most common integrations for different purposes by doing the following:

1. Clicking on **Integrations** in the left-hand navigation menu
2. Clicking on **Discover** in the sub-menu

This will take you to an interface where you can see some options at a single glance, as seen in *Figure 16.1*:

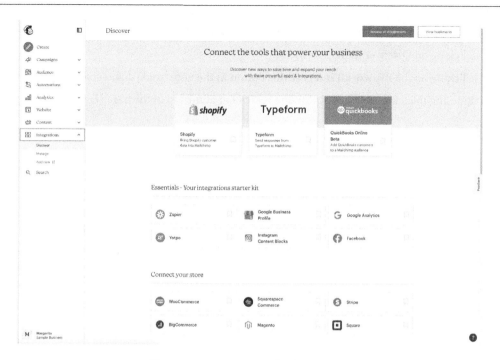

Figure 16.1 – Integrations | Discover page

The most popular CRM is Salesforce and an integration for it can be found on the main **Discover** page under the **Sync your contacts** section. If you are not looking for a CRM-specific integration, another popular option is an integration such as Zapier, also found on the **Discover** page. Zapier is an application that can connect hundreds of applications with one another. It's a really flexible option that I've mentioned previously in other chapters where we've discussed integrations and the data that moves from a platform into your Mailchimp account (*Chapters 12*, *14*, and *15*). With that said, let's talk about how we search for integrations generally and then how we use them.

What the various integration paths are and how to find and use them

In this section, we'll go through the variety of ways you can find integrations either inside of the Mailchimp application itself or through the integration marketplace. But first and foremost, we have to review how to browse for integrations.

Browsing for integrations

Much like in *Chapter 15*, you can search for integrations that may be compatible with the CRM you're leveraging by doing the following:

1. Clicking on **Integrations** in the left-hand navigation menu
2. Clicking on **Discover** in the sub-menu
3. Clicking on the **Browse all integrations** button in the upper right-hand corner
4. Entering the name of your CRM in the search bar at the top of the page (*Figure 16.2*)

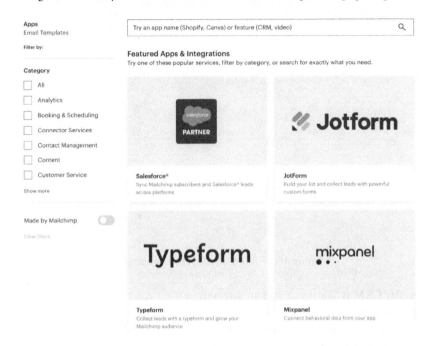

Figure 16.2 – Connect apps and integrations Marketplace page

As noted in *Chapter 15*, even if your preferred CRM doesn't have its own integration listed, you can use really useful applications such as Zapier to act as a go-between to integrate with Mailchimp (a link to the integration directory for Zapier is included in the *Further reading* section of this chapter).

But CRMs tend to be rather large and complex platforms, so while generally speaking they'll still follow the same broad, conceptual we've talked about with other integrations, they may have more for you to map and set up when you think about matching your data in the CRM with how you would like the data to appear on the Mailchimp side.

> **A note about contact data in CRMs**
>
> CRMs are designed to store data about people in all stages of the traditional sales funnel. This means that you may have data for contacts that shouldn't be marketed to just yet and with whom you are still cultivating a relationship. So, keep in mind that not all the contacts in your CRM can or should necessarily be synced over when you first connect your integration of choice.

Once you know the answer to whether there is an integration available for your specific CRM or not, that will largely dictate whether you're able to move forward with a single installation or whether you need to look into the use of a bridge application such as Zapier. This is because in order to leverage the integration for an intermediary application, you would first need to make an account with that secondary application outside of Mailchimp. Next, we'll walk through a sample integration with Salesforce and then Zapier.

Sample integration walk-throughs

Let's say you're already leveraging Salesforce; you would, for example, be able to use the **Mailchimp for Salesforce** integration, which would create a one-to-one connection between Mailchimp and Salesforce. So, if you were looking to install that integration, while logged in to your Mailchimp account, you would do the following:

1. Click on **Integrations** in the left-hand navigation menu.
2. Click on **Discover** in the sub-menu.
3. Scroll down to the **Sync your contacts** section and click on **Salesforce**.
4. Click on the **Connect Now** button.
5. Click on the **Get It Now** button.
6. Log in to your **Salesforce Trailblazer.me** account.

This will then take you to where you begin the installation walk-through. The detailed walk-through can be found in the *Further reading* section (*Connect your Salesforce Account to Mailchimp*). The installation process is fairly hands-off. After you log in, you'll only have a few steps to follow:

1. Click on the **Install in Production** button.
2. Check the box to agree to the terms and conditions.
3. Click **Install for All Users**.
4. Check the **Yes, grant access to these third-party web sites** box.

From there, the installation will proceed automatically. It'll take a minute or so and then you will log in to your Mailchimp account as the final authentication. If you're familiar with Salesforce, their application refers to secondary integrations that help to augment the capabilities of their platform as apps, and they have a menu called **App Launcher**, where applications such as Mailchimp for Salesforce will be available to you after the installation takes place (*Figure 16.3*).

250 CRM and Connectivity Integrations

Figure 16.3 – Salesforce App Launcher menu

When you click on this integration, then click on **MC Setup**, if you skipped logging in to your Mailchimp account previously, you will be prompted to log in before proceeding. From this point, there are four activities that you can engage in with this integration:

- **Lead creation**: This is where you would choose whether you would like Mailchimp to be able to send leads back to Salesforce, essentially making it so that if there is a contact in your Mailchimp account that is not accounted for in your Salesforce account, the integration will pass it from Mailchimp back to Salesforce.
- **Field mapping**: This is similar to the mapping steps we've covered with other integrations. It's the part of the integration where you will match contact fields in Salesforce with the field the data corresponds to in your Mailchimp audience (*Figure 16.4*).

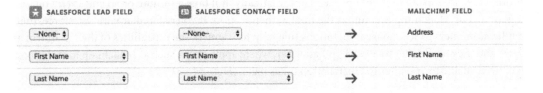

Figure 16.4 – Mailchimp for Salesforce Mappings interface

- **Permission settings**: This is where you would be able to adjust the settings for Salesforce users to be able to leverage the integration. In order to allow a specific Salesforce user (outside of the admin that set up the integration) to work with the integration, you'll want to provide them with **MailChimp Admin** and **MailChimp User** permissions (*Figure 16.5*).

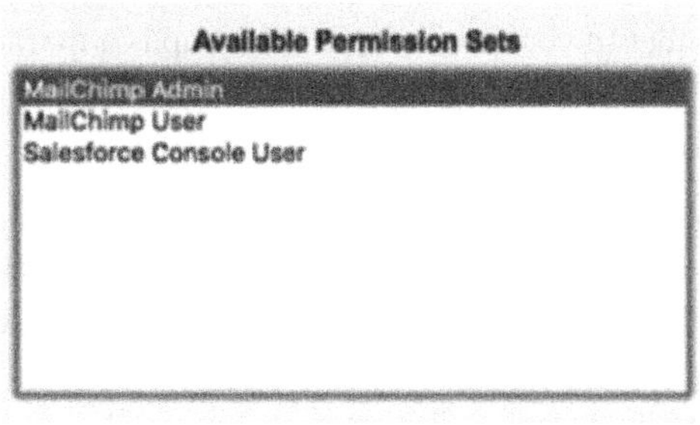

Figure 16.5 – Mailchimp for Salesforce Available Permission Sets interface

- **Sync settings**: The integration is quite flexible in the sense that you can choose how much data you want to keep in your CRM by adjusting how long activity data is maintained. Additionally, you can choose to sync one Mailchimp audience and not another if you would like. For each audience, you will have a drop-down menu where you can choose from options such as keeping all activity, keeping activity for seven days, or even not syncing an audience at all. You can see all the sync options in *Figure 16.6*.

Figure 16.6 – Mailchimp for Salesforce activity sync drop-down menu

The heart of what we're trying to achieve with CRM integrations such as Mailchimp for Salesforce can be encapsulated in the function of features such as the sync settings. Having not only alignment between the data in your different platforms but also access to robust data in your Mailchimp platform means that you can leverage more of the features we covered in earlier chapters.

If you're not already leveraging a CRM, you can largely utilize an audience in your Mailchimp account in a similar way. However, depending on the format of your business and the nature of your audience, there may be a reason you may want to consider a CRM platform. Some reasons include the following:

- **Marketing consent**: Outside of transactional purchases to a store triggering a contact being added as a transactional contact to your audience, Mailchimp is a marketing automation platform, which means that the majority of your audience should be opted in to receive marketing. This is to maintain compliance with different spam laws.
- **Contact data availability**: Because the primary channels for digital marketing revolve around email, a saved audience member within Mailchimp requires at minimum an email address. Typically, within a CRM, you don't necessarily need an email address to create an entry. So, if your business has a case for prospects and perhaps creating contact entries with a physical address and not an email address, a CRM may be a great fit.

Next, let's walk through connecting Zapier.

Zapier integration

For connectivity integrations such as Zapier, what we're conceptually trying to accomplish is the movement of data from a platform into Mailchimp, and Zapier will act as our intermediary. The way Zapier works is that you can establish within their application what they refer to as **Zaps**. Zaps are how Zapier refers to creating an automation workflow. When you set up an automation, Zapier receives the information and then "zaps" that information from one place to another.

If you would like an application you're already using to be connected to your Mailchimp account through a Zapier account, when you are logged in to your Mailchimp account, you can find the Zapier integration by doing the following:

1. Clicking on **Integrations** in the left-hand navigation menu
2. Clicking on **Discover** in the sub-menu
3. Clicking on **Zapier** from the **Discover** page
4. Clicking on **Learn More**

This will take you to a page where you can search for and see the hundreds of applications that Zapier can act as a bridge for, as seen in *Figure 16.7*.

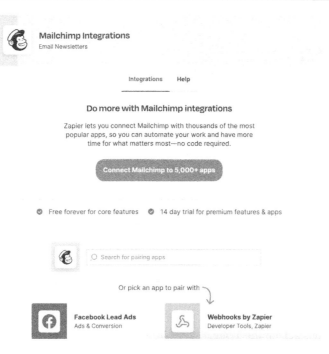

Figure 16.7 – Zapier integration dashboard

From here, when you click on **Connect Mailchimp to 5,000+ apps**, you will be taken to a login page where you can create an account or log in to an existing Zapier account. Once you've logged in to the account, you will see your Zapier dashboard. At the top, you will see a **Make a Zap** interface to help you build out a Zap to connect an app to your Mailchimp account. To provide an example, let's say you want to use Zapier to connect an application such as Typeform. You would do the following:

1. Type `Typeform` in the **Connect this app** field.
2. Type `Mailchimp` into the **with this one!** field.

This will then reveal the next step where you would fill out the trigger and the action you would like Zapier to take. These are essentially the instructions you would like Zapier to follow for you as part of the automation you're setting up. So, for example, I would enter the following:

1. **New Entry** into **When this happens…**
2. **Add/Update Subscriber** into **then do this!**

Once you've set up the action you would like Zapier to take on your behalf, you can then click on the **Try it** button. You can see the interface to create the basis for this Zap in *Figure 16.8*.

254　CRM and Connectivity Integrations

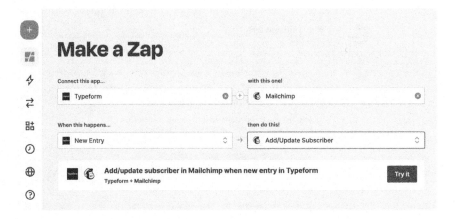

Figure 16.8 – Filling out a sample Zap

Once you've clicked on **Try it**, this will take you to the more robust Zap builder. Within the builder, Zapier will allow you to edit one trigger or action at a time. When you click on one of the items, it will open up the block where you can edit the conditions under which the trigger or action occurs. For example, if you click on the **Trigger** block, it will open up a block where you will be prompted to connect the Typeform account where the trigger you set in *Figure 16.8* should come from, as seen in *Figure 16.9*.

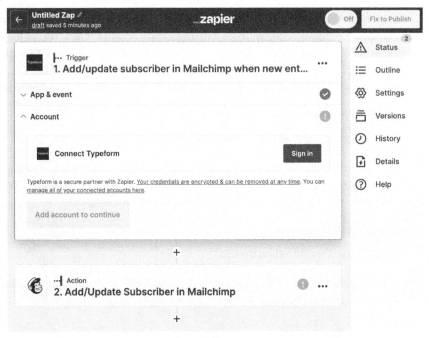

Figure 16.9 – Editing the Typeform trigger

Once you've logged in to your Typeform account, this will then pop up a trigger field where you will select where the form data will come from. Then, when the form is confirmed, you can have Zapier run a test and pull a recent result just so you can see what the data will look like. From there, Zapier will move you on to the action. This is where you tell Zapier what data you would like in your Mailchimp account. You will choose your Mailchimp audience for the data to be moved to. You'll be given options such as whether Zapier should send data for subscribers that already exist so that Mailchimp will update that contact's data or whether you would like only new contacts. You can choose whether the new contacts are added to a group or have a tag added to them when they're moved to Mailchimp. You can see some of these options in *Figure 16.10*.

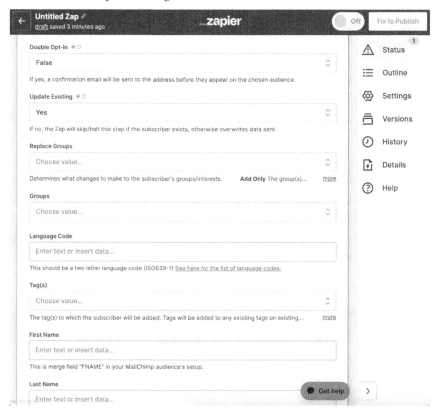

Figure 16.10 – Editing the Typeform trigger

When you've made decisions about how data is handled and what data does and doesn't come with the Zap, you can click on **Continue** and then **Publish**! Once the Zap is published, Zapier will begin handling the movement of data from Typeform to Mailchimp. Zapier offers these types of functions for thousands of integrations you can connect with your Mailchimp account. So, even if you can't find a dedicated integration for your desired application to connect to Mailchimp, you can still get data flowing to help make sure you can make the best use of any data you have elsewhere.

If you're considering a CRM, there are a bunch on the market, though some of the most popular are Salesforce, Zoho, Sage, and HubSpot. Zapier is definitely one of the best connectivity applications for bridging data from one place to another.

Now, let's take a look at how some of the additional data that may come from a CRM or connectivity integration can be leveraged with some of the features we've discussed in previous chapters.

Understanding where data is present when syncing is initiated and associated advanced features

As a reminder, the majority of the data you likely have housed in a CRM is going to be similar or correspond directly to what we discussed as subscriber contact data in *Chapter 3*, and *Chapter 4*. It tends to be data about who that contact is and, as we've covered repeatedly in various places in this book, data on your audience can be very powerful for helping you to engage with them. Referring specifically back to something we mentioned in *Chapter 4*:

> *Using and developing a strategy for personalization, including personalizing things such as the products and services you offer or your website, can increase the impact of your revenue.*

Leveraging more specific and granular data helps you to better refine your marketing strategies. So, ensuring you have access to as much data as possible inside your Mailchimp account from other applications you may have already been using helps to make sure you're maximizing the amount of data you have available for driving your marketing.

To view data about a whole audience, you can view your contact table when logged in to your Mailchimp account by doing the following:

1. Click on **Audience** in the left-hand navigation menu.
2. Select **All contacts** from the sub-menu in the left-hand navigation menu.

This will take you to a table where you can see your contacts and a table of the data associated with those people. By default, it will let you scroll to the right if there are more columns than will fit on your screen, but you also have a **Toggle Columns** option (*Figure 16.11*) where you can choose which pieces of subscriber data are visible all at once in the table for you to scroll through.

Understanding where data is present when syncing is initiated and associated advanced features

Figure 16.11 – All contacts table

This is also where you would go to access the segment-building interface if you would like to build a segment to specifically target a subset of your contacts. For example, let's say I have both a digital store for selling my products and a physical brick-and-mortar location. If I am promoting events at the store, I may want to create a segment for people within a specific number of miles from my store. To do that, when looking at this contact table, I would do the following:

1. Click on **New Segment**.
2. Click on **Regular Segment** from the drop-down menu.
3. Select **Location** from the variable drop-down menu.
4. Enter a city or zip code into the blank field.
5. Click on **Validate Location**.
6. Click on **Use This Location**.
7. Select a number of miles.
8. Click on **Preview Segment**.

We can see a sample using **Atlanta** as an example in *Figure 16.12*.

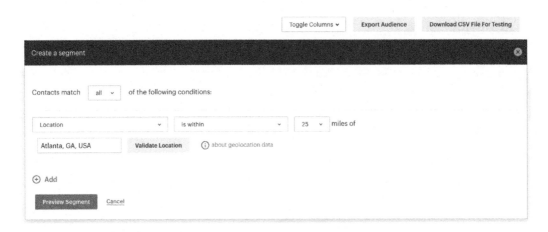

Figure 16.12 – Location segment building

You can then send a targeted email to people who would actually be able to potentially take advantage of an in-person event at your brick-and-mortar location. You may be asking yourself:

Why would I want to do something like that anyway?

Which is a fair question! Let's think of it from two perspectives:

- *From our contact's perspective*, it might be really annoying to receive a marketing email about an event they can't attend even if they really wanted to. If that happens frequently enough, instead of asking themselves whether they're ready to purchase something, they might be wondering, *"Why do I even subscribe to them if there's not really anything for me in these emails in my inbox?"* In a digital marketing-saturated world, people receive so much information constantly, so the less personalized to their interests that content is, the less likely that person is to engage repeatedly.

- *From the perspective of the marketer*, over time, their data on engagement will be very broad and difficult to extrapolate a conclusion from. For example, let's say we're comparing the performance of two email marketing campaigns where both campaigns went to 100% of our audience with no regard for their interest.

    Email 1 was an email about a promotion on our website (so it's accessible to all of our contacts). Email 2 was an email about an in-store-only promotion and had no promotion for people going to our website (so the promotion is only accessible to a percentage of our contacts). If we compare these two, we might hope to see similar amounts of engagement, and if we see much lower engagement on Email 2, we'd be right to wonder why. But the reality is, Email 2 might have experienced similar proportional engagement, but our reporting isn't going to reflect that because the emails went to everyone. We'd be better served to target Email 2 so that we can see what the **rate** of engagement was as opposed to the whole numbers.

Understanding where data is present when syncing is initiated and associated advanced features   259

You can also view the data coming over from your connected CRM within a specific subscriber's profile as well. Let's say you are an agency and you manage your clients and the information they receive through Mailchimp. To prepare for a conversation with them, you may want to view not only their contact data (which is synced for consistency with your CRM through an integration) but also their activity. When logged in to your Mailchimp account, you can either use the **Search** option in the left-hand navigation menu to search for that specific contact or you can click on **Audience** (*Figure 16.13*).

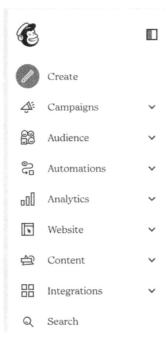

Figure 16.13 – Left-hand navigation menu with Audience and Search

If you want to navigate to them manually, when you click on **Audience**, you would then do the following:

1. Click on **All contacts** from the left-hand navigation sub-menu.
2. Click on the specific email address in the contact table.

Your audience member's contact detail page will provide you with all the known information about that person that has been collected through a Mailchimp form or integration (*Figure 16.14*).

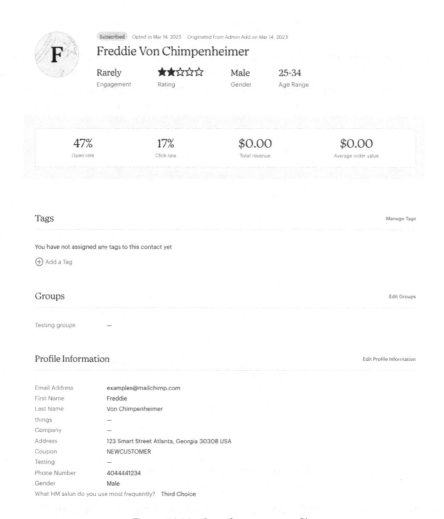

Figure 16.14 – Specific contact profile

In that way, you can use that and any activity data you may need to reference when having a conversation with your client.

You can also refine your **customer journeys** to specifically go to contacts who come over from your CRM. In *Chapter 12*, we covered building a sample customer journey targeting contacts when they're added to our audience. If you wanted, you could even refine those journeys to only be sent to people coming over from specific integrations. You do this by adding a segment to filter the people who qualify for the customer journey, as seen in *Figure 16.15*.

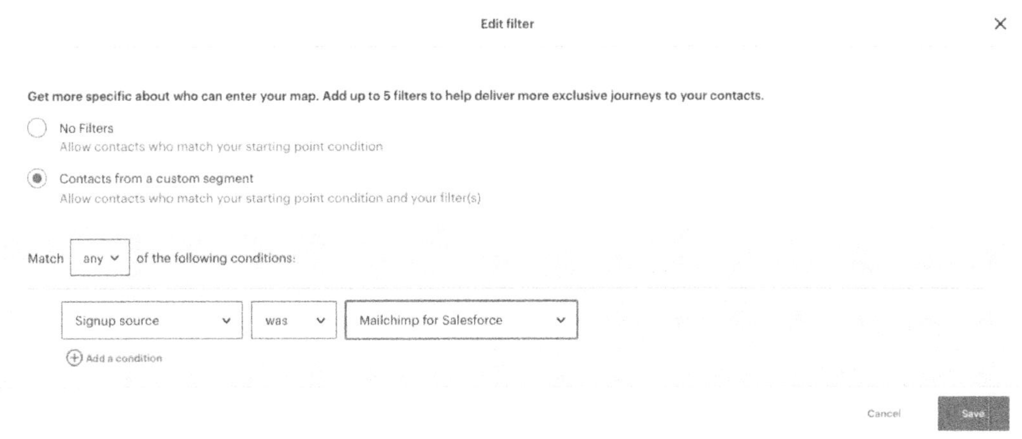

Figure 16.15 – Customer journey subscriber filter

In this example, we can see the **Mailchimp for Salesforce** integration is the selected filter, but you can use any integration that's connected to your account. As you connect integrations, more and more will appear here, including e-commerce integrations and form and survey integrations, as we've covered in previous chapters.

We can see how having access to more data within your Mailchimp account unlocks your ability to leverage more and more of the features we've discussed in the chapters of this book.

Summary

In this chapter, we learned what a CRM is and what distinguishes it from platforms such as Mailchimp. We also covered where within the Mailchimp application you can find integrations for connecting Mailchimp to any existing CRM you might already be leveraging. Walking through where to find the integrations themselves, we also talked through some of the different types of integrations (direct or bridge integrations) and, at a high level, reviewed what the integration process is like for one of the most popular CRM platforms.

From there, we really got down to the heart of why you might consider a CRM external to Mailchimp but, most importantly, how having access to more robust data enables greater utilization of the features that were covered earlier in the book. By leveraging data, you can personalize your content more and more over time, which drives engagement by making your audience feel seen and connected to your brand and/or product.

More accurate and personalized content tends to appear more polished and intimate, which over time makes your contacts feel connected to your brand. Finally, in the next chapter, we're going to roll all of these concepts together and go through some real-world examples of how your channels might work in concert for different businesses/organizations.

Further reading

- *About Integrations*: `https://eepurl.com/dyij11`
- *Manage User Levels in Your Account*: `https://eepurl.com/dyimdf`
- *Zapier integration*: `https://mailchimp.com/integrations/zapier/`
- *Mailchimp for Salesforce integration*: `https://mailchimp.com/integrations/mailchimp-for-salesforce/`
- *About the Salesforce Integration*: `https://eepurl.com/dyikcf`
- *Connect Your Salesforce Account to Mailchimp*: `https://eepurl.com/dyik35`
- *Customize the Salesforce Integration*: `https://eepurl.com/dyilpH`
- *Use the Salesforce Query Builder*: `https://eepurl.com/dyinj1`

17
Use Cases and Real-World Examples

In this chapter, we will focus on some end-to-end real-world examples. Throughout the book, I've provided some examples that explain how to apply specific features to different types of businesses or organizations. However, I think it would be helpful to review some of those types of businesses/organizations together and note which features could be used together within the Mailchimp platform to maximize your usage of the app.

In this chapter, we'll be going over the following categories of businesses/organizations:

- Starting a business or online presence
- Bricks and mortar to a digital presence
- Service-based business models

For each use case, I'll provide you with a scenario and some context on the hypothetical business. From there, we'll discuss which features the business might leverage and for what reason. And finally, we'll discuss some growth areas that might be appropriate for the future of that kind of business/organization.

> **Note on this chapter's format**
>
> This chapter won't go into much detail about setting up each feature, as that information can be found in the chapter corresponding with the feature. Instead, it will go over the role that feature plays in the business's overall marketing strategy.
>
> Additionally, as the saying goes, Rome wasn't built in a day. I will recommend features to engage with in a certain order, but if the use case calls for the use of four features, for example, you do not have to set them up all at once before you start engaging with your audience. Treat your marketing effort as a product development process; iterate and build on a foundation. Even if you start with just the first recommended feature and come back to the second in a week or a month, you're at least setting a foundation and moving forward.

You might remember from *Chapter 1*, we talked a bit about buckets that you can place marketing channels into. So, as we go, I'll suggest how the growth of these businesses view the role of these channels in the scope of the current business. As a reminder, those buckets are as follows:

- **Non-negotiable**: These are the channels that are either already critical to your marketing efforts, or if you have none established yet, it's the biggest channel like emails.
- **Known growth**: These are the channels that you know would be helpful, but you haven't actually attempted to work them into your marketing efforts
- **Curious**: These are the channels you're either unfamiliar with or you haven't previously considered how they would fit into a marketing effort for your needs

In *Figure 17.1*, we can see this hierarchy illustrated as a hierarchy from bottom to top; highest priority to lowest:

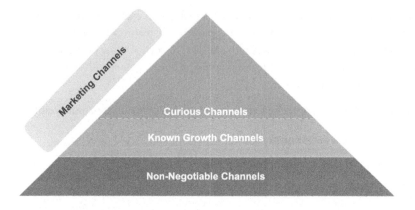

Figure 17.1 – Hierarchy of marketing channel needs

With that said, let's get into our first category of business.

Starting a business or online presence

In this section, we'll be walking through examples where the business or organization has just started getting an initial online presence off the ground and is beginning its digital marketing.

Type of business

For this first business, let's build upon one of our earliest examples in this book. For this example, the business is a small-batch beauty company. It makes bars of soap, shampoos, and conditioners.

Background of the business

This business has the following features:

- **Age**: Less than a year old
- **How have they sold up to this point?**: Limited product sales at local popups around their city
- **Digital presence?**: No online marketing presence yet

Next goals and vision for growth

The owner of this small business largely runs it alone, with some help from members of their family. They're generating some profit from their popups and would like to start shipping their product and not just selling through popups. Their reason for doing this is to create new customers and create a lower-friction avenue for previous customers to become repeat customers. They have some repeat customers who come to their different popups, and they would like to make it easier for those customers to buy from them.

Ideal Mailchimp usage for this business

Considering that this business has a minimal online marketing presence, it's likely that if they have any presence, it's very likely limited to one or a small handful of social media accounts. So, if they're looking for growth, there are a couple initial strategies that a business like this should start with and we'll review why. The following is a breakdown of the channels and phases they can grow in:

Non-negotiable channels:

1. **Audience building**

   Audience determination: With a small or no digital presence, this business probably has a very loose understanding of who its audience is and potentially has absolutely no record or collection of audience members. Even if they have an Instagram account for their business, this wouldn't be the same as having concrete contact information for each audience member. So, priority #1 for a business or organization like this should be to start creating a way to collect and engage with an audience.

   First form: This business should start creating forms for people to begin signing up to engage with whatever their future content might be. Mailchimp will create a form for you as soon as an audience is created, which means that you can create forms in two phases:

   I. While you engage with creating a more robust and aesthetically pleasing form, you can leverage the **Hosted Form** (Form builder seen in *Figure 6.3*). You can then share that form's URL via social media, for example, where you may already be promoting your popups less formally. This allows you to make use of whatever you've already been using to promote your popups informally to gather data for your audience through the form.

II. You can have multiple forms up and funneling data to your single audience. So, while your **Hosted Form** is active and up wherever you've shared it, you can begin building another form, such as a **landing page** or a **website** if you plan on building one long term. These options are equally good. Because this business has no audience with consent to contact for email marketing, the most important step is to establish a funnel. This helps with the first goal of creating new customers and giving the business people to market to.

2. **Campaign Emails**

    Email marketing: With even a small audience, you can begin sending email marketing to those new contacts. While you build out other channels, you can send emails about your popups and how to contact you. This then gives you your second marketing channel to build on whatever you were using prior to Mailchimp and to maintain that relationship with the customer.

Known growth channels:

1. **Store Website**

    Product Pages: Once you have established a funnel, then it's time to move forward with listing your actual products for sale. This gives you something to promote in addition to your popups. You jump right into listing your first product (*Figure 13.3*), likely your best seller. From there, when you complete the creation of a store, you can then move on to editing the remainder of a website.

    Signup page: Once you have set the store up, you would prioritize setting up a contact form somewhere on the website (*Figure 9.11*). This is your opportunity to either replace your **Hosted Form** or just create another form to ensure that even if people don't sign up using the URL for your **Hosted Form**, they'll be presented with the opportunity to sign up again if they visit your website to check out your products.

2. **Welcome Customer Journey**

    Sign up Journey: This is a wonderful first place to automate your marketing channels and communication with audience members. Building a **Customer Journey** using the **Sign up Starting Point** (*Figure 12.3*) creates at least one point of contact that sends an email to new subscribers every time they join your audience through any of your active forms.

Curious channels:

1. **Email Experimentation**

    A/B Testing and Multivariate Testing: As we covered in earlier chapters, experimentation can be a very powerful tool for growing your marketing efforts. So, when you get to the place where you can grow and become curious about how to extend the use of platforms such as Mailchimp, **A/B testing** and **multivariate testing** are the best places to start, as we saw in *Figure 11.1*.

2. **Connect**

    The next growth area is to integrate your Mailchimp account with other platforms that you may have already been using. This can include e-commerce platforms if you chose a different platform in the **Store Website** step, or you can search for other integrations for applications you might be using for your business (*Figure 15.3*).

3. **Refine your Brand**

    An additional growth space you may want to look into is a refinement of the assets you use for your brand. As covered in *Chapter 7*, you can take the assets you uploaded in the past when creating your email campaigns or automations and use the **Creative Assistant** to redesign your brand assets.

As your beauty business grows, this breakdown gives you a high-level overview of how to move through the hierarchy of marketing needs. Next, let's check out another scenario.

From bricks and mortar to a digital presence

In this example, we'll review a business that sells physical goods out of a store and would like to expand its digital footprint.

Type of business

This next business is a bookstore in Atlanta, GA. It has dabbled with a digital presence in social media, and it has some contact information that it has gathered from customers in-store for marketing.

Background of the business

This business is as follows:

- **Age:** 5+ years.
- **How have they sold up to this point?:** It has a physical bookstore in Atlanta, GA, USA.
- **Digital presence?:** It has a social media presence and a simple website with its address and a contact form. It uses a Square point-of-sale device but has not yet expanded to leveraging additional features.

Next goals and vision for growth

The owner of this small business has eight employees and does all of their business in person in their store. They want to grow their business by selling online and shipping from their store. Additionally, they also want to be able to promote events to their audience.

Ideal Mailchimp usage for this business

Considering that this business has an audience to start with, but a small online presence, their best starting place would be to jump right into marketing to their existing audience while growing the online portion of their business. The key deviation here is that as a brick-and-mortar business, it has a separate platform for in-person sales that it can leverage for e-commerce expansion. The following is a breakdown of the channels and phases it can grow in.

Non-negotiable channels:

1. **Audience building**

   Audience import: Because this small business started collecting signup details for marketing in its physical store, it has a list that it can start with. In this scenario, if the list is written out, it'll need to be transcribed into a spreadsheet on a computer, but from there, can be imported into an audience in Mailchimp (*Chapter 3*).

   Form integration: This business already has a simple website with information about the store and a contact form. Depending on the host of their site, from the Integrations Marketplace, it can connect its website to its Mailchimp account so that moving forward, it doesn't have to import contact information just to grow its audience.

2. **Commerce connections**

   Even brick-and-mortar businesses need a way to take payment. And, increasingly, point-of-sale devices are products provided by companies such as Square. This business is already using a physical point-of-sale station, but with the **Square** integration found in the **Mailchimp Integrations Discover** page, the bookstore can sync data in real time from its Square point-of-sale device to the audience in Mailchimp. Square allows the business to take its inventory and create a page listing those products in order to sell its goods online. The role of Mailchimp would be to integrate with Square to allow the business to market changes to their inventory. This integration of their two platforms will empower the business to segment its marketing. It'll allow the business to make use of **Product Content Blocks** in its email campaigns, and it can use more e-commerce-related triggers for its **Customer Journeys** in the future. This is part of the non-negotiable bucket because it serves the business' short-term growth goals of marketing its products through email campaigns and selling digitally, but then leaves the door open for long-term growth into automation and other channels, if desired.

3. **Campaign Emails**

   Email will generally fall into the non-negotiable group of your hierarchy, as it's one of the most popular and engaging marketing channels. The reason is that email is a primary and ubiquitous application used by pretty much any audience member on the internet. Whether the audience member is an inbox-zero kind of person or an inbox-with-thousands-of-emails person, they're looking at their email inbox at the very least a couple of times per week. This means that as people grow their businesses or conduct any organizational marketing activities, landing in people's inboxes is important. So, for this business, if it wants to stay at the top of the minds of its local customers and reel in new customers, cultivating a presence in the email inboxes of its audience is key.

Known growth channels:

1. **Welcome Customer Journey**

   Sign up Journey: Again, this is a wonderful first place to automate your marketing channels and communication with audience members. Building a **Customer Journey** using the **Sign up Starting Point** (*Figure 12.3*) creates at least one point of contact that sends email to new subscribers every time they join your audience through any of your active forms.

   Shopping activity Customer Journey: When a business already has some established sales data, even if it's largely just local to its physical location, a good first growth channel for them to consider is automation based on purchasing activity it is already seeing. Presumably, a business with some number of employees besides the owners is doing daily business to be able to afford a physical location. This means that it is getting sales data daily in its Square account. As this data is synced back to their Mailchimp account when a sale is made to someone who has opted in to receive marketing communications, setting up something like a **Customer Journey** for people who buy a specific product (for example, maybe a featured book of the month or a featured new release) might be a good way for them to drive additional business. For example, perhaps the business wants to send people who purchased a specific New York Times Best Seller an automated email with suggestions of similar books in the same genre as their next read. This is a great way to not only show your customer you're paying attention to their interests, but also to place another product of yours in front of them for a chance at another sale.

Curious channels:

1. **Email Experimentation**

   A/B Testing and Multivariate Testing: This business probably has a good handle on what its customers in the Atlanta area want when they come in, but it's possible, as it builds a wider brand and sells outside of their region, that maybe it'll have more segments of customers with different tastes and may need to figure out how to balance the brand it has built with how that brand might need to evolve to grow a bigger digital market and sales. So, when you get to the place where you can grow and become curious about how to extend your business, **A/B testing** and **multivariate testing** are the best places to start, as we see in *Figure 11.1*.

Finally, let's check out how an established business that predominantly provides services might leverage Mailchimp.

Service-based business model

Service-based businesses are ones where the entrepreneur may offer an intangible product, such as consultations, and we're going to review what channels and strategies might be most helpful to them.

Type of business

This business is a consultation business. It provides services such as consultation and creates digital content related to digital marketing for its clients.

Background of the business

This business is as follows:

- **Age:** 10 years
- **How have they sold up to this point?:** As a digital content creator, it predominantly sells intangible services in the form of affiliate marketing services through its social media and email campaigns. It sells courses through its website, and it sells consultation services to those looking to break into the same field. As with most digital content creators, varied income and marketing streams are key to their sustainability.
- **Digital presence?:** Prior to leveraging Mailchimp, it had a robust but fractured digital presence. Its data was housed in a variety of different applications, which meant that it was sometimes difficult to keep track of the business and its growth.

Next goals and vision for growth

This content creator has three employees. The four people believe they are leveraging the different platforms they use effectively, but it's difficult to maintain a holistic view of their impact over time. So, their goal is to consolidate some of their streams of work into one platform and, secondly, ensure their data is syncing to Mailchimp so they can leverage it to review their marketing impact for an affiliate pitch deck.

Ideal Mailchimp usage for this business

As a marketing company, it is already leveraging various platforms to deliver services to its different revenue streams. For its affiliate work, it is leveraging its social media to deliver on some of these campaigns, as well as Gmail (through GSuite) to deliver partnered emails. For its courses, it has also predominantly leveraged GSuite to house the recordings of its courses and has manually sent emails to those who have purchased courses through its website on Squarespace. And for consultations, it has similarly manually sent a follow-up email with a Calendly link for people to schedule an appointment with her when they have purchased or signed up for a consultation. Its upfront needs will be pretty robust and may vary depending on what it wants to consolidate into Mailchimp first. For the purposes of this example, we'll say the value of its revenue streams will inform the order and, from the largest percentage of revenue to the smallest, they are as follows: digital marketing courses, consultations, and affiliate content. The following is a breakdown of the channels and phases they can grow in:

Non-negotiable channels:

1. **Audience building**

   Website connection: Because this business is already not just receiving consent to market, but also selling specific courses through its website, task number one should be to integrate its Squarespace account. This can be done through the **Integrations Discover** page (*Figure 14.1*). This will get data about its contacts, purchases, and location synced to its audience in Mailchimp and ensure that anyone who signs up for its content through the site as the business builds out anything else through Mailchimp can be included in the marketing.

2. **Campaign Emails**

   Branded marketing: Up to this point, the business was using a much simpler email builder. While Gmail is synonymous with sending emails, it does not specialize in marketing emails that are designed to be sent to multiple people at once without risking leaking the data of one audience member to another. Most importantly, marketing automation platforms such as Mailchimp have more robust builders that enable their users to design emails that appear more polished when they land in their audience member's inboxes. For a content creator, this is actually a two-fold benefit because it doesn't just ensure that they're able to market in general, but because the service that they sell is the creation of digital content, the more polished they're able to make their own marketing appear, the greater the value they can assign to the content that they're providing in the form of courses and affiliate services in the future.

3. **Customer Journey**

   A. **Buys a specific product Customer Journey:** Because digital content creators tend to have smaller teams than larger businesses, this business will want to lean into automation a little harder than another business may. Its need will be greater. Up to this point, the business was pre-recording content and then scheduling emails to send in a specific cycle. For example, it may sell a week-long course once per month. The sale opens for the first week of the month and then the course is sent to those who purchase it in the third week of the month. However, the fact that the course is pre-recorded enables this revenue stream to stay open constantly instead of manually creating communications, by establishing a **Customer Journey** specifically for customers who purchase a specific course through their website. The business can design a journey map that automatically sends a beautiful email with a video content block each day of the week-long course.

   B. **Sign up Journey:** If it's not clear yet, a signup journey is a must for automating your marketing channels and communication with audience members. This gives this business in particular a single welcome email where they can promote and provide context on all of the services that they offer. Building a **Customer Journey** using the **Sign up Starting Point** (*Figure 12.3*) creates at least one point of contact that sends emails to new subscribers when they join your audience through any of your active forms or other integrated platforms.

Known growth channels:

1. **Rethinking consultation bookings**

   I. This business owner has two options for automation to simplify their life. If they like the platforms they're using for scheduling consultations when people purchase them through their existing Squarespace site, then they can create another **Customer Journey** to send a follow-up email with a link to their Calendly instead of doing it manually, as they currently do. If they want those purchases and appointments to be handled all through Mailchimp, they can leverage the **Appointments** option under **Websites** to build a page to sell them. Both options are equally good, depending on the preference of the business. In the long term, it may be beneficial for the business to consider whether the cost of using more platforms outweighs the preference for the platforms themselves, but from a functional perspective, they're both functional and professional looking.

   > **Note on consultation bookings as a "curious" growth space for this type of business**
   >
   > If the business prefers to build a **Customer Journey**, that wouldn't necessarily be a channel it's *curious* about; that would be something it would want to consider in the previous bucket when it was building **Customer Journeys** for the purchases of specific courses. Each product, whether course or consultation, would have its own Customer Journey map that would be built in that section.

   II. **Set up appointments:** The first growth area this business might consider is creating a store page for appointments as a sellable service. Again, in the interest of consolidating its data into Mailchimp, but also automating more of its work so that when a customer purchases a consultation, the customer can select the time, make the payment, and receive details about their booking all at once. And from the business's perspective, it can edit its available times, view or cancel appointments, and view customer data about these appointments all in one place.

2. **Email Experimentation**

   A/B testing and multivariate testing: This business thrives on understanding trends in digital marketing and content. Staying in tune with what its audience is connecting with and what they are not is exactly their business. So, experimenting with its own content not only provides insights into its own customers, but the business can take that data, depersonalize it so they're not revealing the customer's personal data, and turn it into a lesson for a marketing course, or even include it in a pitch deck when they approach affiliates to grow that segment of their business. So, as they get to the place where they can grow and look at how to extend their business and build their weakest revenue segment, **A/B testing** and **multivariate testing** are the best places to start, as we can see in *Figure 11.1*.

Curious channels:

Because this business is already relatively robust, its curious channels will largely begin to stretch into channels where the business would be asking itself the question about whether it would make the most sense to move some segment of its business from one platform to Mailchimp:

1. **Website Migration**: The concern for this business is the question of whether its Squarespace site serves it well enough, and whether there would be an intrinsic benefit in consolidating its digital presence more entirely into Mailchimp or if things are satisfactory as they are. This question isn't really cut and dried. The business will want to weigh the effort and the cost of that move. Some questions it might seek to answer to understand and investigate that option include the following:

   - Is it cheaper to stay on separate platforms?
   - Do I or any of my employees have the availability soon for that migration?
   - Which features do I most treasure about my website platform?

   With a sense of these answers, if the value is there, setting up a website and making the move would bring the little remaining data outside of Mailchimp into one platform, which gives them just one platform to primarily use to run their business.

With that, we've gone over some real-world examples, from a small nascent business to a more established business looking to make a pivot into more robust, all-in-one marketing. Let's wrap things up.

Summary

In this chapter, we covered three types of businesses and how they might use Mailchimp immediately and as their business grows. Referring to our first chapter to bring this full circle, we talked about three utilizations of the Mailchimp platform. First, we went over a small, new business looking to break into e-commerce and build a digital presence for the very first time and what its growth into the platform might look like. Then we talked about a brick-and-mortar store that was looking to make the pivot from hyper-local to shipping its products and developing its digital marketing presence. And finally, we talked about a business that was older and managing multiple revenue streams that it wanted to both maintain and grow. This last business covered a lot of utilizations, including content creation, more advanced marketing, and providing services.

Even in the absence of physical products, the first little business could get off the ground, begin marketing, and take pre-orders to begin to get a sense of how it could grow. And similarly, even our largest business example had space for growth and experimentation by letting the platform handle some of its manual tasks so that it could focus on the more creative parts of the job, such as creating more content and revenue streams, while the Mailchimp platform handled other parts of the business.

That's ultimately the goal and main takeaway with any marketing platform. Your growth won't necessarily be linear or identical to every other business using Mailchimp or any other platform, but as you grow your business or organization, ask yourself what can you automate and hand over to your marketing platform so that you're empowered to do what you do best: creating the content and products that your audience comes to you for. Even if platforms can provide suggestions through machine learning and data they've aggregated over time, as we discussed in *Chapter 10*, when we talked about predicted demographics and content optimization through suggestions, you're still the brains behind your business. If you can free yourself up to do more creating for your business, you're letting your platforms empower you to do your best work.

Index

A

A/B testing 22, 63, 167-169
account management 18, 19
Account Overview page, Settings drop-down menu
   Details section 20, 21
actions 178, 188
activities, for engaging with integration
   field mapping 250
   lead creation 250
   permission settings 251
   sync settings 251
audience/contact activity 181, 182
audiences 25
   building, with form and survey integrations 234-238
   combining 41-44
   exporting 44
   importing 44
   setting up 25, 26
audience settings page
   Campaign defaults 29, 30
   Form settings 28, 29
   New subscriber notifications 30, 31
automations 64, 178, 179

B

branching logic 185
brick and mortar 8
bricks and mortar, to digital presence scenario
   background 267
   goals and vision for growth 267
   Mailchimp usage 268
   type 267
business 264
   background 265
   goals and vision for growth 265
   Mailchimp usage 265
   type 264

C

calls to action (CTAs) 157
Campaign Editor
   using 111-117
Campaign reporting 144-147
   Comparative Reports 159
   expanded/advanced features 156-159
   interpreting 153-155
   using 153-155
campaigns 6

campaign scheduling
   batch delivery 118
   pop-up modal scheduling options 118, 119
   send at specific time 118
   Send Time Optimization 118
CAN-SPAM 34
central list
   versus various list 31
channel 6
Classic Automation 7, 8, 177, 185
   setting up 186-195
Click performance interface 151
Combine Audiences tool 42-44
comma-separated value (CSV) file 38
commerce data
   used, to expand marketing efforts 229, 230
commerce feature 198
Comparative Reports 143, 159-163
connectivity integrations 246, 247
contact
   bounced 25
   subscribed 25
   transactional 25
   unsubscribed 25
contact dataset
   expanding, to include commerce/purchasing data 209-213
contact statuses
   knowing, significance 26
Content Optimizer 156
Content studio 89
   Creative Assistant 91-94
   Giphy 95
   Instagram 95
   My Files 94
   My Logo 96
   Products 95

Courier
   URL 23
Customer Journey Builder 7, 8, 64, 177, 185
   setting up 186-195
customer journey map 7
customer journeys 260
   subscriber journeys 213
   transactional journeys 213
Customer Journeys API trigger 184
customer relationship management (CRM) 245, 246
   contact data 248
customer relationship management (CRM) integrations 246, 247
   additional data, using 256-261
   associated advanced features 256-260
customer relationship managers (CRMs) 38

D

date-based events and data 183
Default Email Builder section 23
digital content creator 8, 120, 121
domain 125
   authentic appearance, having 127
   deliverability, improving 127
   entry point, to brand 126
   obtaining 127-133
   private domain 126
   public domain 126
   settings, personalizing 126
   sign-up portal 126

E

e-commerce
   specific automations, setting up 213-216
e-commerce activity 182, 183

Index 277

e-commerce marketer 9, 121-123
email campaign
   experimental design 167-171
   information, taking from results to understand audience 171-174
Email from Mailchimp section 23
email inboxes 101
embedded forms 83, 84
events 178
experimenting
   with engagement 165, 166

F

featured commerce integrations 220, 221
   enabling 227
form and survey integrations 237
   used, for building audience 234-238
forms
   creating, on landing page 78-81
   need for 69, 70

G

General Data Protection Regulation (GDPR) 65
group category 50
   setting up 51, 52
group names 50
groups 49, 50
   considerations 53
   importing to 55

H

Help us improve your stats section 21, 22
hero images 80
hosted form builder 71, 72

hosted forms 71
   editable categories 74-77

I

inactive contacts 61
   archive 64, 65
   definition, developing 62-64
   removing, considerations 65
   unsubscribe 64, 65
Integration and API events 184
integration connection, phases
   authentication 221
   installation 221
   setup 221
   syncing 221
integrations 219, 245
   availability 221
   browsing for 247-249
   connecting 243
   discovering 238-242
   overview 249-252

J

journey point 178
journeys 179

L

landing page 266
   form, creating on 78-82
list
   importing 37-41
   information, required for making 26, 27

Index

M

Mailchimp 4, 5, 143
   account, creating 9-12
   online marketing, using with 4
   URL 125

Mailchimp for Salesforce integration 249, 261

Mailchimp reporting
   accessible information 144-147

Mailchimp-specific terms
   campaigns 6
   channels 6
   Classic Automations 7
   Customer Journey Builder 7

Mailchimp Store
   setting up 199-209

Mailchimp usage, bricks and mortar to digital presence scenario 268
   curious channels 269
   known growth channels 269
   non-negotiable channels 268

Mailchimp usage, business 265
   curious channels 266
   known growth channels 266
   non-negotiable channels 265, 266

Mailchimp usage, service-based business model 270
   curious channels 273
   known growth channels 272
   non-negotiable channels 271

Mailmunch 235

Manage automatic replies section 24

marketing automations, creating in Shopify
   reference link 223

marketing channel activity 184

marketing channels
   curious 5, 264
   known growth 5, 264
   non-negotiable 5, 264

marketing efforts
   expanding, with commerce data 229, 230

marketing, targeting
   higher engagement 48, 49

Mensa marketers 8

Merge Tags 34, 35
   default merge tag value 36, 37
   Put this tag in your content 35, 36

Multivariate Testing 167, 169

O

online marketing 4
   using, with Mailchimp 4

opens and clicks
   Click performance interface 151
   Predicted Demographics interface 151, 152
   stats overview 148-150

P

platforms
   information, passing between 227-229

pop-up forms 83-86

post-sending actions 64

Predicted Demographics interface 151, 152

private domain 126

public domains 126

Q

queue 178

R

reCAPTCHA 29
referral badges 84
responsive email 103
rules 188

S

segment 56
  creating 57-59
segmenting 49, 56
  conditions 56
  logic 56-58
  tools 56
service-based business model 269
  background 270
  goals and vision for growth 270
  Mailchimp usage 270
  type 270
Shopify
  connect 222
  pre-installation checklist 222
  sync 222
Shopify connection process 221
Shopify integration setup
  App Settings 223
  Merge Tag Mapper 223, 226
  Shopify Customer Tag Mapper 224
  sync overview 226, 227
  Sync page 225
  Tags & Groups step 224
Snapshot feature 159
SurveyMonkey 235
synced contacts 228

T

tags 49, 53, 54, 85
  importing to 55
Template Editor 100-103
Template Marketplace 105-110
templates 99, 100
  selecting 103-105
traditional sales funnel 70
triggers 178, 180
TXT (plain-text) file 38
Typeform 235

U

U.S. CAN-SPAM Act 26

V

vCard 109

W

website 125, 266
  making 133-139
  sections 137
  settings, editing 139, 140
website integrations 237
Welcome campaign 158

Z

Zapier 247
Zapier integration 252-256
Zaps 252

Packtpub.com

Subscribe to our online digital library for full access to over 7,000 books and videos, as well as industry leading tools to help you plan your personal development and advance your career. For more information, please visit our website.

Why subscribe?

- Spend less time learning and more time coding with practical eBooks and Videos from over 4,000 industry professionals
- Improve your learning with Skill Plans built especially for you
- Get a free eBook or video every month
- Fully searchable for easy access to vital information
- Copy and paste, print, and bookmark content

Did you know that Packt offers eBook versions of every book published, with PDF and ePub files available? You can upgrade to the eBook version at packtpub.com and as a print book customer, you are entitled to a discount on the eBook copy. Get in touch with us at customercare@packtpub.com for more details.

At www.packtpub.com, you can also read a collection of free technical articles, sign up for a range of free newsletters, and receive exclusive discounts and offers on Packt books and eBooks.

Other Books You May Enjoy

If you enjoyed this book, you may be interested in these other books by Packt:

Digital Marketing with Drupal

José Fernandes

ISBN: 9781801071895

- Explore the most successful digital marketing techniques
- Create your digital marketing plan with the help of Drupal's digital marketing checklist
- Set up, manage, and administer all the marketing components of a Drupal website
- Discover how to increase the traffic to your Drupal website
- Develop and implement an e-commerce marketing strategy for your Drupal Commerce store
- Manage your daily marketing activities using Drupal
- Get started with customizing your consumers' digital experienceFind out what's next for Drupal and digital marketing

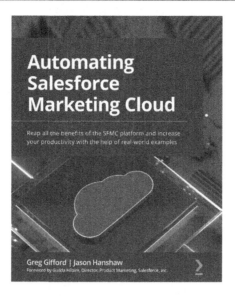

Automating Salesforce Marketing Cloud

Greg Gifford, Jason Hanshaw

ISBN: 9781803237190

- Understand automation to make the most of the SFMC platform
- Optimize ETL activities, data import integrations, data segmentations, email sends, and more
- Explore different ways to use scripting and API calls to increase Automation Studio efficiency
- Identify opportunities for automation with custom integrations and third-party solutions
- Optimize usage of SFMC by building on the core concepts of custom integrations and third-party tools
- Maximize utilization of employee skills and capabilities and reduce operational costs while increasing output

Packt is searching for authors like you

If you're interested in becoming an author for Packt, please visit `authors.packtpub.com` and apply today. We have worked with thousands of developers and tech professionals, just like you, to help them share their insight with the global tech community. You can make a general application, apply for a specific hot topic that we are recruiting an author for, or submit your own idea.

Share Your Thoughts

Now you've finished *Marketing Automation with Mailchimp*, we'd love to hear your thoughts! Scan the QR code below to go straight to the Amazon review page for this book and share your feedback or leave a review on the site that you purchased it from.

`https://packt.link/r/1-800-56173-3`

Your review is important to us and the tech community and will help us make sure we're delivering excellent quality content.

Download a free PDF copy of this book

Thanks for purchasing this book!

Do you like to read on the go but are unable to carry your print books everywhere? Is your eBook purchase not compatible with the device of your choice?

Don't worry, now with every Packt book you get a DRM-free PDF version of that book at no cost.

Read anywhere, any place, on any device. Search, copy, and paste code from your favorite technical books directly into your application.

The perks don't stop there, you can get exclusive access to discounts, newsletters, and great free content in your inbox daily

Follow these simple steps to get the benefits:

1. Scan the QR code or visit the link below

https://packt.link/free-ebook/9781800561731

1. Submit your proof of purchase
2. That's it! We'll send your free PDF and other benefits to your email directly

Made in United States
Orlando, FL
09 January 2024

42294659R00167